T·H·E
AUGSBURG
CONFESSION

A
Commentary

L E I F
GRANE

Translated by John H. Rasmussen

AUGSBURG Publishing House • Minneapolis

THE AUGSBURG CONFESSION
A Commentary

Published in Danish 1981 by G•E•C Gads Forlag, Copenhagen, under the title *Confessio Augustana*.

Copyright © 1959 Leif Grane, © 1981 G•E•C Gads Forlag. English translation copyright © 1987 Augsburg Publishing House, Minneapolis.

Scripture quotations unless otherwise noted are from the Revised Standard Version of the Bible, copyright 1946, 1952, and 1971 by the Division of Christian Education of the National Council of Churches.

The English translation of the Latin text of the Augsburg Confession is that of Theodore G. Tappert, in *The Book of Concord,* © 1959 by Fortress Press, and is used by permission.

Library of Congress Cataloging-in-Publication Data

Grane, Leif.
   THE AUGSBURG CONFESSION.

   Translation of: Confessio Augustana.
   Bibliography: p.
   Includes indexes.
   1. Confessio Augustana. I. Rasmussen, John H.
II. Confessio Augustana. III. Title.
BX8069.G7313   1987   238'.41   86-28832
ISBN 0-8066-2252-0

Manufactured in the U.S.A.   APH 10-0519

     4   5   6   7   8   9   0   1   2   3   4   5   6   7   8   9

• CONTENTS •

Preface to the English Edition 5
Translator's Preface 7
Abbreviations 9

Introduction 11
Preface (to the Augsburg Confession) 24

Part I: Chief Articles of Faith 29
   1. God 31
   2. Original Sin 40
   3. The Son of God 50
   4. Justification 58
   5. The Ministry of the Church 69
   6. The New Obedience 81
   7. The Church 89
   8. What Is the Church? 99
   9. Baptism 103
  10. Lord's Supper 113
  11. Confession 127
  12. Repentance 134
  13. The Use of the Sacraments 145
  14. Ecclesiastical Order 151
  15. Ecclesiastical Rites 159
  16. Civil Affairs 166
  17. The Return of Christ for Judgment 178
  18. Free Will 181
  19. The Cause of Sin 190
  20. Faith and Good Works 194
  21. The Cult of Saints 205

Part II: Articles in Which an Account Is Given of the
    Abuses Which Have Been Corrected 211
    Introduction 213
    22. Both Kinds 215
    23. The Marriage of Priests 217
    24. The Mass 221
    25. Confession 226
    26. The Distinction of Foods 228
    27. Monastic Vows 234
    28. Ecclesiastical Power 241

Conclusion 250

Selected Bibliography 252
Index of Subjects 254
Index of Names (Selected) 255

• PREFACE TO THE •
ENGLISH EDITION

Some years ago, while offering a course of lectures on the Augsburg
Confession at the Theological Faculty of the University of Copenhagen,
I looked in vain for a short commentary on the confession that I could
recommend to the students. It was then that the idea of my writing
such a commentary took shape. My aim was rather unpretentious: to
write a book in which students and other persons who were interested
in the doctrinal traditions of the Lutheran church could find useful
information to accompany the reading of the confession itself. I was—
and still am—convinced that every reading of this document is less
than useful without a basic knowledge of the origin of the confession
and of the doctrines of the reformers which are briefly stated in it. I
wanted to give students of the Augsburg Confession some tools by
which their understanding of the text could be facilitated and, at the
same time, to make its use as an "eternal" document outside history
more difficult. Those who desire a more detailed study of the confession
should consult the bibliography for further reading.

Against all expectations—the publisher's and my own—the book
was not only well received, but even rather quickly sold out. New,
more or less revised editions have been printed continually ever since

the first Danish edition came out in 1959. In 1967 the book was translated into Swedish, and in 1970 into German. In both countries it has been reprinted and is still in print. The book probably owes its relative popularity to its modest aim, which leaves room both for more specialized historical study and for theological reflection on the current significance of the confession.

The 450th anniversary of the Augsburg Confession in 1980 gave occasion for a number of books, many of them collections of articles. The more important of these are listed in the bibliography. This literature has certainly increased our knowledge about many historical details and, especially, has contributed to the ecumenical dialog. These books have different purposes but, since they all seem to contribute to detailed study, or to take part in the kind of theological discussion which is beyond the scope of this commentary, I have not found it necessary completely to revise this book in such a way as to include the results of this research or this discussion. This translation is based on the latest Danish edition, that of 1981, which was completed before the publication of many of these works. I have learned much from this literature, but it has not convinced me of the necessity for revision of the framework and scope of my book, and a discussion of the new literature—for example, in the notes—seemed to me a presumptuous idea totally beyond the simple aim that has been determinative throughout all editions, regarding both form and content.

Over the course of several years I have had the pleasure of becoming familiar with several American universities and theological seminaries. The contact with American Reformation scholarship is something that I appreciate very much. For this reason, and for many others, I welcome the English edition of my first—and probably most widely read—book with warm greetings to those of my American colleagues who have given me not only knowledge and insight but—what is even more important—friendship.

Leif Grane

• TRANSLATOR'S •
PREFACE

This translation of Leif Grane's *Confessio Augustana* was undertaken in order to provide the English-speaking reader with a short commentary on the Augsburg Confession, one that emphasizes the importance of viewing it in the light of its historical and theological context. Professor Grane treats each article, tracing it back to its roots in earlier sources and setting forth the principal issues articulated by it in light of the writings of the reformers and their opponents.

The translation of the Latin text of the Augsburg Confession is the one most widely used among English-speaking persons today, that of Theodore G. Tappert in *The Book of Concord* (Philadelphia: Fortress, 1959), pp. 23-69. Tappert chose to publish in parallel form the translations of the German (on the top half of the page) and the Latin (the lower half of the page). Citations of Luther's writings are taken, when possible, from *Luther's Works,* American Edition (see bibliography). For other citations, existing English translations are used whenever possible, and are acknowledged in the notes. Scripture references, except for those in Tappert's translation of the Augsburg Confession, are from the Revised Standard Version.

I would like to express my gratitude to Justin Pierce, S.D.S., of Silver Lake College, Manitowoc, Wisconsin, for assisting me in the translation of Latin passages for which published English translations are unavailable, to the editor of academic and professional books at Augsburg Publishing House for his fine editorial work, to my mother, Margaret Rasmussen, for her assistance in typing the manuscript, and to my wife, Jami, for her love and support throughout the project. Finally, I would like to dedicate my contribution to the memory of my grandfather, John M. Jensen, whose work as a translator has provided the inspiration for my efforts to follow in his footsteps.

John H. Rasmussen

• ABBREVIATIONS •

AC	Augsburg Confession
Ap	Apology of the AC, in *BC*
BC	*The Book of Concord,* ed. T. Tappert
BK	*Die Bekenntnisschriften der Evangelisch Lutherischen Kirche,* ed. Heinrich Bornkamm
Clemen	*Luthers Werke in Auswahl* (see bibliography)
ET	English translation
FC	Formula of Concord, in *BC*
GT	German text of the AC
LC	Luther's Large Catechism, in *BC*
LW	*Luther's Works,* American Edition (see bibliography)
Mel. W.	*Melanchthons Werke*
Migne, *PL*	*Patrologia Latina,* ed. J. P. Migne
SA	Smalcald Articles, in *BC*
SC	Luther's Small Catechism, in *BC*
WA	(Weimarer Ausgabe) *D. Martin Luthers Werke* (see bibliography)
WA, DB	WA, *Deutsche Bibel*
ZThK	*Zeitschrift für Theologie und Kirche*

· INTRODUCTION ·

The great upheaval during the 1520s which led to what we call the Reformation was not motivated by any desire to create new confessions of church doctrine. On the contrary, what Martin Luther and his friends in Wittenberg wished to abolish was precisely that which, according to them, was *new* in the church. Initially, the matter was simply a theological conflict. Luther struggled as long as possible to maintain the notion that he was not in conflict with the Roman church but only with some of its theologians. As is well known, however, this notion quickly proved to be an illusion. The famous 95 Theses on indulgences of October 31, 1517, brought the question of church authority into the debate, and eventually what began as a theological controversy escalated into a full clash with canon law. The resulting legal battle progressively became more heated until it reached its climax on December 10, 1520, when Luther, in effect, burned the canon law at the stake. There the papal bull threatening his excommunication also went up in the flames, demonstrating that it was the canon law, according to Luther, which was the true injustice. After this he could await with a clear conscience the arrival of the papal bull (January 3, 1521) which expelled him from the Roman church. When a few months later, at the Diet of Worms, the emperor declared him an outlaw, expelling him from secular society as well, the preparatory phase of the Reformation was in one sense brought to a close.

These actions on the part of pope and emperor put Luther's followers and sympathizers in a new predicament. Continuing to follow Luther was tantamount to rejecting the authority of both church and emperor. It was to acknowledge that Luther had not been "convinced by the Word of God or by clear reason," the conditions he laid down at Worms for retracting his books. It was to declare, in effect, that legal right had become a sham, while true right was on the side of the supposed heretic.

It is only against this background that one can seriously speak of the Reformation—if a change in the church's situation is meant thereby. At first the Reformation was a preaching movement. The first outward signs that more was happening than "inner" spiritual reforms were the marriage of priests and the exodus of monks from the cloister. Next, changes in the worship services were instituted, especially distribution of the Supper in both kinds. In Wittenberg and electoral Saxony, naturally, these changes were made largely as a result of Luther's preaching and writings. The reforms were understood as obedience to "God's Word," corrections of existing church law and practice on the grounds that they lacked scriptural justification and could be viewed as mere human traditions. Most of what was happening was unorganized, of course, or at least locally determined. In spite of this, reforms were widespread, even where princes were ill-disposed toward the Reformation. The upheaval had become so pervasive that intervention was considered dangerous, for fear that reprisals could lead to insurrection. The result was that the Reformation grew. A good part of it grew wild, however, and often there was no one at hand to prune the wild branches. The diets that followed Worms (1521) had little effect, due to the emperor's absence. The Diet of Nuremberg (1524) adjourned with a vague declaration that the Edict of Worms should be executed—to the extent possible.

In order to understand the situation, one must be clear that no one had oversight of the conditions. One may speak only tentatively of "evangelical" princes or cities up until the Peasants' War (1524–1525). Experiences during the Peasants' War, however, made it clear to the rulers that it was necessary either to suppress the Reformation altogether or to give it a publicly acknowledged shape in the form of an evangelical church entity. The papally minded princes from both north and south

Germany had already in 1524 formed alliances to defend the traditional faith, and after the Peasants' War a number of evangelically minded princes emerged. In 1526 the Gotha Alliance was formed between Elector John of Saxony and Landgrave Philip of Hesse as the principal partners, but with the consent and participation of a number of others. This decision, jointly to defend themselves against attack for the sake of their faith (the basis of their agreement), already contained an essential prerequisite for the development of an evangelical confession. The Peasants' War had demonstrated the necessity to create order in the new ecclesial entity. Along with order, however, a clear conception of its doctrinal basis was also necessary.

After the Peasants' War, the Reformation ceased having the character of a spontaneous, freely expanding movement, and was gradually transformed into a true evangelical church entity. Many city councils found themselves forced by public opinion to take legal action to make the Reformation official. Often, in such cases, tendencies of the late Middle Ages were perpetuated. In the princely territories the introduction of the Reformation prompted governmental initiatives which assumed episcopal duties that seemed to require a theoretical foundation. "The Word of God" (i.e., evangelical preaching and writings) had, as Luther once expressed it, spread over the land as in a downpour. But what happens now when the magisterial authorities have assumed the place of the downpour? How does one relate to authorities who use coercive means to force people to take part in evangelical worship services, receive the Supper in both kinds, and abandon a number of medieval devotional practices? How does one justify prohibiting pastors from continuing in the old way? Philip of Hesse persuaded Archbishop Albert of Mainz to surrender to him the regular ecclesiastical jurisdiction in Philip's land. In Saxony, one could eventually come to view—as did Luther—the intervention of the authorities as an emergency measure necessitated by the desertion of the bishops. Such intervention, therefore, was executed not by *right* of the authority, but by the *duty* of the Christian authority. The means of intervention employed almost everywhere was visitation. Commissioners composed of jurists and theologians were sent out into the parishes, as in Saxony during the years 1526–1530. These commissioners were exposed to a wide range of problems, such as questions concerning the life and teaching of individual pastors, the resources of individual churches, the disposition of monastic property, and much more.

The visitation experiences accelerated the attempt to create an acceptable model of instruction for the people and thus a model for the proclamation of pastors as well. While the Catechisms of Luther and others were written mainly to provide easily understood summaries of central Christian teachings, the *Instructions for the Visitors* of 1528, written essentially by Melanchthon but reviewed and provided with a preface by Luther, went significantly further. Here already is one of the sources of the Augsburg Confession (AC). Certain areas already then were on the verge of true confessional formulation, intending to create a common basis for proclamation within defined localities. On a broader scale, however, when larger cities and territories were involved, no true confessional formulation came about until the political situation sharpened toward the close of the 1520s.

The Diet of Speyer (1526) provided the environment for the development of a true evangelical church entity. As it was unfeasible to execute the Edict of Worms during the emperor's continuous absence, the various estates of the realm agreed that until the coming council, each estate should conduct itself "wie er es gegen Gott und kaiserliche Maiestät zu verantworten sich vertraue" (as it thinks itself able to defend before God and the imperial majesty). In practice, this was simply an acknowledgment that no agreement could be reached and that each city or territory was in reality a free agent. After the second Diet of Speyer in the early spring of 1529, however, the situation changed dramatically. Not only was the decision of 1526 abrogated, but any expansion of the Reformation was forbidden, Catholic worship services were to be permitted everywhere, and the sacramentarians (i.e., the Zwinglians and the Anabaptists) were to be extirpated. The distinctive thing about the well-known protest which some estates posted in appeal to the absent emperor was not its character as a minority protest against a majority decision. The protest was, rather, a legal action in which the protesters, in proper juridical form, offered another interpretation of imperial law than the one expressed in the verdict of the diet. In defending the harmony of evangelical preaching with Scripture and the legality of the reforms, the "protesting estates" maintained that they in reality were the ones who had imperial law on their side in every respect.

On the 22nd of April, the day of the imperial diet's adjournment, certain of the evangelical estates concluded a secret alliance led by electoral Saxony and Hesse. In order to have an effective alliance, however, there had to be agreement about the faith which was jointly to be defended. Such agreement was long in coming. Up to this point the evangelicals had taken Zwingli and the Swiss under their protection, but shortly after the diet a reversal took place. Luther and Zwingli had been in conflict about the Lord's Supper during previous years. Luther had closed his latest contribution, the extensive *Vom Abendmahl Christi (Concerning Christ's Supper)* (1528), with a *Bekenntnis (Confession)* which also happens to be an important source of the AC. Luther's *Bekenntnis* gained added significance when a shift in Saxon politics took place shortly after the diet. The Saxons were fearful of Philip of Hesse's ambitious plans for a comprehensive alliance, which would include the Swiss, and of what his intentions might be for such an alliance. Consequently the time it took to ratify this alliance, which was formed as the diet adjourned, was drawn out further and further. During the summer, under circumstances about which we know nothing specific, the so-called Schwabach Articles appeared; they now became the basis of electoral Saxony's politics. The Schwabach Articles took a sharply Lutheran position on the question of the Lord's Supper, and so it did not matter significantly that Luther met with Zwingli in October of 1529 in Marburg. More progress, in fact, was made in those discussions than had been anticipated. Even so, a few days after the 15 Marburg Articles were signed, the Elector of Saxony and Margrave George of Brandenberg-Ansbach agreed to consider the Zwinglians as "ungodly and subject to God's wrath." The allies from Speyer met on October 16–19, but the cities Ulm and Strasbourg were forced to reject the Schwabach Articles. Their exposed position in southern Germany, which was overwhelmingly Roman, made it too dangerous to break every tie with the Swiss. Thereafter the alliance had to be abandoned. The evangelicals were quite ill-prepared, therefore, when Charles V summoned the diet to Augsburg. The emperor's summons of January 21, 1530, called upon the princes and cities to give an account of their faith.

In the spring of 1530 the elector gathered the leading Lutheran theologians together to prepare a defense brief which could be presented at the diet. The main emphasis was to be on changes in church order which had taken place in the elector's land, along with their theological justification. Regarding proclamation, the Schwabach Articles were to be adhered to. These first negotiations, from March to April of 1530, resulted in the series of drafts which are known as the Torgau Articles. At the end of April, the theologians and the elector embarked from the castle Coburg and headed for Augsburg, leaving Luther behind.

Upon his arrival in Augsburg, Melanchthon learned of the 404 Articles just published by John Eck, in which 384 sentences extracted from the writings of the reformers were labeled heretical. Melanchthon sensed some risk in this, and immediately began reworking the material he had brought with him.

It appears that the elector had consequently thought to turn further work over to Luther. Luther looked over what was forwarded to him from Augsburg but disavowed any responsibility. Melanchthon was forced to continue on his own because Luther's answer, which contained the well-known words about his own lack of ability to tread so "softly and lightly," was not particularly instructive.

All of these preparations on the part of the elector of Saxony apparently took place without closer contact with the other evangelical estates. The breakdown in October of the previous year of negotiations for an alliance made it politically urgent for Saxony to be on good terms with the emperor. Lacking the added security a strong alliance would have provided, a conciliatory approach seemed to be the only feasible one. In line with this policy, the elector sent an envoy to the emperor at Innsbruck, intending to assure the emperor of the elector's loyalty and to present the Schwabach Articles as a testimony to Saxon orthodoxy. The emperor, however, rejected the articles, ordered the envoy to return to the elector, and reasserted his prohibition of evangelical preaching laid down at the diet. This reaction, which clearly indicated that the emperor had no intention of appearing to be an impartial arbitrator between two parties in a religious conflict, created a sense of panic in the camp of the elector of Saxony. Now it was no longer possible to be content with the Schwabach Articles and simply present the articles about changes in church usages. Since the emperor would not even consider receiving the Schwabach Articles as testimony to the elector's unshakable Catholic faith, these articles became politically useless, and the elector's party was forced to express this faith with greater precision. Melanchthon now faced the clear task of demonstrating the *catholicity* of the evangelical faith, for it was upon this that the legitimacy of the elector's legal claim depended. It was in the rulers' interest, therefore, when the AC stated that the confession is not in opposition to the catholic church or even the Roman church as it is known through the church fathers. Thus it could be contended that princes and cities that adhered to the AC were not in violation of imperial law and had in no way forfeited their legal status within the empire.

The history of the origin of the AC is extremely complicated. The extent to which the preparation and editing of the Confession was determined by the shifting political situation is best illustrated by an examination of the work done on the Preface. The three extant drafts are all composed by Melanchthon (all are printed in *Bekentnisschriften der evangelisch-lutherischen Kirche*). The oldest draft, the fragment *Wa,* and the manuscript *Ja,* which contains a complete Preface, both presuppose the optimism with which the emperor's summons was read in electoral Saxony. Both drafts must have been written before news of the emperor's belligerent attitude toward the Saxon envoy was received in Augsburg in the middle of May.

The last extant draft, the manuscript *Na,* clearly considers the emperor an opponent. It must stem from the end of May. Since Elector John the Steadfast had laid great weight in earlier negotiations on preserving a tolerable relationship with the emperor, while Philip of Hesse's plans clearly were antiimperial, it was necessary to express the elector's loyalty. The tone is appealing, even imploring. Obviously, the point here is to demonstrate how harmless the Protestant cause in reality is.

After observing how the Preface changed from the first confident draft to something in the direction of a plea for understanding, it seems remarkable that what became the final Preface had once again a changed tone. The reason for this, however, is easily found. On June 15 the emperor arrived in Augsburg. During the following days Melanchthon held secret negotiations with the imperial secretary Valdés. At the imperial court it seemed for a few days that there was hope for a quick and peaceful solution. This hope characterized the proposition of the diet of June 20 concerning the religious controversy. The emperor expressed his willingness to hear both parties on the basis of writings in German and Latin from each side. Such an accommodating gesture that returned completely to the attitude held earlier during the year of the summons was naturally a pleasant surprise after the rejection at Innsbruck and a provocative command to participate in the Corpus Christi procession in Augsburg. The Confession, therefore, had to be recast once again in light of the new atmosphere.

This time the task was not entrusted to Melanchthon but to Gregor Brück, the Saxon exchancellor. Not a trace of the nearly whimpering tone of *Na* remains. Now instead of meekly defending the Elector of Saxony's churchmanship and loyalty to the emperor, it is self-consciously asserted, "we, in any case, are completely in step with the emperor." This confident tone which characterizes the Preface recurs in the Conclusion after Article 28. Here it is briefly stated that this is the signatories' confession presented in compliance with the emperor's summons and, in response to any objection, they are prepared to give further proof from Holy Scripture. Clearly, they believe it appropriate to let the Confession stand as a simple, straightforward account of proclamation and church order in the signatories' lands and cities. Every trace of anxious apologetic has disappeared.

It is reasonable to assume that this attitude on the part of the confessors should be considered in interpreting the AC. The Preface and Conclusion provide a framework within which the 28 articles are to be understood, i.e., the spirit and background for their interpretation. When reading the Confession, we must not ignore the historical circumstance that the AC presents itself as a statement that soberly but self-consciously relates what is being proclaimed in the confessors' congregations, how these congregations have been ordered, and which abuses have been abolished; otherwise, a free-floating autonomy is imposed upon it which it never claims for itself. The AC does not intend to initiate anything. It does not intend to create any new church doctrine. Rather, its purpose is simply to reproduce what is taught in the Christian church. Its entire design is alien to any sense of what we have come to understand as confessionalism. Thus, it is not without irony that with the formation of the Smalcald League (1531) the AC became the symbol of unity for a special group of princes and cities, and later, as confessionalism spread throughout Europe (e.g., with the Peace of Augsburg, 1555), became the distinctive symbol of the so-called Lutheran church.

In order to understand the origin and development of the AC, it must be recognized that it is the product of two parallel objectives, one represented by theologians, the other by politicians. The theologians are primarily concerned with the content of proclamation. This means that in the development of the Confession they are occupied with doctrinal formulation. It is characteristic in this respect how Luther renounced all fellowship with Zwingli during the eucharistic controversy. The other objective is not only political but determined by judicial considerations as well. It was all-important for the princes that the case on behalf of the instituted reforms be made so that it would still be possible to understand the faith controversy as a legal conflict. These two objectives were of course closely related, since the law, even imperial law, was theologically based. The princes could not simply give the theologians a free hand, however, because their very legitimacy as estates of the realm was at stake.

The AC is thoroughly colored by this "double-mindedness." The final edition of the Confession is even further complicated by the fact that a number of other princes and some cities obtained the elector's permission to be cosigners. This permission naturally implied that they also obtained a voice regarding its content.

On June 25 the finished Confession was read to the emperor in German. During the following weeks it was critically examined by the papal theologians in attendance. Agreement about a refutation, the *Confutatio* (the Confutation), was reached only after extensive negotiations. It was read aloud on August third, and Melanchthon in rebuttal wrote his famous Apology which, however, the emperor refused to accept, having declared the issue closed with the Confutation. During the ongoing negotiations about the form and content of the Confutation, which bore the stamp of the papal legate Campeggio, the emperor was forced to abandon his desire for the other side to present a confession as well. The imperial court did, however, prevent the Confutation from being formulated in a manner which would preclude the possibility of further negotiations. When the protestants refused to submit to the emperor's decision, further negotiations were the only alternative. Despite great efforts on both sides, however, these negotiations, held during August and September, proved fruitless.

Melanchthon throughout his life considered the AC his own work, and undertook continuous revisions. Best known of these is his Latin edition of 1540, the *Augustana Variata,* which eventually played an especially important role in the doctrinal controversies following Luther's death. Even though the AC came to enjoy great authority, there was no opposition to Melanchthon's mode of procedure. Some time would have to pass before the AC would gain preeminence. During the conciliar negotiations of 1536–1537, for example, the elector assigned Luther the task of preparing the so-called Smalcald Articles which, despite his authorship, were not accepted by the Smalcald League. The south German cities considered them too sharp, especially on the eucharistic question. In addition, Melanchthon schemed against them. Nevertheless, they still gained a certain authority because of Luther, as is evidenced by their inclusion in the *Book of Concord* (1580). Among the factors which led to the formation of the Lutheran Confessions, although in a negative manner, was the *Tridentinum.* The conclusions of the Council of Trent, therefore, will be brought into the discussion where it seems germane. Each of the writings listed here comprises part of the theological-historical context within which the AC must be seen.

It is clear that the AC must not be viewed only in relation to the documents which expose its obvious presuppositions and consequences, but also in relation to the entire theological work of Luther, which is one of its principal presuppositions. This factor is given extensive—some will say, too much—consideration here. This, of course, is open for discussion. A historical understanding of the AC, however, is patently impossible apart from a rather thorough aquaintance with Luther's theology. This premise is generally accepted in contemporary interpretation of the AC. The uniqueness of the AC over against Luther's writings I hope will be made clear by pointing out the more important differences between Luther and Melanchthon. Fundamentally, however, our position is that, despite all differences, the AC expresses the essentials of Luther's reformation concerns. It would be imprudent, I believe, to put major emphasis on the differences. To be sure, Luther's consent to the AC was not given without reservation, as shown by his letters from May to July in which he reacts to the AC in its various stages of development. His criticisms, however, had to do not so much with the contents, but with the lack of sharpness against the opponents. He also misses the treatment of some subjects, such as purgatory, indulgences, and papal authority. Admittedly, however, in the Apology Melanchthon covers to some extent what the Confession itself neglects.

As far as is possible in a book of this size, Luther's theology is dealt with from historical and chronological perspectives. Here the concern is to attempt to sketch some lines of development rather than to expound Luther's thought from any predetermined viewpoint. Thus it will be stressed that the heavy consideration given Luther is based upon a specific perspective on the place of the AC within the history of the Reformation rather than upon one or another form of "Lutheran" theology which prescribes the "correct" understanding of the AC. Our concern, in other words, is not how contemporary dogmatics deals with the AC as a confessional writing, but how the Confession fits into the theological-historical context to which it belongs. The fact that an investigation such as this always involves some dogmatic presuppositions is self-evident to all who have lost their "innocence," in the sense of positivism.

In recent years, as is known, the AC has become of interest to certain theological circles within the Roman Catholic church. The question of a Roman Catholic "acknowledgment" of the AC has been widely discussed. Even though it is outside the scope of this book to take a position on this question, there is reason briefly to mention the problem. Perhaps those who would welcome such an acknowledgment are convinced that differences between "Lutheran" and "Roman Catholic" are being emphasized in a manner that is detrimental to eventual unity. In response to this it must be insisted that any agreement about the AC for which it is necessary to suppress or minimize the conflicts of the time of the Reformation would not be worth the effort. Any eventual acknowledgment, whatever else it may signify, can have meaning only if it is done with complete awareness not only of the actual conflicts of 1530 but also of the interpretive context created by the development of Lutheran doctrine after 1530. The first prerequisite for any serious consideration of the question of an acknowledgment, therefore, is a perspective which refuses to obscure the difficulties encountered at the time of the Reformation.

Perhaps it is not completely superfluous to remind ourselves that the Wittenberg reformers did not uphold confessionalism for its own sake.

When Melanchthon, not only in 1530, but also in the religious discussions of the following years, displayed great obligingness, it was hardly due to his temperament alone, but also to his deep conviction that the *one* church was also found under the papacy—despite abuses and false teaching. Luther also adopted this ecumenical attitude without hesitation. It never occurred to him to identify the one, holy church with the Lutheran church. Quite the contrary, against the Anabaptists he energetically rejected the absurd notion that the church did not exist under the papacy. In practicing this type of ecumenism, however, Luther never felt constrained to discontinue his polemic against false teaching. One does not, therefore, serve ecumenism by minimizing the conflicts of the time of the Reformation. Whatever may happen with respect to an acknowledgment, the eventual result will be meaningless if a decision is made without seriously considering the historical and interpretive context of the AC.

The Text

The basis for the notes and commentary is the Latin text, edited by Heinrich Bornkamm in *Die Bekenntnisschriften der evangelisch-lutherischen Kirche* (=*BK;* published in the anniversary year of the Augsburg Confession, 1930; several editions have appeared subsequently). The German text (GT) is occasionally introduced where it appears to cast light on the Latin. In addition, the more important deviations from the Latin version are noted. The two texts were written simultaneously; sometimes the German, sometimes the Latin, was composed first. It has not been possible to deal with the text-critical problems, and the texts cited above are used without discussion. The text-critical apparatus in *BK* notes all the important variants. Since the early editions of *BK,* new textual discoveries have been made, especially for the Preface.[1] Since the variant readings, however, are of little significance and are completely without theological relevance, I have not considered it necessary to rehearse them here, but have confined myself to the text form which is readily accessible to all who are interested.

---

1. H. Bornkamm, *Der authentische lateinische Text der Confessio Augustana (1530),* Sitzungsberichte der Heidelberger Akademie der Wissenschaften (Heidelberg: Carl Winter Univesitätsverlag, 1956).

Textual Comments

Accompanying each article are clarifying remarks and notes on the content of the text itself. Those textual relationships which are sufficiently illuminated by the critical apparatus of *BK* are touched on in only a few instances. Only the most essential aspects are dealt with in Articles 22–28, the so-called abuse articles. To attempt to deal with them even somewhat thoroughly would have taken far too much space. Perhaps in the commentary on Articles 1–21, where the other articles are discussed and placed in historical context, there is a partial compensation for this apparent lack. The numerical division of the text in *BK* is printed in the right-hand margin.

Commentary

A commentary on each of Articles 1–21 seeks to situate the article historically in its theological-historical context, and theologically within the thought of the Lutheran reformers.

• PREFACE •

Text

Most serene, most mighty, invincible Emperor, most gra-   1
cious Lord:

A short time ago Your Imperial Majesty graciously summoned a diet of the empire to convene here in Augsburg.
In the summons Your Majesty indicated an earnest desire
to deliberate concerning matters pertaining to the Turk, that
traditional foe of ours and of the Christian religion, and how
with continuing help he might effectively be resisted. The   2
desire was also expressed for deliberation on what might
be done about the dissension concerning our holy faith and
the Christian religion, and to this end it was proposed to
employ all diligence amicably and charitably to hear, understand, and weigh the judgments, opinions, and beliefs of
the several parties among us, to unite the same in agree-   3
ment on one Christian truth, to put aside whatever may not
have been rightly interpreted or treated by either side, to   4
have all of us embrace and adhere to a single, true religion
and live together in unity and in one fellowship and church,
even as we are all enlisted under one Christ. Inasmuch as   5
we, the undersigned elector and princes and our associates,

24

have been summoned for these purposes, together with other electors, princes, and estates, we have complied with the command and can say without boasting that we were among the first to arrive.

In connection with the matter pertaining to the faith and in conformity with the imperial summons, Your Imperial Majesty also graciously and earnestly requested that each of the electors, princes, and estates should commit to writing and present, in German and Latin, his judgments, opinions, and beliefs with reference to the said errors, dissensions, and abuses. Accordingly, after due deliberation and counsel, it was decided last Wednesday that, in keeping with Your Majesty's wish, we should present our case in German and Latin today (Friday). Wherefore, in dutiful obedience to Your Imperial Majesty, we offer and present a confession of our pastors' and preachers' teaching and of our own faith, setting forth how and in what manner, on the basis of the Holy Scriptures, these things are preached, taught, communicated, and embraced in our lands, principalities, dominions, cities, and territories.

If the other electors, princes, and estates also submit a similar written statement of their judgments and opinions, in Latin and German, we are prepared, in obedience to Your Imperial Majesty, our most gracious lord, to discuss with them and their associates, in so far as this can honorably be done, such practical and equitable ways as may restore unity. Thus the matters at issue between us may be presented in writing on both sides, they may be discussed amicably and charitably, our differences may be reconciled, and we may be united in one, true religion, even as we are all under one Christ and should confess and contend for Christ. All of this is in accord with Your Imperial Majesty's aforementioned summons. That it may be done according to divine truth we invoke almighty God in deepest humility and implore him to bestow his grace to this end. Amen.

If, however, our lords, friends, and associates who rep-

6

7

8

9

10

11

12

resent the electors, princes, and estates of the other party do not comply with the procedure intended by Your Imperial Majesty's summons, if no amicable and charitable negotiations take place between us, and if no results are attained, nevertheless we on our part shall not omit doing anything, 13 in so far as God and conscience allow, that may serve the cause of Christian unity. Of this Your Imperial Majesty, our 14 aforementioned friends (the electors, princes, and estates), and every lover of the Christian religion who is concerned about these questions will be graciously and sufficiently assured from what follows in the confession which we and our associates submit.

In the past Your Imperial Majesty graciously gave assur- 15 ance to the electors, princes, and estates of the empire, especially in a public instruction at the diet in Spires in 1526, that for reasons there stated Your Imperial Majesty was not 16 disposed to render decisions in matters pertaining to our holy faith but would diligently urge it upon the pope to call a council. Again, by means of a written instruction at the last 17 diet in Spires a year ago, the electors, princes, and estates 18 of the empire were, among other things, informed and notified by Your Imperial Majesty's viceroy (His Royal Majesty of Hungary and Bohemia, etc.) and by Your Imperial Majesty's orator and appointed commissioners, that Your Imperial Majesty's viceroy, administrators, and councilors of the imperial government (together with the absent electors, princes, and representatives of the estates) who were assembled at the diet convened in Ratisbon had considered the proposal concerning a general council and acknowl- 19 edged that it would be profitable to have such a council called. Since the relations between Your Imperial Majesty and the pope were improving and were progressing toward a good, Christian understanding, Your Imperial Majesty was sure that the pope would not refuse to call a general council, and so Your Imperial Majesty graciously offered to promote 20 and bring about the calling of such a general council by the

pope, along with Your Imperial Majesty, at the earliest opportunity and to allow no hindrance to be put in the way.

If the outcome should be such as we mentioned above, 21
we offer in full obedience, even beyond what is required, to
participate in such a general, free, and Christian council as
the electors, princes, and estates have with the highest and
best motives requested in all the diets of the empire which
have been held during Your Imperial Majesty's reign. We 22
have at various times made our protestations and appeals
concerning these most weighty matters, and have done so
in legal form and procedure. To these we declare our con- 23
tinuing adherence, and we shall not be turned aside from
our position by these or any following negotiations (unless
the matters in dissension are finally heard, amicably weight-
ed, charitably settled, and brought to Christian concord in
accordance with Your Imperial Majesty's summons) as we
herewith publicly witness and assert. This is our confession 24
and that of our associates, and it is specifically stated, article
by article, in what follows.

The Latin text is here a translation of the German. The Saxon chan-
cellor Brück is the author. Justus Jonas prepared the translation.

The Preface provides certain useful guidelines for a historical understanding of the AC. First, it reminds us emphatically of the AC's
character as an occasional writing. The AC is an expression of the
Lutheran princes' willingness to comply with the imperial edict of
January 21, 1530. As such, it is intended to be the groundwork for
negotiations in the attempts of this particular diet to settle the dispute.
Second, it should be noted in this regard that the Preface consistently
characterizes the dispute as a party conflict. Strongly relying on the
imperial edict, Brück deftly manages to begin from the premise that
the discussion involves two parties with equal rights in a negotiation
about mutual differences. Third, the emperor is held to his declaration
that he will not act as final judge of the matter.

This brings us to the principal tactic in the policy of the evangelicals,
to stress that the correct forum for settling the matter is a council. Here

again, the declarations of the emperor and imperial resolutions are mustered in support. The importance given to the proposed council reveals that, understandably enough, the expressed hope that the discussions of the diet would lead to positive results was not particularly strong.

Thus, from a political standpoint, the Preface proceeds astutely. The primary goal is that the diet result in an amicable conclusion. Should this prove impossible, the matter must be referred to a free and general council. In this way, a repetition of the events at the Diet of Speyer (1529) could be avoided. Of course, the appeal to a council was of major importance for the evangelicals from the very beginning. In the years after 1530, however, faith in this possibility quickly diminished. The preface to the Smalcald Articles demonstrates that by 1537 Luther had lost all confidence in such a solution. In 1530, however, it was still politically feasible to entertain the thought, since it had not yet become clear how unrealistic it was.

Part I

CHIEF ARTICLES
OF FAITH

Article 1

• GOD[1] •

Text

Our churches teach with great unanimity that the decree   1
of the Council of Nicaea concerning the unity of the divine
essence and concerning the three persons[2] is true and
should be believed without any doubting. That is to say, there   2
is one divine essence, which is called and which is God,
eternal, incorporeal, indivisible, of infinite power, wisdom,
and goodness, the maker and preserver of all things, visible
and invisible. Yet there are three persons, of the same es-   3
sence and power, who are also coeternal: the Father, the
Son, and the Holy Spirit. And the term "person" is used, as   4
the ancient Fathers employed it in this connection, to signify
not a part or a quality in another but that which subsists of
itself.

---

1. The article headings are not original, but were added at the printing of the AC. When the headings simply duplicate the initial words of the article (headings for Articles 9–16, 18–19, 21) Tappert omitted the words from his translation of the text; they are included here in brackets so that the English may more fully correspond to the Latin [trans.].

2. The German text (GT) adds: "Gott Vater, Gott Sohn, Gott heiliger Geist" (God the Father, God the Son, God the Holy Spirit).

Our churches condemn all heresies which have sprung   5
up against this article, such as that of the Manichaeans, who
posited two principles, one good and the other evil, and also
those of the Valentinians, Arians, Eunomians, Mohammedans, and all others like these. They also condemn the Sa-   6
mosatenes, old and new, who contend that there is only one
person and craftily and impiously argue[3] that the Word and
the Holy Spirit are not distinct persons since "Word" signifies
a spoken word and "Spirit" signifies a movement which is
produced in things.[4]

The Council of Nicaea: The AC refers here to the Nicene Creed,
which was the symbol of church orthodoxy from the time of the early
church. The unity of God's being and the three persons, however, are
described in a manner more reminiscent of the Athanasian Creed.
Which is called and which is God: This phrase expresses a reality
which is not merely a "name." It refers, no doubt, to the continuation
that follows the enumeration of the divine attributes, **yet there are
three persons. Infinite** (or "unlimited"): cf. the Athanasian Creed,
line 9. The three attributes **power** (*potentia*), **wisdom** (*sapientia*), and
goodness (*bonitas*) during the Middle Ages corresponded to the three
persons—not in such a manner so that *potentia* applied only to the
Father, *sapientia* only to the Son, etc., yet so that *potentia* properly
should be "appropriated to" the Father, *sapientia* to the Son, etc. **The
maker and preserver of all things, visible and invisible**: cf. the
Nicene Creed. The word *preserver* (conservator) is added here. **Of the
same essence and power, who are also coeternal**: cf. the Athanasian
Creed, lines 6, 11, 13, and 14.

The term **"person"**: The first part of the article closes with a
explanation of how the concept "person" is used. It must not be understood as a part or characteristic, but rather it should be understood in
the same way as the church fathers understood it: as **that which subsists
of itself.** That is, the divine persons are not merely various aspects of

---

3. *Rhetoricari* (argue) here signifies the use of false modes of speech.
4. GT has: "erschaffene Regung in Kreaturen" (a movement induced in creatures).

God's being, but are real and distinct, yet without shattering the unity of the divine being.

A "catalog of heresies" follows: **the Manichaeans** are condemned because of their pervasive dualism. **The Valentinians,** a gnostic school of the second century, considered Christ and the Holy Spirit to be aeons, and thus came to understand them as parts of the divine emanation. It is natural for the **Arians** to be named in a Confession which relies upon the Nicene Creed. The **Eunomians** received their name as followers of the Arian Eunomius toward the close of the fourth century. The **Mohammedans** are included simply because they are among those who deny the Trinity. The **Samosatenes** were followers of Paul of Samosata who denied that the Logos was distinct in relation to God in any respect. The question of the identity of the **new Samosatenes** is discussed in the commentary which follows.

Commentary

By referring to the Nicene, or more correctly, the Nicene-Constantinopolitan Creed, the confessors claim to stand on the doctrinal ground of the early church. The Preface attempted to establish the position that the conflict is between two parties within the church. Precisely for this reason it is important to demonstrate from the beginning that the orthodoxy of the early church is undisputed by the reformers. The Confutation offers no further comment on Article 1 except to declare that this confession *acceptanda est* (must be accepted).[5] Thus in the Apology Melanchthon is content with reaffirming the unity of God's being. He adds that anyone who does not hold to this faith stands outside the church of Christ.[6]

When Melanchthon in 1521 published his *Loci Communes,* he included no formal presentation of trinitarian doctrine because, as he claimed, the mysteries of the Trinity and the Incarnation had been treated by the scholastic theologians through the centuries with no other result than futile speculation. It is in this context that the famous and

---

5. The Confutation (*Confutatio pontificia*) is cited from *Die Confutatio der Confessio Augustana* (Münster, 1974); ET, M. Reu, Part 2.
6. The Apology 1.

often quoted sentence, "We do better to adore the mysteries of the Deity than to investigate them,"[7] belongs. If this sentence is to be seen correctly, however, it must also be seen in connection with the words that follow: "The Lord God Almighty clothed his Son with flesh that he might draw us from contemplating his own majesty to a consideration of the flesh, and especially of our weakness."[8]

Here, however, historical developments necessitated a stronger underscoring of the fact that the confessors stood on the confessional ground of the early church. In part this was due to the fact that certain enthusiasts had appeared as antitrinitarians, but also because John Eck in his 404 Articles had accused Luther of being in conflict with the doctrine of the Trinity. Thus it became important to isolate oneself from the spiritualistic heretics and to rebuff Eck's attack. Eck focused his attack on this sentence from Luther's treatise *Rationis Latomianae— Lutheriana confutatio (Against Latomus)* of 1521: "Even if my soul hated this word, 'homoousion,' and I refused to use it, still I would not be a heretic."[9] Eck cites this sentence as being among the Lutheran heresies (Article 82),[10] even though he quotes only the first half and then comments: "[*homoousion*], which means that the Father and the Son are of the same essence." It does seem that Luther turns against the idea of the unity of the Father and the Son here. Luther's true meaning, however, becomes clear by the words with which he continues in the treatise *Against Latomus:* "For who compels me to use the word, providing I hold to the fact defined by the council [namely, the Nicene] on the basis of scripture?" "The integrity of scripture must be guarded, and a man ought not presume that he speaks more safely and clearly with his mouth than God spoke with his mouth." In other words, expressions from Scripture in which God himself speaks must take precedence over concepts fashioned by human beings. In the

---

7. "Mysteria divinitatis rectius adoraverimus, quam vestigaverimus. . . . Et carne filium Deus optimus maximus induit, ut nos a contemplatione majestatis suae ad carnis adeoque fragilitatis nostrae contemplationem invitaret" (Melanchthon, *Werke* 2/1: 6, 16ff.).

8. Ibid.

9. WA 8:177; *LW* 32 (Philadelphia: Fortress, 1958), p. 244.

10. Eck's Articles are found in W. Gussmann, *Quellen und Forschungen zur Geschichte des Augsburgischen Bekenntnisses* 2 (1930); ET, Reu, 2:97-121, especially p. 100.

Church Postil Luther similarly criticizes the word *Trinity*, because it is not found in Scripture but was invented by humans.[11] Eck's accusation, therefore, was utterly groundless. Nevertheless, once it had publicly appeared, it had to be refuted. The Marburg Articles which, like the AC, refer to Nicea also begin with the doctrine of the Trinity as do the Schwabach Articles and Luther's *Confession concerning Christ's Supper* of 1528.[12] The same is true of the Smalcald Articles.[13]

Concerning the development of the doctrine of the Trinity itself in AC 1, it should be noted that most of the expressions are not in fact from the Nicene-Constantinopolitan Creed but rather from the Athanasian. It is not a case of direct copying but rather of complete agreement with all the essentials of the early church confessions. The AC introduces nothing new. It is better formed, however, than the trinitarian teaching of the Schwabach Articles which simply states "dass in dem einigen wahrhaftigen, gottlichen Wesen drei unterschiedenlich Personen seind" [that in the one, almighty, divine Being, there are three distinct persons].[14] Bucer had directed the criticism against the Schwabach Articles that, "crudely taken," the word *person* could be understood as an independent being. Bucer, in other words, was afraid of tritheism.[15] Even so, in composing the AC Melanchthon seems to have been more apprehensive of the opposite extreme. Thus, the clarification of the word *person* which concludes the first part of Article 1 is clearly intended to preclude a modalistic interpretation. Unity in the concept of God, however, emerges strongly when creation is attributed to the

---

11. "It is indeed true that the name 'Trinity' is nowhere to be found in the Holy Scriptures, but has been conceived and invented by man. For this reason it sounds somewhat cold, and we had better speak of 'God' than of the 'Trinity' " (*Luther's Works,* Lenker ed., vol. 12 [Minneapolis: Lutherans in All Lands, 1910], p. 406).

12. Clemen 3:508, 11ff.; WA 26:500; LW 37 (Philadelphia: Fortress, 1961), pp. 151-372.

13. In his comments on the Schwabach Articles (Reu, 2:49-50), Bucer criticizes the doctrine of the Trinity set forth there with exactly the same argument as Luther's against the words *Trinity* and *homoousion*. It is much better to confine oneself to Scripture! Thus Luther is played against himself here.

14. Approximately the same formulation as in *Confession concerning Christ's Supper;* see note 12.

15. Cf. note 13.

whole triune God instead of the Father alone,[16] which is the case even in the Nicene Creed to which the Confession refers! Luther also frequently emphasizes the unity. One need simply think of the hymn "A Mighty Fortress" to find a clear example in the following words: "ER heisst Jesus Christ, der HERR Zebaoth, Und ist kein ander Gott" [HIS name is Jesus Christ, the LORD of hosts, And there is no other God]. Luther does not intend to imply here that there is no difference between God as creator and as savior. He simply wants to emphasize that it really is God himself who has acted in Christ. In the Catechisms, with their directly pedagogical aims, he expresses himself differently. Here the works of God are distributed among the three persons. It is not, however, a matter of contradiction, but merely of different nuances.

Despite the fact that external factors were partly responsible for the development of Article 1, one cannot conclude that we are here dealing with a subject which was of no interest to the reformers. Luther's critique of the classical formulae reveals, to the contrary, that the accusation so often leveled at the reformers that they simply appropriated the dogma of the Trinity "undigested" is not justified.[17] As is clear from the passage cited above in the treatise *Against Latomus,* Luther was far from being opposed to dealing with the "issue itself." He was only opposed to a treatment of it which went outside of and beyond the Holy Scriptures. Luther found repeated occasion through the years in both lectures and sermons to delve into the doctrine of the Trinity, and when he did he showed no reservation.[18] For him the question was always one of setting the teaching in context with scripture. He rejects scholastic speculation because he wishes to know nothing about God which is not revealed in God's works. Practically speaking, this means that primary emphasis will be placed on the

---

16. The background to this is, of course, the conclusion of the development of the doctrine of the Trinity which took place after Nicea. Fear of tritheism gave impetus to the attempt to assert the unity of God's activity in relation to the creation to the highest degree possible.

17. See K. Thieme, *Die Augsburgische Konfession* (1930), pp. 144ff., where a series of these accusations is listed.

18. For references to Luther's writings, see R. Seeberg, *Lehrbuch der Dogmengeschichte* 4/1 (1930), pp. 230ff., and R. Prenter's enlightening treatment of Luther's relationship to the doctrine of the Trinity in *Spiritus Creator,* trans. J. M. Jensen (Philadelphia: Muhlenberg, 1953), pp. 173ff. Jan Koopman, *Das altkirchliche Dogma in der Reformation* (Beiträge zur evangelischen Theologie 23 [1955]), reinforces this interpretation.

"economic" Trinity as is clearly expressed in the language of God as creator, redeemer, and sanctifier in the Catechisms. Luther does not reject trinitarian language which attempts to express the inner being of God, but simply emphasizes that the inner being of God is known only through his works in revelation. Luther does not depart from the classical doctrine of the Trinity in any way by this perspective. He does just the opposite: he returns to it by rejecting the deviations brought about by the speculations of Scholasticism. In the trinitarian battles of the early church, the issue at stake was always salvation. Denying the divinity of the Son and the Spirit threatened the understanding of salvation as an act of God. Luther is interested in the doctrine of the Trinity for precisely the same reason. In the Large Catechism he says: "As we have explained before, we could never come to recognize the Father's favor and grace were it not for the Lord Christ, who is a mirror of the Father's heart. Apart from him we see nothing but an angry and terrible Judge. But neither could we know anything of Christ, had it not been revealed by the Holy Spirit."[19] These words succinctly express what the doctrine of the Trinity meant for Luther. First, the three persons are clearly distinguished, eliminating any form of modalism.[20] Second, it is clear to what degree everything in a person's relationship to God is determined by the initiative of God himself. This makes it obvious, however, that it is impossible to speak as if Luther considers the doctrine of the Trinity merely a piece of tradition to be perpetuated. Rather, it is a leading premise of his whole theology. In *Spiritus Creator,* Regin Prenter writes: "Scholastic theology retained all its traditional confession of the eternal divinity of the Son and the Spirit. But because of the synergistic doctrine of salvation it gave man's free will a significance which was really a limitation of the domain of the work of both the Son and the Spirit."[21] In contrast to Scholasticism, the statement of Melanchthon (cited above) that God, through the incarnation, would guide us to the contemplation of our flesh and weakness expresses the reformers' point quite nicely—that confession of the triune God is intimately linked with the confession of humanity's

---

19. Large Catechism 4 §65 (*BC*, p. 419).

20. Cf. Prenter's interesting refutation of Karl Holl's claim that Luther holds a modalistic view of the Trinity (*Spiritus Creator*, pp. 180ff.).

21. Ibid., p. 177.

utter powerlessness. Thus, the doctrine of the Trinity was freed from speculation about the relationship of the human soul as *imago trinitatis* (the image of the Trinity) and the eternal inner being of God, returning towards an understanding of the living connection between the doctrine of the Trinity and the way salvation itself was viewed. The dogmatic struggles of the early church are expressions of the latter. Despite the fact that the reformers failed to find new or better words,[22] their trinitarian teaching marked a renewal in comparison with scholasticism because there was a return to the original connection between the Trinity and historical revelation.[23]

Against this background, it is clear that the second part of Article 1 cannot be reduced to a purely church-political arrangement either. The degree to which "heresy" was still equated with rejection of early church dogma for the reformers is illustrated by the fact that §1 in the new faculty statutes for the Wittenberg theologians in 1533 prescribed that pure doctrine was to be taught in harmony with the AC, and that the ancient heresies condemned at the Councils of Nicea, Constantinople, Ephesus, and Chalcedon should be combatted as strongly as possible.[24] In the "catalog of heresies" of Article 1, special interest is focused on the term "new Samosatenes." Most important here is the thought of Johann Campanus who arrived at the Elector of Saxony's court in Torgau during March of 1530 and presented his viewpoints. He taught that the Holy Spirit was not a person and that Christ was not of the same essence as the Father. He attacked Lutherans on a number of other points as well. Besides this, he established connections with the Anabaptists and won acclamation for his antitrinitarian views. At Torgau he was, of course, rejected.[25] He had drawn so much attention, however, that it was deemed necessary specifically to reject him and his followers. Antitrinitarian teaching won wide acceptance among the enthusiasts. Denck also was an opponent of trinitarian teaching. The specific teaching rejected in Article 1 seems not to be confined

---

22. In the treatise *On the Councils and the Churches* (1539), Luther himself acknowledges that the word *homoousion* is necessary (WA 50:572f.; *LW* 41 [Philadelphia: Fortress, 1961], pp. 82ff.).

23. Melanchthon also revised his view on the theological treatment of the doctrine of the Trinity. From the 1535 edition on, the *Loci* begins with the doctrine.

24. See Köstlin-Kawerau, *Martin Luther* 2 (1903), p. 281.

25. See Köstlin-Kawerau, 2:148, 322f.; cf. *BK,* p. 51, n. 7.

to the teaching of Campanus. The precise occasion, therefore, for the specific formulation of the rejection is unknown. In 1530 the various antitrinitarians were still extremely cautious about advocating their thought publicly. From the language of Article 1 it seems that the rejected doctrine was thought to be one which would define both "the Word" and "the Spirit" as expressions for what occurs within a person upon being "born again" or receiving the "outpouring of the Spirit." This is most easily seen in relation to "the Spirit." Obviously, the Holy Spirit here is identified with a person's spiritual renewal. It is more difficult to decifer what is meant in saying that "the Word" is "the spoken word." Could it be that a type of "pneumatic speech" is meant here? Most certainly it is not the proclamation of the gospel in the understanding of the Reformation. Regardless of how this might be explained, however, the decisive element in the rejection of the heresy is that for the reformers to deny the divinity of the Son and the Spirit meant giving up the gospel itself.[26]

---

26. There is no doubt that the AC refers to a specific teaching here. Despite persistent research, however, it has been impossible to determine exactly what it means. No scholar known to the author who has commented on Article 1 has contributed to the solution of the problem.

Article 2

• ORIGINAL SIN •

Text

Our churches also teach that since the fall of Adam all   1
men who are propagated according to nature are born in
sin. That is to say, they are without fear of God, are without
trust in God, and are concupiscent.[1] And this disease or vice   2
of origin[2] is truly sin, which even now damns and brings
eternal death on those who are not born again through Baptism and the Holy Spirit.

Our churches condemn the Pelagians and others who   3
deny that the vice of origin is sin and who obscure the glory
of Christ's merit and benefits by contending that man can
be justified before God by his own strength and reason.[3]

---

1. GT: "Dass sie alle von Mutterlieb an voll boser Lust und Neigung seind" (That is, all men are full of evil lusts and inclinations from their mother's wombs).

2. *Hic morbus seu vitium originis* (this disease or vice of origin): *originis* (of origin) modifies both antecedents.

3. From a purely linguistic standpoint, the clause beginning with *ut* (who) either denounces the intent to obscure the glory of Christ (in which case one would translate: "and who, to obscure the glory of Christ's merit and benefits, contend that," etc. [trans.]), or simply states the consequence of false confidence in humanity's own powers. The latter is probably the most logical.

Since the fall, all who are **propagated according to nature** are **born in sin.** This qualification, of course, serves to exclude Christ, who was born in a supernatural manner. Next, a more precise definition of the phrase **in sin** is given: **That is to say. . . .** Two negative definitions of sin, **without fear of God** (i.e., without acknowledging God as Lord of one's life) and **without trust in God** (i.e., without the complete confidence characteristic of faith) are followed by a positive definition: **and are concupiscent.** Augustine had previously made use of the term *concupiscentia* in connection with original sin. For him, the term's principal connotation was sensuality (more on this later). Here in the AC, as in the Apology later, the term is used in harmony with Luther's understanding of it and covers much more than sensual desire. It includes also a person's entire spiritual existence insofar as it is not produced by faith. After this follows the second part of the reformers' teaching: **And this disease or vice of origin is truly sin** (*vere sit peccatum*). Couched in traditional language, this phrase means that original sin is not merely one's inexplicable fate, but also guilt. Condemnation and **eternal death** accompany it, therefore, as punishment. This is true **even now,** after Christ. The last sentence restricts this punishment to those who have not been reborn in **Baptism** through which they receive **the Holy Spirit.**

The second section condemns **the Pelagians and others** who deny that original sin is really sin, holding that a person can be justified before God **by his own strength and reason.** This last contention has catastrophic effects on how one sees Christ.

Commentary

The most noteworthy aspect of this article is its definition of the word *sin:* "without fear of God . . . , without trust in God, . . . and concupiscent." This definition is new over against the Middle Ages: Original sin cannot be described as mere defects in certain human attributes or as a lack of supernatural endowments. Rather, the human situation has been completely changed by it.

In early Scholasticism we meet two different perceptions of original sin. Anselm defines it in a purely negative manner as lacking the original righteousness which Adam had in paradise (*carentia* or *de-*

fectus iustitiae originalis ["lack of" or "eclipse of original righteousness"]).[4] Peter Lombard, on the other hand, perceives original sin as
concupiscence, which for him refers to the lower powers in human
nature seeking to break free from the control of reason and the will.[5]
Both hold that original sin is completely removed in Baptism. After
Baptism concupiscence becomes the "tinder of sin" (*fomes peccati*),
which in itself cannot be considered sin. While the foremost theologians of high Scholasticism, for example, Alexander of Hales,[6]
Bonaventura,[7] and Thomas Aquinas,[8] sought to reconcile these two

---

4. Anselm, *De conceptu virginali et originali peccato,* cap. 27 (Migne, PL 158,
461): "Hoc peccatum, quod originale dico, aliud intelligere nequeo in eisdem infan-
tibus, nisi ipsam quam supra posui, factam per inobedientia Adae justitiae debitae
nuditatem per quam omnes filii sunt irae . . ." (In regard to these infants, I cannot
understand this sin I am calling "original" to be anything else than that same depra-
vation of the required justice, which I described before as the result of the disobedience
of Adam, by which all are children of wrath . . .; *Why God Became Man and The
Virgin Conception and Original Sin,* trans. Joseph M. Colleran [New York: Magi
Books, 1969], p. 208).

5. Peter Lombard, *Sententiarum Libri IV,* Lib. II, Dist. 30, 7 (Migne, *PL* 192, 722):
"Quid ergo originale peccatum dicitur? Fomes peccati, scilicet concupiscentia vel
concupiscibilitas, quae dicitur lex membrorum, sive languor naturae, sive tyrannus
qui est in membris nostris, sive lex carnis; unde August., in lib. de Baptismo par-
vulorum, tom. 7: Est in nobis concupiscentia, quae non est permittenda regnare. Sunt
et ejus desideria, quae sunt actuales concupiscentiae, quae sunt arma diaboli, quae
veniunt ex languore naturae" (What, then, can original sin be said to be? It is the
"tinder" of sin, that is, concupiscence or lust which is called the very "law" of our
members, or the "feebleness" of our "nature," or the "tyrant" which resides in our
members, or the very "law" of "the flesh"; hence Augustine, in the treatise *On the
Baptism of Infants,* vol. 7, says: "There is concupiscence in us, which must not be
permitted to rule us. There are its desires, which are actual concupiscences, the weapons
of the devil, which arise from the feebleness of our nature" [trans. Justin Pierce]).

6. *Summa Theologica,* II-II, Inq. II, Tract. III. Quaest. II, cap. III, art. III: "Cum
ergo quaeritur utrum originale peccatum secundum idem sit culpa et poena, dicendum
est quod secundum carentiam debitae iustitiae est culpa, secundum concupiscentiam
vero est poena" (When, therefore, it is asked whether original sin according to the
previously stated perspective is both a fault and a penalty, it must be said that in
respect to the lack of the required justice it is a fault, and in respect to concupiscence
it is indeed a penalty [trans. Justin Pierce]). Tom. 3 p. 240. *Ad claras aquas,* 1930.

7. *Commentaria in IV Lib. Sent. II* dist. 30, art. II, q. 1 concl.: "Peccatum originale
est concupiscentia, prout in se claudit debitae iustitiae carentiam" (Original sin is
concupiscence, insofar as it locks in the lack of the required justice [trans. Justin
Pierce]). *Opera Omnia,* Tom. 2, p. 722. *Ad claras aquas,* 1885.

perceptions, Duns Scotus[9] and later William of Ockham[10] held to the "Anselmian" line. For these last two, original sin is nothing more than a kind of debt for which humans are liable by the will of God, even though they are not personally touched by it. Consequently, humanity's natural powers were considered wholly intact and could be emphasized in the doctrine of justification.

Luther had already in 1515 turned his full strength against this notion (especially in the *Lectures on Romans*). If human powers are intact, then Christ is unnecessary. Sin is unbelief, and true acknowledgment of sin comes from God alone as he reveals himself. In justification the person acknowledges his or her sin and has it forgiven. Sin is forgiven by grace, because it is not imputed by God, but it does not disappear before death. The real sin is not any sinful deed but original sin, which comes into being at the same time as the person, and which through the will's consent becomes the person's own sin. Concupiscence is not merely sensual desire. It is an expression of all self-centered human striving, including that related to spiritual matters.[11]

This perception emerges clearly in the AC, as does the danger of a false doctrine of original sin, namely, that Christ's glory is nullified as trust in humanity's own power is enhanced. In this Article 2 follows the Marburg and Schwabach Articles very closely.[12] The authors of the

---

8. *Summa Theologica*, II-I q. 82, art. 3: "Peccatum originale materialiter quidem est concupiscentia; formaliter vero, defectus originalis iustitiae" (original sin materially is concupiscence, yet formally it is the lack of original justice; trans. T. C. Obrien, O.P., vol. 26, p. 39).

9. *Opera omnia*, Tom. 13 (Opus Oxoniense) in Sent. II d. 30 q. 2, Paris 1893: "Peccatum originale non potest esse aliud quam ista privatio [i.e., iustitiae originalis]; non enim est concupiscentia" (original sin cannot be anything other than this privation [i.e., of original justice], it is not, therefore, concupiscence [trans. Justin Pierce]).

10. *Super IV libros Sententiarum annotationes*, Lyon, 1495, II q. 26 U: "Item ad questionem de peccato originali. . . . Nam de facto est sola carentia iustitiae originalis cum debito habendi eam" (Likewise with regard to original sin. . . . For in reality it is only the lack of original justice along with the obligation of having it [trans. Justin Pierce]).

11. The *Lectures on Romans* are permeated by these thoughts. See, e.g., WA 56, 229, 1ff.; 271, 1ff.; 285, 1ff.; ET, *LW* 25:213ff., 259ff., 272ff.

12. The tone is sharper in the Smalcald Articles. Here Luther states that original sin is a corruption of nature so deep and terrible that human reason is wholly unable to comprehend it; it must be believed according to the revelation of Scripture. This is followed by a detailed and sharp rejection of the teaching of the incorruptibility of nature and the ability of natural powers (SA 3.1; *BK*, pp. 433f.; *BC*, pp. 302-303).

Confutation are quite clear about where to direct their rebuttal. The sentence which claims that original sin really is sin is acknowledged without argument. The AC is rejected, however, on two other points. First, the idea that original sin consists in the absence of fear of God and trust in God is denied. It is argued that this notion is more closely related to the personal guilt of an adult (*culpa actualis*) than to the offense of a newborn child. Second, the Confutation notes that to speak of concupiscence as sin can be understood to mean that original sin remains also in the baptized. This notion is rejected by referring to the papacy's previous condemnation of two statements of Luther about sin remaining after Baptism.[13] The first objection reveals that while the authors of the Confutation recognize where the conflict lies, they have still completely misunderstood the AC. They construe the words "without fear of God, . . . without trust in God" to be descriptions of a psychological state and thus are bound to consider it unfair to speak this way of small children who "do not as yet possess the full use of reason." The German text of the AC, however, proves that the AC's point is completely different: "dass sie alle . . . keine wahre Gottesfurcht, kein wahren Glauben von Natur *haben können*" (that they all . . . *are unable* by nature to have true fear of God and true faith in God). Whether one is a child or an adult is beside the point, because the "corruption" of original sin is precisely that human beings are unable—*and unwilling*—to know God. By this understanding of original sin it is also shown that Article 1 is taken seriously. There is no other God than the triune God who can be known only as he reveals himself.

In the Apology, Melanchthon vigorously rebuts the Confutation, declaring that the AC teaches nothing new but simply repeats the teachings of the New Testament and the church fathers. He attempts to prove that, correctly understood, the definition of original sin as lack of

---

13. At issue are the two following sentences from Leo X's bull against Luther, *Exsurge Domine*, of June 15, 1520: 2. "In puero post baptismo negare remanens peccatum, est Paulum et Christum simul conculcare" (He who denies that after Baptism sin remains in every child tramples upon Christ and St. Paul). 3. "Fomes peccati, etiamsi nullum adsit actuale peccatum, moratur exeuntem a corpore animam ab ingressu coeli" (The tinder of original sin, even without actual sin, bars the entrance to the kingdom of heaven); Denzinger (34th ed., 1967), 1452–1453; ET, *LW* 32:19, 29.

original righteousness says the same thing as the AC.[14] He also considers Augustine's doctrine of original sin. "Concupiscence" refers to the fact that humans seek and love "carnal things" (*carnalia*) instead of God. *Carnalia* are not limited to the sensual here, but include all human wisdom and righteousness. According to Melanchthon, the very same thing is expressed in Article 2. Correctly and in harmony with the church fathers, Article 2 covers both sides of the doctrine: original sin as lack and as desire. Those who advocate the scholastic teaching that concupiscence is not sin but merely penalty[15] not only have Scripture against them, but the whole church as well.[16]

If one is to be clear about what was at stake for the reformers, it must be borne in mind that they confronted a theology that thought in metaphysical terms and was tied to concepts of a nonpersonal character. The objective for Scholasticism was correctly to define the being and place of humanity within creation as a whole. The word *nature*, therefore, which played no role at all in the New Testament, became a key term in medieval theology. At creation, humanity had been given a specific nature. The task of the doctrine of original sin was to determine the extent to which this original nature had been changed. Then, in the doctrine of justification humanity's new *status*, the state of grace, was defined. All three stages, *status integrae, naturae lapsae,* and *gratiae* (the state of intact nature, of fallen nature, and of grace), were of interest for anthropology. Generally, the object was to determine which capacities and possibilities are held by humans in each state. Luther, however, had no interest in such neutral, "static" attempts at determining capacities. He viewed everything from the perspective of a person's relationship with God. Everything a person has or is must

---

14. *Iustitia originalis* (original righteousness), says Melanchthon, is nothing else than the right relationship to God itself, identical with *similitudo Dei* (the likeness of God). Original sin, therefore, means not only that the submission of the lower powers ceases, but that *notitia* (knowledge) and *fiducia Dei* (trust in God) are lost. It is certainly possible to interpret the concept *carentia iustitiae originalis* (lack of original righteousness) in this manner, but it is also clear that this was not the intention of the Scholastics as they applied the term to original sin.

15. And thus, an adiaphoron, as long as the will does not give its consent to the desire.

16. One cannot avoid the fact that Melanchthon reaches this "agreement" with medieval theology also only by interpreting it in a foreign manner.

be qualified by this basic premise, the person's relationship with God or lack of it. To understand how crucial this difference is, further clarification is necessary. The polemical situation forced the reformers to stress that original sin had ruined human nature over against assertions of the incorruptibility of the powers of humanity. If one forgets that there are different modes of thought operating here, however, one misses the reformers' intentions completely. When one continues in the scholastic mode of presenting the problem, the reformers' teaching becomes nothing but a deprecation of humanity to the point where humanity is no longer even human. The fact that Luther himself, for want of a better term, occasionally used the word *habitus* (condition) in connection with original sin has not helped in clarifying the situation. This has likely contributed to the fact that the same line was pursued in later Lutheran theology.[17] To attain further clarity on this question, however, we must turn to the Confutation's second objection.

As noted previously, the point of the second objection is that to identify original sin with concupiscence can be understood to mean that original sin remains even after Baptism. In the Apology, Melanchthon refuses to sidestep the question and admits that this is precisely the meaning of Article 2. Grace does not mean the removal of original sin but its forgiveness. Luther has said this, he continues, to show that even after Baptism humans are dependent on Christ for the nonimputation of sin, and upon the Spirit for its eradication. A central point in the reformer's perception of humanity is at stake here. Baptism bestows no new *habitus* as such so that now, objectively considered, the person is a different and better human being. Rather, Baptism initiates a new relationship with God so that, insofar as the person clings to Christ, that person partakes in his righteousness. The reformers have no teaching about humanity in and of itself, but only about humanity in relation to God. Thus, to teach that sin remains after

---

17. In the Apology, Melanchthon also lets himself be drawn onto his opponents' ground by speaking of *potentia* (potency) and *actus* (act) in connection with the Confutation's objection regarding the innocence of the newborn in reference to their lack of the fear of God, so that one might receive the impression that his doctrine of sin follows the old lines. Besides this the Apology's statement is very clear. There is nothing to imply that the reformers' doctrine of original sin is simply a sharpening of the scholastic doctrine, as Roman Catholic polemics has incorrectly perceived it. It is another question whether this polemic hits the mark over against Lutheran orthodoxy.

Baptism has nothing to do with a devaluation of humanity. Assertions about human "nature" are of little interest. What is decisive is the fact that humans receive their lives as gifts from God's hand, or in various ways assert their self-sufficiency. Human nature, if one must use the term at all, is nothing more for the reformers than what the Creator has determined it to be: a life of faith and obedience to God, renouncing every form of self-assertion, even when it takes the form of righteousness. Thus, it is possible, after all, to speak of a corruption of nature if it is understood that something entirely different is meant by the word *nature* here than a metaphysical definition of being. Much preferable to the term *sinful nature*, therefore, is the term frequently used by Luther, *personal sin*. By this it is expressed that the key aspect of original sin is each individual human being's personal relationship to God and the self and not merely a hereditary fate or sickness. In the second part of Article 2, the "Pelagians and others" who do not consider original sin to be real sin are condemned. In addition to Scholasticism (more or less rightly), this part is also addressed to Zwingli, who considered original sin to be a sickness in which humanity is involved without fault.[18]

When at the general Council of Trent the Roman church sought to establish its teaching, it was clear that the doctrine of original sin had to be treated. The decree which was adopted on this matter[19] is summarized briefly below:

1. When Adam disobeyed God's commandment, he lost the holiness and righteousness with which he had been endowed, incurred the wrath of God, death, and captivity under the power of the devil, and was changed for the worse in both body and soul.[20]

---

18. Zwingli: *De peccato originali declaratio, Corpus Reformatorum* 92, 372; 4: "Sic ergo diximus originalem contagionem morbum esse, non peccatum, quod peccatum cum culpa coniunctum est" (Therefore we say that the original contagion is a sickness, not a sin, because sin is inseparable from fault [trans. Justin Pierce]).

19. Fifth Session, decree concerning original sin.

20. 1. "Si quis non confitetur, primum hominem Adam, . . . sanctitatem et iustitiam, . . . amisisse, incurrisseque . . . iram et indignationem Dei, atque ideo mortem, . . . et cum morte captivitatem sub (diaboli) potestate, . . . totumque Adam per illam praevaricationis offensam secundum corpus et animam in deterius commutatum fuisse: anathema sit" (If anyone does not confess that the first man, Adam, . . . lost the holiness and righteousness in which he had been constituted . . ., incurred the wrath and indignation of God, and thus death, . . . and together with death, captivity under the power of the devil, . . . and that the entire Adam through that offense of prevarication was changed in body and soul for the worse, let him be anathema). ET, Schroeder, p. 21.

2. This act had the same consequences for the whole human race after him.[21]

3. This sin, transmitted to all by propagation, not imitation, can be removed by the merit of Jesus Christ our mediator, in whose merit we partake through Baptism.[22]

4. Newborn infants should also be baptized since they too are carriers of original sin, even though they have committed no sin and must be cleansed by Baptism in order to partake of eternal life.[23]

5. Through baptismal grace the guilt of original sin is forgiven, and everything that has the character of real sin is removed. A curse is pronounced on those who deny this by saying that sin is not removed, but merely not imputed. What remains is concupiscence or "tinder," which the Catholic Church has understood to be called sin, not at all because it truly and actually is sin in the reborn, but because it is of sin and leads to sin. The blessed Virgin is not included in what is said here about original sin.[24]

Conflict with the reformers does not actually emerge clearly until number 5, the principal point being the question of what happens to original sin in Baptism. Since this question is not even addressed in the AC, the two confessions may not seem to be as far apart as might be expected; and yet one must remember that in the Apology Melanchthon agrees with Luther. The final characterization of Adam after

---

21. Reference is made to Rom. 5:21.

22. "3. . . . Hoc Adae peccatum, quod origine unum est, et propagatione, non imitatione, transfusum omnibus inest unicuique proprium . . ." (. . . this sin of Adam, which in its origin is one, and by propagation not by imitation is transfused to all, which is in each one as something that is his own . . .). ET, Schroeder, p. 22.

23. "4. . . . Ex traditione Apostolorum etiam parvuli, qui nihil peccatorum in semetipsis adhuc committere potuerunt, ideo in remissionem peccatorum veraciter baptizantur, ut in eis regeneratione mundetur quod generatione contraxerunt . . ." (From the faith handed down from the Apostles, even infants who could not as yet commit any sin of themselves are for this reason truly baptized for the remission of sins, in order that in them what they contracted by generation may be washed away by regeneration . . .). ET, ibid., pp. 22-23.

24. "5. Si quis . . . reatum originalis peccati remitti negat, aut etiam asserit, non tolli totum id, quod veram et propriam peccati rationem habet, sed illud dicit tantum radi aut non imputari: Anathema sit" (If anyone denies that . . . the guilt of original sin is remitted, or says that the whole of that which belongs to the essence of sin is not taken away, but says that it is only cancelled or not imputed, let him be anathema). ET, ibid., p. 23.

the Fall, "was changed for the worse," repeats an Augustinian citation from the Synod of Orange in 527[25] and is a very weak definition. On the other hand, the Council of Trent clearly keeps itself free of Pelagianism. The difference between Trent and the AC is not clarified until we examine the different ways in which the concepts are applied. This means that until the center of the controversy is reached in the issue of justification, the differences will remain hidden. At that point, however, the consequences drawn by each party from its doctrine of original sin will be exposed.

---

25. Denzinger, 371.

Article 3

• THE SON OF GOD •

Text

Our churches also teach that the Word—that is, the Son   1
of God—took on man's nature in the womb of the blessed
virgin Mary.[1] So there are two natures, divine and human,   2
inseparably conjoined in the unity of his person, one Christ,
true God and true man, who was born of the virgin Mary,
truly suffered, was crucified, dead, and buried, that he might   3
reconcile the Father to us[2] and be a sacrifice not only for
the original guilt but also for all actual sins of men. He also   4
descended into hell, and on the third day truly rose again.
Afterward he ascended into heaven to sit on the right hand
of the Father, forever reign and have dominion over all creatures, and sanctify those who believe in him by sending the   5
Holy Spirit into their hearts to rule, comfort, and quicken
them[3] and defend them against the devil and the power of
sin. The same Christ will openly come again to judge the   6
living and the dead, etc., according to the Apostles' Creed.

---

1. GT: "Dass Gott der Sohn sei Mensch worden, geborn aus der reinen Jungfrauen Maria" (that God the Son became man, born of the virgin Mary).

2. GT: "Gottes Zorn versohnet" (to propitiate God's wrath).

3. GT: "Dass er . . . durch den heiligen Geist heilige, reinige, stärke und troste, ihnen auch Leben und allerlei Gaben und Guter austeile" (that through the Holy Spirit he may sanctify, purify, strengthen, and comfort . . . that he may bestow on them life and every blessing).

The article begins with the incarnation: Christ **took on man's nature.** This use of classical language makes it natural to refer to the Athanasian Creed, line 33: "Unus (Christus) autem non conversione divinitatis in carne, sed assumptione humanitatis in Deo" (one [Christ], that is to say, not by changing the Godhead into flesh but by taking on the humanity into God). After mentioning the virgin birth, a short rehearsal of the orthodox doctrine of the two natures (two natures in one person) is followed by an affirmation of the humanity of Christ in language reminiscent of the Apostles' Creed: **born of the Virgin Mary,** etc. Once it has been stated who he is, the purpose of the incarnation can be given: **that he might reconcile,** etc. He is to reconcile the Father to us; God is the object of reconciliation here. His death is to be a sacrifice for **all** human sin, not only for original sin (see below). The rest of the article continues, enlarging upon **the Apostles' Creed. The same** (*idem*): it is the same Christ, God and man, who rose and took his place at the right hand of the Father who will judge the living and the dead. The kingly work of Christ includes dominion over all creatures and also the sanctification of all believers. The latter is accomplished through the Holy Spirit, whose work is described in the relative clauses. He is the comforter, life-giver, and defender against the evil powers—the devil and sin. There is no separate article on the Holy Spirit in the AC. It is not necessary, because the work of the Holy Spirit is presented in general here in Article 3, and because most of the remainder of the Confession is actually nothing but a further exposition of the Spirit's work.

Commentary

The purpose of this article, as that of Article 1, is first and foremost to testify that the confessors are in harmony with early church orthodoxy. Polemics recede into the background as expressions taken either from the Apostles' Creed or from other early church confessions are used. The article covers both the person and the work of Christ. Initially its concern is to establish the incarnation. God's Son "took on man's nature in the womb of the blessed virgin Mary." The German text indicates that overly much significance ought not be attributed to the words "took on." They mean no more than "sei Menschen worden" (became man). After this, the doctrine of the two natures is summarized in terms reminiscent of the Chalcedonian formula: "inseparably conjoined."[4] Then, without pausing, the article describes the work of Christ in the words of the Apostles' Creed. Not only the suffering, crucifixion, death, and burial of Christ, but the incarnation itself took place "that he might reconcile the Father to us." The confession of Christ as true God and true man is not a theme for speculation, but is intimately connected with the confession of Christ as redeemer. We shall return to this shortly. The merest hint of critique against the Roman church occurs in connection with the atonement, where the text reads: "that he might . . . be a sacrifice not only for original guilt but also for all actual sins of men." As far as the atonement is concerned, the distinction between original sin and actual sin disappears. Only Christ, true God and true man, can atone for sin. This is the only consequence that can be drawn from the Christological dogma. As Article 24 makes clear, this critique is aimed at the idea of the sacrifice of the mass. Responding to Article 24, the Confutation insists that it is a misunderstanding to assume that the Roman church considers the sacrifice of the mass to be an atoning sacrifice. According to the Confutation, the critique thus misses the mark. Here, however, the Council of Trent contradicts the Confutation, as in the council it is expressly stated that the sacrifice of the mass effects atonement for sinners.[5] The rest of the article uses traditional language and contains nothing unique to the reformation.

It is deliberate, of course, that the AC states its teaching on Christ in close connection with the dogma of the early church. As will hopefully become clear in the treatment of the following articles, however,

---

4. The corresponding section in the Chalcedonian Latin text reads: "In duabus naturis, inconfuse, immutabiliter, indivise, inseparabiliter . . . (in two natures, without confusion, without change, without division, without separation . . .).

5. Session XXII, Doctrine concerning the Sacrifice of the Mass, chap. 2: "Docet sancta Synodus, sacrificium istud vere propitiatorium esse. . . . Quare non solum pro fidelium vivorum peccatis, poenis, satisfactionibus et aliis necessitatibus, sed et pro defunctis in Christo, nondum ad plenum purgatis, rite iuxta Apostolorum traditionem offertur (Denzinger, 1743); (. . . The holy council teaches that this sacrifice is truly *propitiatory*. . . . Wherefore according to the tradition of the Apostles, it is rightly offered not only for the sins, punishments, satisfactions, and other necessities of the faithful who are living, but also for those departed in Christ but not yet fully punished; Schroeder, p. 146).

the paths separate not least here, on the question of how the incarnation is understood. A whole series of the articles that follow builds on the opponents' divergent perceptions of the incarnation. In Article 3, the differences are simply not expressed. Both in its formulation and in its aim (apart from the one point mentioned), the article is unpolemical. It is intentionally structured to emphasize the connection between the incarnation and the atonement, between Christ's person and work.[6] The doctrine of the two natures, therefore, does not stand in isolation, but is framed within the statements on Christ's work. While the central statement on the atonement stresses Jesus' death as a sacrifice, it is significant that the article does not end here, but continues equally to stress the kingly rule of Christ, the goal of which is the sanctification of every believer. Since this aspect of Christ's work is executed through the Holy Spirit, the confession of the Spirit must also be made here rather than leaving it for a later article on God the Holy Spirit. Later in the AC, there is, of course, extensive discussion of the Spirit's work in the church. The confession of the Spirit as God, however, is made here in conjunction with statements on the kingly rule of Christ. Here also belongs the final part of the article, the return of Christ for judgment. Indeed, it may even seem superfluous after this that a special article be devoted to the second coming. Since, however, the reformers typically consider the work of Christ to be one work from the incarnation to his return, the confession of Christ is incomplete if the consummation is not included. It is emphasized twice that it is always "the same Christ" that is spoken of, namely, the incarnate one in whom the divine and human natures are "inseparably conjoined in the unity of his person." Despite the fact that all this is said in complete harmony with early church orthodoxy and without any explicit polemics, there is little doubt to whom it is addressed: it is Zwingli whom the reformers have in mind here. Thus it comes as no surprise that the Confutation approves the article without further comment. In the Apology Melanchthon simply notes this approval without discussing the

---

6. Cf. Luther's treatise *The Three Symbols or Creeds of the Christian Faith* of 1538, where he states that the devil attacks Christ from three sides: (1) denial of his divinity; (2) denial of his humanity; (3) denial of his work. All three articles are equally important. To lack one of them is to lack all of them, "denn der Glaube soll und muss ganz und rund sein" (for the faith is supposed to be and must be whole and complete); WA 50, 269; ET, *LW* 34:210.

problems any further. This attitude conforms completely to Melanchthon's main objective in the AC, which is to confine the conflict within the narrowest possible bounds.

While the doctrine of the Trinity had merely to be defended against certain enthusiasts, Christology had been the subject of a heated debate between Luther and Zwingli. The occasion for the debate was their disagreement about the doctrine of the Lord's Supper, which developed into a major argument about the concept of "nature" and "person" in Christological dogma. The words "two natures, divine and human, inseparably conjoined in the unity of his person" are written with Zwingli in mind. Zwingli too, of course, professes the classical teaching, but because his theology is governed by the fundamental opposition of God and humanity, this opposition inevitably manifests itself in his view of the relationship between the two natures of Christ. Consequently, he finds it extremely difficult to bring them together in any real unity. He distributes each individual aspect of Jesus' life between the two natures separately to the point that the integrity of Christ's person is threatened. One might illustrate how this distribution is carried out with the following examples: according to his divine nature Christ knows everything; according to his human nature he says that no one knows the day or the time; according to the divine nature he is with the Father from eternity to eternity, untempted and immortal; according to the human, he thirsts, is tempted, suffers, and dies.[7]

Zwingli had developed a distinctive hermeneutical theory to support this Christology.[8] He claims that in the Bible, the designations for each of the two natures can be inverted so that when one nature is named it must be understood to mean the other, or so that an expression which appears to include both natures actually designates only one of them. This use clears the way for pure arbitrariness. For example, John 1:14 reads, "the word became flesh," or "God became flesh." Since God cannot "become" anything without being imperfect, the meaning must

7. These ideas appear wherever Zwingli speaks about the person of Christ. See, e.g. *Hauptschriften Bd. II* (Zurich, 1948), pp. 309ff. (*Fidei christianae expositio*), and *Bekenntnisschriften der reformierten Kirche,* 1903, pp. 80-81 (*Fidei ratio*); ET, Jacobs, pp. 160-162. Cf. G. Plitt: *Einleitung in die Augustana* 2 (1868), pp. 88ff., where a series of such examples are listed.

8. Zwingli asserts that in the Gospels Christ employs a figure of speech, "alleosis," which must be understood in the manner described below. See Plitt, p. 93.

be: man became God. According to the "inversion rule" the subject and predicate must be exchanged. Since each nature remains just as it is, the meaning of the sentence must be that the human is brought into union with the person of God's Son. Consider another example, John 12:32: "When I am lifted up from the earth, I will draw all men to myself." In both cases it seems as if the "I" should be understood as referring to both natures, but in reality, according to Zwingli, the "I" in the clause about Jesus being "lifted up" refers only to the human nature which alone can die, while the other "I" in the reference about "drawing all to myself" applies to the divine nature alone.

Thus, no matter how much Zwingli insists that he is in agreement with early church orthodoxy, he fails to maintain any real unity in the person of Christ.[9] His assumption that the divine and the human stand in opposition to each other makes it impossible for him to allow the same manifestations of Christ's life to be true expressions for both the divine and the human natures. For Zwingli, the union of the two natures properly occurs through an act of the intellect from the human side: "we transfer that which properly belongs to the one onto the other."[10] The unity is made dependent upon this "transfer." It could not be more plainly stated that the unity is not a real unity.

In the treatise *Confession concerning Christ's Supper* (1528), Luther deals extensively with this theory. He is adamantly opposed to it because it has no basis in Scripture. It is the devil's invention, because it constructs a Christ who is no holier than anyone else. If only the human nature suffered for me, then Christ himself needs a savior.[11] It

---

9. See, e.g. *Fidei ratio* 1, *Bekenntnisschr.* p. 80, 1ff.; ET, Jacobs, pp. 160ff., cf. Plitt, p. 89.

10. Cited in Plitt, p. 93.

11. Clemen 3, 390, 37ff.(WA 26, 319f.; ET, *LW* 37:209-210): "Hüt dich / Hüt dich / sage ich / fur der Alleosi / sie ist des teuffels larven / Denn sie richtet zu letzt ein solchen Christum zu / nach dem ich nicht gern wolt / ein Christen sein / Nemlich / das Christus hinfurt nicht mehr sey / noch thu / mit seinem leiden und leben / denn ein ander schlechter heilige / Denn wenn ich das gleube / das allein die menschliche natur fur mich gelidden hat / so ist mir der Christus ein schlechter heiland / so bedarff er wol selbs eines heilands / Summa / es ist usaglich / was der teuffel mit der Alleosi sucht" (Beware, beware, I say, of this "alleosis", for it is the devil's mask since it will finally construct a kind of Christ after whom I would not want to be a Christian, that is, a Christ who is and who does no more in his passion and his life than any other ordinary saint. For if I believe that only the human nature suffered me, then Christ would be a poor Savior for me, in fact, he himself would need a Savior. In short, it is indescribable what the devil attempts with this "alleosis"!).

is the Son of God himself who was crucified, and to Reason one must reply: "The Deity cannot suffer and die—that is true; but since the divinity and the humanity are one person in Christ, the Scriptures ascribe to the divinity, because of this personal union, all that happens to humanity, and vice versa. Therefore, it is also correct to say: the Son of God suffers, for this person who suffers, Christ, is truly God." [12]

Luther considered the Swiss to be deluded when they allowed the two natures to stand apart from one another in Christ. In Christ it is impossible to find one single place where God is present and not man. Where Christ is, there is God and man. What Christ does and suffers applies to both natures. Mary gave birth not only to Christ the man but also to the Son of God. For Zwingli, Christology is a metaphysical problem. For Luther it must be seen in context with the whole story of salvation, where there is simply no room for speculation on how two opposite modes of being (i.e., the human and the divine) can be united. The only thing that means anything is that God in Christ suffered death for us, for upon that depends salvation. Zwingli's teaching in fact means that revelation itself disappears, because if God ultimately remains in heaven, then we do not meet him in the man Christ.

Just as some have claimed that the reformers were not really interested in the doctrine of the Trinity, it has also been charged that Christology proper, i.e., the doctrine of the two natures, was of little interest to them. The famous sentence from Melanchthon's *Loci* is often cited in this vein: "To know Christ means to know his benefits." [13] In his understanding of these words, Ritschl has exerted much influence. He interprets the sentence to mean that the doctrine of the two natures is a matter of indifference when one learns to know Christ according to his benefits. [14]

---

12. Ibid., 391, 19ff. (WA 26, 321; ET, *LW* 37:210). Cf. 406, 35ff. (WA 26, 341f; ET, *LW* 37:229f.).

13. "Hoc est Christum cognoscere beneficia eius cognoscere, non, quod isti (scholastici) docent, eius naturas, modos incarnationis contueri" (To know Christ means to know his benefits, and not as they [the scholastics] teach, to reflect upon his natures and the modes of his incarnation). *Melanchthons Werke,* vol. II, 1, p. 7; ET, *Library of Christian Classics,* vol. 19, pp. 21-22. A parallel to this passage is found in AC 24 §31; *BC,* p. 59.

14. See Karl Thieme, *Die Augsburgische Konfession,* pp. 148ff., where Ritschl's interpretation is rehearsed.

Article 3 is supposed to have been written for apologetic reasons apart from any "religious interest" Melanchthon may have had in the doctrine. This interpretation forces Melanchthon to conform with Ritschl, according to whom the divinity of Christ is not an expression of his *being,* but merely corresponds to his *worth* to the believer as savior. There can be no doubt that Ritschl's interpretation is in error. Melanchthon's words must be understood from the perspective of his polemical posture against the speculative explanations of the scholastics. The point is that Christology must not be isolated. It must be seen in context with the *work* of Christ. It is the preoccupation with how God could become man (*modus incarnationis*) which he rejects as leading to useless speculation. The fact itself, on the other hand, *that* God became man is for Melanchthon, too, an essential premise for every true acknowledgment of Christ.

Since Luther's whole polemic against Zwingli shows clearly how much was at stake for him in the teaching on Christ's person, it is strange that Ritschl also claimed that Luther was disinterested in the doctrine of the two natures.[15] True, Luther was as little interested as Melanchthon in the doctrine of the two natures for speculative purposes, but it is certain that in the dogma of the early church he found an unimpeachable "case" for his own expression of the doctrine. It was clear to him that false teaching on the person of Christ inevitably leads to false teaching on the atonement. His battle with Zwingli offers clear testimony to this. The intimate connection between Christology and the doctrine of the atonement forbids any attempt to isolate the teaching on Christ's person, and this is why the reformers reject speculation. This does not mean, however, that it is essentially the "work" which constitutes the "person," but rather that the "person" is known only in the "work." In addition, the doctrine of Christ's person, as stated previously, is comprehended only in the statement of purpose in Article 3, which presents the goal of the incarnation—that Christ should be "a sacrifice for all our sins."

---

15. See ibid., p. 163.

Article 4

• JUSTIFICATION •

Text

Our churches also teach that men cannot be justified[1]   1
before God by their own strength, merits, or works but are
freely[2] justified for Christ's sake through faith when they be-   2
lieve that they are received into favor[3] and that their sins are
forgiven on account of Christ, who by his death made satisfaction for our sins.[4] This faith God imputes for righteous-   3
ness in his sight (Romans 3;4).

The issue here is only justification **before God** (*coram Deo*), not
justification before humans (*coram hominibus*). As Article 18 con-
cedes, humans are able by their free will to attain a degree of civil
righteousness (*iustitia civilis*). Before God, however, humans cannot

---

1. The GT emphasizes "Vergebung der Sünde" (forgiveness of sin).

2. GT: "Aus Gnaden" (by grace).

3. GT: "Gerechtigkeit und ewiges Leben geschenkt" (righteousness and eternal life are given).

4. GT: "Glauben, dass Christus fur uns gelitten habe. . ." (when we believe that Christ suffered for us. . .).

be justified **by their own strength,** that is, with the aid of their own natural endowments, reason, and will. Original sin makes this impossible. **Merits**: the whole idea of merit is completely rejected. Before God humans have no merit. **Works**: for the sake of completeness, works are also mentioned even though the two previous concepts have already nullified any thought of works-righteousness. Now that these things have been rejected, justification can be described: **but . . . freely.** Justification is pure gift. It happens **for Christ's sake**. The expression is further clarified in the following sentence which simultaneously explains the expression **through faith**: Christ is the source, faith the way to justification. Faith's content is the conviction that sinners are forgiven for Christ's sake. The reason justification can occur for Christ's sake is bound up with the fact that his death makes **satisfaction for our sins**. This righteousness which is won by faith is an imputed righteousness (*imputat*).

Commentary

The doctrine of justification must be understood in context with Articles 2 and 3. As original sin does not mean that humanity has "changed for the worse" (Council of Trent), but that it has torn itself apart from its Creator so that now all its life's relationships are *self*-determined, any talk of human ability to prepare itself for justification is pointless. It must happen *freely*. No judgment is made here about humans' spiritual abilities. The point of Reformation teaching is not, as Catholic polemics often suggests, that humanity's natural powers have been so corrupted that any sort of moral achievement is impossible. Original sin is not a quantitative "something" which has rendered a specific, measureable portion of humans' natural powers useless while what is left over can be used by grace. The point is that the very moment in which our original dependence upon God ceases, we come under the power of sin with all that we have and all that we are. This also applies to our "highest" powers, which in reality are the most dangerous. To characterize justification as "free" is to assert that just as sin is a total determination of the human being, so is righteousness. It is a renewal of the *whole* person. Therefore, it must be given; one who is subject to sin can only sin. God alone can work renewal. To speak of a preparation for grace, understood as a human achievement, is for the reformers nothing else than to advocate presenting one's sins to God. The atonement, therefore, is much more than merely the objective basis for justification. It is identical with it in the sense that the righteousness which becomes humanity's righteousness can be none other than Christ's righteousness. Thus, "for Christ's sake" does not merely name the condition which must be met for justification to be possible. "Without merit, for Christ's sake" designates the Christian life in its entirety, not merely the beginning of justification. As Melanchthon states in the Apology: "Christ does not stop being the mediator after our renewal" (Apology 4 §162). He continues to say that if it is only "initial grace" which is given us for Christ's sake, while the increase of grace is dependent on good works (i.e., on human cooperation with grace), then salvation, in the final analysis, does not depend on Christ, but on ourselves. All merit, even in the state of grace, detracts from the works of Christ.

Since justification is completely God's work, it happens "by faith." What this means, of course, depends completely upon what one means by "faith." Article 4 says nothing about what this faith consists of, only what it clings to. In Article 20, however, we learn that justifying faith is faith that not merely believes the "history" but also the "effect of the history," namely, the forgiveness of sins. What is referred to here is what Luther often calls "the right application of the personal pronoun." It does me no good to believe that Christ died for sinners, if I do not believe that he died for me. Even the devil has a purely historical faith.[5]

The claim that humans are justified when they believe in the forgiveness of sins might seem to imply that faith is understood as a condition for justification. Such is not the case, however. In the Apology, Melanchthon points to the connection of the concepts of "promise" and "faith." Faith justifies not because it is worthy of justification as a good work, but because it clings to the promise (Apology 4 §56). Justifying faith, therefore, is not a human virtue or quality, but the

---

5. It is in this context that Luther's sharp rejection of the concepts *fides acquisita* (acquired faith) and *fides informis* (unformed faith) must be understood. Both concepts are confined to mere intellectual assent to the content of the faith. Regarding further elucidation of these problems, see the treatment of Articles 6 and 20.

relationship with God itself. To say that faith is reckoned as righteousness does not mean that faith is anything in and of itself. Rather, it means that the only conceivable righteousness before God, the righteousness of Christ, is grasped by faith. Thus, the popular notion that the difference between the reformers and the Roman church is that the reformers wish to speak "only" of faith while the Roman church would include works together with faith is misleading. According to this understanding it would seem that the only difference is that the reformers have weaker demands. This, however, completely misses the point of "faith alone." The point is that the right relationship with God which has been ruined by original sin consists in giving up one's self-mastery and abandoning oneself completely to God's mercy. Behind this understanding lies a completely different concept of grace. Grace is the very way God expresses himself.[6] The godlessness of original sin is abolished and human nature is recreated by faith in the forgiveness of sins. "This is how God wants to be known and worshiped," says Melanchthon, "that we accept his blessings and receive them because of his mercy rather than because of our own merits" (Apology 4 §60). Since humanity's relationship with God has been ruined by original sin, his mercy must take the form of forgiveness. What is decisive, however, is that it is precisely God's will that one live completely by his mercy. This is what happens in the faith that abandons itself to Christ. In faith, therefore, a person is restored to a right relationship with the Creator. Faith, as Luther says, is the fulfillment of the First Commandment.

Article 4 closes by stating that God imputes this faith for righteousness. The idea of imputation (*imputatio*) had been a decisive element in Luther's doctrine of justification from the very beginning. Here, to a certain extent, he may have been influenced by Ockhamism, which taught that ultimately it is God's free acceptance (*acceptio*) which

---

6. Cf. the GT of Article 5: "ein gnadigen Gott haben" (we have a gracious God). As early as the first *Commentary on the Psalms* (1513–1515), one finds literally hundreds of places where Luther glosses "misericordia [mercy], i.e., gratia [grace]." One must be careful, however, to avoid the common misapprehension that the idea of grace as divine favor was a new discovery by Luther. Scholasticism was also well aware of this. It had always insisted that the prerequisite of infused grace was God's gracious will itself.

makes a person pleasing before God. Here it should be noted that even though acceptance by grace is the way to salvation, it is so, not as a matter of necessity, but only because God has so willed it. With Luther, however, the idea is more than one last proviso in defense of God's sovereignty, but expresses the constitutive factor in a person's relationship with God.[7] Martin Bucer criticizes the use of the concept in the Schwabach Articles, objecting that we cannot merely be reckoned godly or holy, but that we must also *become* so.[8] This objection, found also in Roman Catholic polemics, is typical of a total misunderstanding of the idea of imputation.

Behind the objection, of course, lies the notion that the goal of justification must be that a person obtains a righteousness which can really be called his own. That, however, is just the misunderstanding that imputation language is meant to prevent. It is meant to emphasize the contention that Christian righteousness is always Christ's righteousness. Justification has nothing to do with a person's gradual progress toward "real" godliness in which imputed righteousness covers the ever-diminishing part of the person that remains corrupt. The reformers utterly reject such quantitative calculations. Imputation does not mean that imputed righteousness is a fictitious righteousness set alongside of one's own. Rather, it means that imputed righteousness is a renewal of the whole person. This renewal can never take place through the gradual improvement of the sinner, but consists in the fact that now a person has righteousness only in Christ. The fact that this righteousness is "outside myself" (*extra me*), as Luther says, does not make it incomplete. Rather, it is here and here alone that the Creator's decision about the person is realized.

This understanding of justification compels the reformers to assert that a Christian is simultaneously sinner and righteous (*simul iustus et*

---

7. Regarding the concept of *acceptatio* in Ockhamism, see my article "Gabriel Biels Lehre von der Allmacht Gottes," *ZThK* 53 (1956): 63-65.

8. "Der funft artikel. Dieser artikel ist allerding christenlich, ains allain ausgenommen, dass die red also geet, als ob uns Gott, so wir glauben, fur frum und hailig rechent und wir aber nit auch soliche leut werden mussten" (The Fifth Article. This article is Christian throughout with the one exception that from the terminology one might conclude that God reckons us, if we believe, as godly and holy, but that we need not become such godly persons) (*Bucers Gutachten,* in Gussmann, 1/2: 293; ET in M. Reu, *The Augsburg Confession: A Collection of Sources* [Chicago, 1930], 2:52).

peccator)—in and of oneself a sinner, righteous by faith in Christ. Since sin and righteousness are not related to each other in the sense that a person is righteous to the same degree that he or she has ceased to be a sinner, the reformers must also assert that sin does not disappear with Baptism. If humans were exempt even to the slightest degree from having to live in forgiveness, they would to the same degree have a righteousness of their own to put in the place of Christ's righteousness. The implications of this will become clear when we deal with the Council of Trent's treatment of justification. First, however, we will examine the contribution of the Confutation to the discussion.

The Confutation begins by applauding the AC's condemnation of Pelagianism. The remainder of the article is content with drawing attention to the concept of merit (*meritum*). If anyone would deny that merits are acquired by the assistance of grace, he would be more in agreement with the Manichaeans than with the catholic church. A series of scriptural proof texts is then cited in support of the merit concept. Even though our works are not meritorious in themselves, God's grace makes them worthy of eternal life. The idea of merit is subordinated to the idea of grace. The Confutation has no more to say. The issue of justification is not addressed at all. One might even wonder why the authors bother to express themselves conditionally in reference to the concept of merit, for there is no doubt that Article 4 excludes every kind of merit regardless of whether it has been caused by grace or not.[9]

The differences become much more clear when one moves to the Council of Trent, which especially in this area is negatively determined by the Reformation. The extremely detailed decree on justification begins with a rejection of Pelagianism (chap. 1). Justification is always initiated by God's prevenient grace (*gratia praeveniens*). This divine initiative, however, must always be followed by a preparation which takes the form of a cooperation between God and humanity. Since human beings have free will, they can reject grace. On the other hand, apart from grace a person cannot become righteous. As the decree continues to describe this preparation in all its phases, it becomes clear that the main interest is focused on the psychological, i.e., what happens "inside" the person during justification. This question is a secondary one to the reformers. They are aware, of course, that humans

---

9. Regarding the concept of merit see the commentary on Article 20.

are involved psychologically in justification. From that point on, however, they refuse to pursue any distribution between the roles of grace and nature.

In the description of justification itself (chap. 7), the council asserts that it is not only the forgiveness of sins, but a renewal of the inward person, for in justification love (*caritas Dei*) is infused by virtue of the merits of Christ. It is stressed that faith does not unite a person perfectly with Christ until hope and love are added. Thus, when Trent states (chap. 8) that a person is justified "by faith," it means that faith is the beginning of salvation, the root of all justification. Behind the entire decree lies Trent's opposition to the Reformation's "faith alone." Accordingly, the reformers' language about faith as trust (*fiducia*) and as certainty of salvation is rejected (chap. 9). Justification does not consist in "naked faith" any more than grace consists only in God's gracious will (chap. 11, canons 9, 10, 11, 12, 13, 14, 19, 20). Through grace, love is infused, by virtue of which the Christian now progresses towards a real righteousness which is increased by the observance of the commandments of God and the church (chaps. 10, 11). A strong warning is issued against considering oneself certain of salvation. Of course one must place one's hope in Christ, but one must also work toward the increase of righteousness with fear (chaps. 12, 13). Since this increase happens through good works understood as merits, the concept of merit is made the subject of some remarks. The council maintains that works are merits only by virtue of grace, and thus it never speaks of relying upon one's own righteousness. On the contrary, it is in fact a grand expression of the unique character of God's divinity that he permits his gifts to be our own merits. Moreover, it is continuously emphasized that everything is grace, even when it is a matter of human cooperation with God, of merits, of the increase of righteousness, etc.

The decisive elements in the Council of Trent's doctrine of justification may be summarized as follows:

1. God's prevenient grace is always the beginning. This beginning, however, must be followed by a preparation which requires human cooperation since, because one has a free will, one is able to reject the proferred grace.

2. Nevertheless, justification itself is undeserved, for it is not the preparation but Christ that merits the grace of justification. This grace

infuses faith, hope, and love so that the justified is not merely reckoned as righteous but truly is righteous.

3. This initial righteousness is increased by the observance of the commandments of God and the church as faith cooperates with grace through good works. Growth in justification both can and must occur.

4. No one can be certain of salvation, but one must place one's hope in Christ and work with fear.

5. The Christian's good works are true merits since God in his divinity permits things which are his gifts of grace to be our merits.

While the teaching is undeniably anti-Pelagian, the distance between it and the AC is great. The critical posture over against the reformers, which constantly emerges not only in the anathemas of the canons but also in the decree itself, is based on the premise that righteousness before God must be a human quality which progresses toward greater and greater perfection. Consistent with this premise, the reformers are criticized because they are "content" with the forgiveness of sins. To borrow a phrase that has become popular today, one could say that Trent accuses the reformers of "cheap grace." "Faith alone" leaves nothing to humans. That is what is intolerable. From a Reformation viewpoint, however, this criticism is nothing but the protest of human reason against the gospel. It is inconceivable to reason that righteousness before God can be anything else than a human quality which makes one pleasing to God, since with this inherent righteousness, one performs acts which make one worthy of eternal life. If this is true, however, it is no longer the gospel of Christ which gives salvation but works of the law, whether they are accomplished by human strength or by divine assistance. For Luther, this means that the gospel is turned into law, and faith in Christ is abolished. The difference between the Roman and Lutheran positions is not that in the first case the law and good works are taken seriously while, in the other, one is content merely with faith. Luther also realizes that the law belongs to God and that there are works which must be done. The law and works, however, have their rightful place only on earth. In heaven, that is, before God, they have no function whatsoever. There, only one thing is valid, faith in Christ. In the Roman view of justification, the law is brought in to justification. It happens by faith *and* works. Accordingly, it is God *and* humans, grace *and* free will which create salvation. For Luther, this notion is nothing less than the theology of the Antichrist, for where the law reigns, faith cannot be found. Where humans are compelled to do good works for the sake of salvation, faith dies, and the Spirit, the forgiveness of sins, together with the rest of Christ's gifts disappear. In place of this comes the inevitable consequence, judgment, for the law does not give, it demands, and where the demand is not fulfilled punishment must follow. When one considers the law to be the way to righteousness there is nothing else to say. Thus, to give works any place at all in justification is a rejection of God's grace in Christ.

The law, therefore, is never to function as a way to justification, not even together with grace. It has no place at all in the conscience, where faith alone must rule. When the law does enter the conscience, it is never to save, only to condemn. In the conscience, the law reveals and increases sin so that a person comes to despair of self and is driven to Christ. This, the spiritual use of the law is its most important use. As mentioned previously, however, the law also rules on earth, directing the whole of civil existence. While even the Christian, as sinner, is subject to the law in its civil use for the discipline and chastisement of the flesh, this does not affect his freedom under the gospel. Viewing such a doctrine of justification as Trent's from this perspective, it becomes obvious that the spiritual use of the law which drives a person to acknowledge his sin is shunted off to the side while what Luther calls the civil use of the law occupies the center. Furthermore, these "civil" works of the law now become a factor in one's relationship to God. In other words, a confusion of the law and the gospel has taken place. From a Lutheran perspective, the following conclusions may be drawn:

1. The righteousness which is perceived as a cooperation between grace and free will may well be able to create many externally "good" works. Before God, however, they are worth nothing. God, of course, can and does exploit such "righteousness" to maintain order in the world, but this has nothing to do with the actual fulfillment of the law. The law must not merely be kept externally, but also spiritually. This is something which only Christ can accomplish, and it is precisely for this reason that faith in him is the only true fulfillment of the law.

2. It follows from this that the notion of being able to prepare oneself for grace must be rejected. All works done apart from faith are sins, even if they might be respectable from a human perspective.

3. When a sinful person is confronted by the law, that person will always attempt to take possession of it as a tool with which to acquire righteousness. Thus, from a Lutheran perspective, Trent's notion of a cooperation between grace and humanity is from the outset nothing else than an invitation to use the law for self-serving ends which rob God of his glory. To permit works to have a role in justification is to use the law, whose demand is love of God and neighbor, directly against its purpose—for self-assertion before God. It is precisely in the circumstances in which humans believe themselves able to fulfill the law where it can be seen that they have been ignorant of sin and of Christ all along.

4. The law itself is not to blame for this. In itself, the law is good and holy. Human misuse of the law, however, gives it a corrupting effect. Since sinful humanity seeks its own advantage in everything, each zealous attempt to fulfill the law is perverted into using the law as an accomplice to gain independence from God, precisely the opposite of what the law demands!

5. When Luther says that a person is unable to fulfill the law, therefore, he is not making a general moral appraisal of humanity. Instead, he is expressing his conviction that it is precisely in attempting to fulfill the law that one comes to violate it. The life of love demanded by the law and for which humans were created can only begin, according to Luther, when humans give up every last vestige of self-sufficiency, living entirely upon what they receive from God. This is nothing else than to say that the law points to Christ. In him the law is fulfilled, because faith is just what the law requires, full dependence upon Christ alone.

6. Thus, to speak of faith *and* works is not simply a harmless expression which further elaborates the meaning of justification. Rather, it is to transform the Gospel into law. This is not because it is forbidden to speak of good works. It is because to speak of faith *and* works obscures the fact that the law, according to its own self-understanding, is fulfilled only when what it demands is freely given as a gift. This is precisely what happens in faith. Whenever something else is added, the inevitable result is once again to abandon faith in Christ in favor of one's own good works. In faith the law is fulfilled and thereby comes to its end. One might express it this way: what the law requires is

freedom from the law! I.e., the law desires nothing else than its own cessation when what it demands is freely given in faith.

As far as works are concerned, they have their place on earth, as has been said. The relationship between faith and works will be treated further in Articles 6 and 20. In a sense, it could be claimed that the entire AC is about this one article alone, justification by faith. Here the question concerned the article's foundation. The problems addressed here, however, will resurface occasionally in the remainder of the AC and will hopefully be clarified more satisfactorily than has been possible here. Together with Article 3, the article on justification constitutes the center of the AC. It is upon Christ and faith that everything else depends. In what follows it will be seen how the conflict about the understanding of this eventually determines the perspective from which every other issue is dealt with.

Article 5

• THE MINISTRY OF •
THE CHURCH

Text

In order that we may obtain this faith, the ministry of teach- 1
ing the Gospel and administering the sacraments was in
stituted.[1] For through the Word and the sacraments, as 2
through instruments, the Holy Spirit is given, and the Holy
Spirit produces faith, where and when it pleases God, in
those who hear the Gospel. That is to say, it is not on account 3
of our own merits but on account of Christ that God justifies
those who believe that they are received into favor for
Christ's sake.[2] Gal. 3:14, "That we might receive the promise
of the Spirit through faith."

Our churches condemn the Anabaptists and others who 4
think that the Holy Spirit comes to men without the external
Word, through their own preparations and works.

---

1. GT: "Hat Gott das Predigtamt eingesetzt, Evangelium und Sakrament geben"
(God instituted the office of the ministry, that is, provided the gospel and the sacraments).

2. GT: "Dass wir. . .ein gnädigen Gott haben, so wir solchs glauben" (That we
have a gracious God. . .when we believe this).

69

The introductory clause ties the article to what precedes it. Now the discussion turns to the question of how justifying faith is obtained. The **ministry of teaching** (*ministerium docendi*) . . . is the means. **Was instituted**: the expression is neutral only from a purely linguistic perspective; "By God" must be inferred, or the article loses its meaning. The German text makes this inference explicit. The centrality of the ministry derives from the belief that **the Holy Spirit**, who creates **faith, is given through the Word and the sacraments. Where and when it pleases God**: where God through the Spirit creates faith, it is always his free gift. The Holy Spirit works faith, when God wills, **in those who hear the Gospel;** here again it is emphasized that the Spirit works through the Word. The explanation of what **the Gospel** is reestablishes the connection with Article 4. The gospel is simply the doctrine of justification which has already been set forth in the article mentioned.

The second paragraph opposes **the Anabaptists and others,** that is, Anabaptists and other enthusiasts (*Schwärmer*). Characteristic of their teaching is the belief that the Holy Spirit comes **without the external Word,** without the oral and visible Word of proclamation and the sacraments. Instead, they rely upon **their own preparations and works.** Specifically, this phrase has in mind the teaching about certain spiritual exercises called "Langeweile" (self-abstraction), "Gelassenheit" (concentration), and others, with which a person prepared for the coming of the Spirit. In addition, any notion of mortification of the flesh as a condition for the Spirit's regeneration is rejected here.

Commentary

After justification itself is established in Article 4, it is now explained how a person obtains this justifying faith. The article is actually not so much about the ministry as it is about the means of grace. Nevertheless, it is still possible from this perspective to see what place the ministry holds in a church where the means of grace occupy the place suggested here.[3] Article 5 corresponds exactly to Article 7 of the

---

3. Here we must confine our dealings to the function of the ministry. The place of the ministry with respect to ecclesiastical order and related questions should properly be dealt with under Article 14.

Schwabach Articles and to the main thrust of the Marburg Articles. Faith is given by the Spirit through the external Word while the Spirit nevertheless still remains free with respect to the Word. The fact that the article's main concern is to emphasize the external Word is reinforced by the negative paragraph which expressly directs its criticism against the Anabaptists. Not directly but implicitly, as is typical of the AC, this article also deals with the position of the Roman church. The authors of the Confutation seem not to notice the radical change which the notion of the ministry must undergo. They approve the statement that the Holy Spirit is given through "words and sacraments" (*verba et sacramenta*)! The fact that the plural form of "word" (*verba*) is used in the Confutation, however, reveals that its authors have failed to understand that "Word" here has a special meaning. Most likely they are thinking about the various sacramental formulas. Moreover, they state their reservations about the language that refers to faith as the gift of the Holy Spirit, adding that it must be faith formed by love (*fides formata*), since in Baptism, not only faith, but also hope and love are infused. Clearly, from a Roman perspective this must be a central objection. The contrast between the AC and the Confutation comes through especially clearly in the German text. The German reading which corresponds to the Latin, "who believe they are received into favor for Christ's sake," reads, "dass wir durch Christus Verdienst, nicht durch unser Verdienst, ein gnädigen Gott haben, so wir solchs glauben" (that we have a gracious God, not by our own merits but by the merit of Christ, when we believe this). It is strange that the authors of the Confutation failed to recognize what a fundamental difference this is. When "grace" is identified with having a gracious God instead of with being infused with a new supernatural *habitus*, then the issue is not merely "faith," on the one hand, as opposed to "faith formed by love," on the other, but the whole character of both ministry and sacraments is radically changed. It means, moreover, that the proclamation of the gospel ceases to be mere exhortation. Proclamation itself becomes a means of grace, together with the sacraments.

The historical context of Article 5 is the battle against the enthusiasts and Anabaptists which had been forced upon the Lutheran reformers ever since the beginning of the 1520s. The principal point of contention had been the understanding of the relationship between the Spirit and the Word. From the very beginning Luther had referred to the *verbum vocale,* the external, spoken word which meets people through proclamation and the sacraments as the means through which the Holy Spirit's gifts are mediated. The conflict with the enthusiasts, however, forced him to examine the question further.[4] The doctrine of the Word and the Spirit now became the criterion for distinguishing the true church from all heretics. In the treatise of 1525, *Against the Heavenly Prophets,* Luther deals with the enthusiasts. Their talk of communing with the Spirit apart from proclamation and the sacraments is for him a rejection of God's ordinance. What God has ordained to be a matter of inward faith and spirit, they convert into a human work, and what God has ordained as an external word and sign, they convert into an inner spirit, since in defiance of God's ordinance they put the mortification of the flesh ahead of faith.[5] If one presses them about how one gains access to this high spirit, they do not refer to the proclamation of the gospel but to inner experience. If one inquires even further about this, continues Luther mockingly, then one will find that they know about as much about this as Dr. Carlstadt knows of Greek and Hebrew.[6] According to the Lutheran reformers' understanding, the enthusiasts' perception of the Spirit contained a dangerous subjectivistic element which would not only dissolve the church, but which implied a denial of the incarnation. To teach that the Spirit is given after a preparation consisting of the mortification of the flesh was to teach that it was a person's own works and not Christ himself, present through proclamation and the sacraments, which was the way to salvation. Therefore the Smalcald Articles also emphasize strongly that no one is given the Spirit or grace by God except through and with the external Word which comes first. This must be maintained against the enthusiasts who boast of possessing the Spirit independently of the Word. Among these Luther includes not only the enthusiasts, but also the pope who thinks he can rule over the church by his own power. Enthusiasm infects

---

4. Regin Prenter, in *Spiritus Creator,* trans. J. M. Jensen (Philadelphia: Muhlenberg, 1953), has clearly demonstrated that one cannot speak of any innovation in Luther's thought as he battled against the enthusiasts. His argument was simply sharpened by the polemical situation.

5. WA 18:139, 1ff; *LW* 40 (Philadelphia: Fortress, 1958), pp. 148-149.

6. WA 18:137, 5ff.; *LW* 40:147.

Adam and his children from the Fall to the end of the world. It is the source of all heresy. Anything that claims to be of the Spirit apart from the spoken Word and sacraments is of the devil himself.[7]

The same understanding is expressed in Article 5. Yet the issue is still far from being exhausted. Martin Bucer's comments on the Schwabach Articles' formulation that the oral word is the only way to faith[8] is most enlightening. Bucer protests against the claim that God's grace and the Spirit are necessarily bound to the external word. Such a claim appears to him to be a restriction of God's omnipotence.[9] In answering such an objection from the perspective of the AC one might counter that if God's decision to come to sinful humanity through Christ is a restriction of his omnipotence, then Article 7 of the Schwabach Articles and Article 5 of the AC are as well. If it is true, however, that the incarnate Christ is the only way to salvation, then it is also true that the Spirit is given only through the Word, for the Word is Christ himself. While one must acknowledge that the AC permits no possibility of the Spirit's mediation apart from the Word, the relationship between the Word and the Spirit is scarcely so unambiguous in another respect. To hold that the Spirit comes only through the Word does not imply that the Spirit is bound to the Word. The phrase "where and when it pleases God" preserves God's freedom. In this context, too, the relationship parallels the incarnation. It is precisely because Christ came as a man that God remains *hidden* even in his revelation, so that only the Spirit can disclose the fact that God is here, in this man. Similarly, the proclaimed word does not become God's Word until the Spirit makes it into an inner word. In itself, the proclaimed word is merely the letter, and therefore dead. That is to say, the connection between the Word and the Spirit must not be taken to imply that God has completely surrendered himself to us in his revelation.

---

7. Smalcald Articles, Part 3, Article 8 §§3ff.; *BC*, p. 304.

8. Article 7 of the Schwabach Articles closes with these words: "Sonst ist kein ander Mittl noch Weise, weder Wege noch Stege, den Glauben zu bekommen; dann Gedanken ausser oder fur dem mundlichen Wort, wie heilig sie scheinen, seind sie doch eitel Lugen und Irrthumb" (Other than this there is no means, mode, or way to receive faith. For thoughts outside of or before the oral word, however holy and good they appear, are nevertheless nothing but lies and error).

9. W. Gussmann, *Quellen und Forschungen zur Geschichte des Augsburgischen Bekenntnisses* (1930) 1/2: 295; ET in M. Reu, 2:53-54.

We are accustomed to taking the phrase "where and when it pleases God" in a predestinarian sense. Melanchthon, however, wrote in a letter to Brenz that he had completely avoided the subject of predestination in the AC. He adds, "throughout I speak as if predestination follows our faith and works."[10] If the above-cited phrase from Article 5 is interpreted in harmony with Melanchthon's letter, its intention must be to preclude the notion that the relationship between the Word and the Spirit is a matter of necessity. The Spirit does not simply follow the Word automatically. The purpose of this would be to emphasize that when God pours out his Spirit, it is always an act of his free grace. Apart from Melanchthon's statement it is of course possible to understand the words as predestinarian. Whether it is correct to discuss predestination in this context is a question to which we shall return shortly.

While the Lutheran position over against the enthusiasts was quite clear, Zwingli had considerably more difficulty in divorcing himself from them because of his essential agreement with their doctrine of the Spirit. According to Zwingli's doctrine of predestination, even the pious heathen can belong to the church. Election is completely separated from participation in the Christian community. In actuality, therefore, Zwingli has no place for the means of grace. Faith does not come through the Word. The elect are instructed by the Spirit directly and thereby brought to faith. It is only after being instructed by God through the Spirit that one becomes able to understand the proclamation; proclamation itself is unable to call forth faith.[11] Thus for Zwingli there is no inner connection between the Word and faith. He can only observe that in the New Testament it appears as if outward proclamation always precedes faith. The reception of the Word, however, is ascribed to the

---

10. See *BK*, p. 58, note 3.

11. "Nos putamus, fidem ex verbis hauriri non posse, sed fide magistra quae proponuntur verba intellgi. . . .Fides ergo magistra et interpres est verborum. Quomodo igitur ex verbis tandem fidem hauriremus, quum nonnisi fide muniti ad scripturae interpretationem debeamus accedere?" (We believe that faith cannot arise from words, but that it is by faith as teacher that we understand what the words mean. Faith, therefore, is the teacher and interpreter of the words. How then can faith be said to arise from the words, since it is only armed by faith that we ought to approach the interpretation of the Scriptures? [trans. Justin Pierce]) (*Amica Exegesis, Opera 3*, p. 517, cited in Plitt, 2:177).

work of the Spirit alone.[12] Zwingli seeks to establish the necessity of proclamation with this argument, despite his peculiar understanding of the work of the Spirit. Zwingli, just as adamantly, holds that the sacraments similarly cannot confer grace.[13]

The Lutheran doctrine of the Word and the Spirit as set forth in Article 5 also has two points to make with respect to the Roman understanding of the means of grace. First, it asserts that proclamation is a means of grace. The two most important functions of the ministry of the church are "teaching the Gospel" and "administering the sacraments." Correspondingly, the words "through the Word and the sacraments" clearly mean "through *proclamation* and the sacraments." In *The Babylonian Captivity of the Church* and in many other places Luther asserts that the first duty of a priest is to proclaim the gospel. During the Middle Ages proclamation had been reduced to a pedagogical tool with which to deepen and secure a person's acknowledgment of the grace which could be obtained only through the sacraments. With Luther it is *the Word* that is held up as the true means of grace. By this it is not only emphasized that proclamation itself is a means of grace, but also that it is *the Word* in the sacrament that constitutes the sacrament. The decisive element in both proclamation and sacraments is whether the promise brought by the word of proclamation and the sacramental word, respectively, is received in faith, for one can "have a gracious God" only as the Spirit works faith in the promise. Therefore the charge of *the Word being absent* applies not only to the Roman perspective on proclamation but equally to the Roman *sacramental praxis* in which the sacramental word is not understood as the Word of the promise—the Word spoken to the person receiving the sacrament in which Christ himself comes with his gifts—but merely as a consecration through which the sacramental signs are changed into

---

12. "Canonice enim sive regulariter loquendo videmus apud omnes populos externam praedicationem Apostolorum et Evangelistarum sive Episcoporum praecessisse fidem, quam tamen soli spiritui ferimus acceptam" (For in speaking canonically or regularly we see that among all nations the outward preaching of evangelists or bishops has preceded faith, which we nevertheless say is received by the Spirit alone) (*Fidei Ratio, Bekenntnisschriften der reformierten Kirche,* p. 92; ET, H. E. Jacobs, 2:176).

13. Regarding Zwingli's teaching on the sacraments, see under Articles 9, 10, and 13.

supernatural elements.[14] On this basis, Luther's bitter struggle against the so-called private masses is easily comprehended. In a "private mass" no one is present to receive the sacramental word as the Word of promise.[15]

The second point which the Lutheran doctrine of the Word and the Spirit has to make against the Roman understanding focuses upon the character of the means of grace. On the question of the relationship of the means of grace to the Holy Spirit, a new divergence emerges sharply. Roman teaching on the sacraments is nondialectical. It knows nothing of the AC's "when and where it pleases God." Here the Spirit is truly bound to the means of grace. This means that the sacraments are sufficient in and of themselves, by which the danger of perceiving them magically is apparent. It would be incorrect, of course, to claim that Roman sacramental theology is magic. This pitfall is avoided by the teaching that in order for the sacrament to be efficacious, the recipient must not "bar the door" (*obicem ponere*), which means that he must not be in any mortal sin and must intend to receive the sacrament in the manner in which the church wishes to give it. Even so, it is obvious that the teaching about the sacrament working *ex opere operato* (i.e., by virtue of its being correctly performed) can easily lead in the direction of magic. Here any consideration of God's sovereignty has been completely overlooked. Zwingli, on the other hand, in his zeal to emphasize God's sovereignty has reduced the Word and the sacraments to empty signs. In the final analysis, both of these results can be traced back to diverging understandings of the incarnation. From the perspective of Article 5, both Rome and Zwingli must be charged with the attempt to avoid the offense of Christ's lowly appearance. Zwingli cannot seriously entertain the belief that God's revelation really *enters* this world so that it is *God himself* we encounter through Word and sacraments. Rome, of course, intends to preserve a real encounter between God and humanity in the sacraments, but an encounter on a supernatural plane. In a certain sense it might be said that Lutheranism takes a middle ground between Rome and Zwingli. At the same time,

---

14. Cf. Regin Prenter's treatment of the subject in "Luther on Word and Sacrament," in *The Word and the Spirit: Essays,* trans. Harris E. Kaasa (Minneapolis: Augsburg, 1965), pp. 125-148.

15. Especially *The Abrogation of the Private Mass,* 1521.

however, it is clear that both must defend themselves on the same issue, the incarnation.

On exactly the same basis that both Zwingli and Rome were able to avoid the offense of the incarnation, it becomes possible for them to make their understanding of salvation nondialectical as well. Emphasizing the Spirit's sovereignty, as in Zwingli, leads to a clear theology of predestination. Emphasizing the Spirit's bondage to the means of grace, of course, makes the sacraments sufficient in and of themselves. Precisely for that reason, however, it becomes necessary for the Roman church to stress the human role in justification by describing the psychological process which the justified person goes through. The alternative, predestination or human responsibility, cannot be avoided, once one overlooks the fact that the Word is the true means of grace. When this occurs, the coming of grace to human beings is less than a real encounter between the God who became man in Jesus Christ and the sinful person. Rather, one either is left with no encounter at all since God in his eternal wisdom gives the Spirit directly through some sort of inner transformation (Zwingli), or one construes this encounter by painstakingly determining how the roles in the process of salvation must be distributed between God and humanity (Rome). In the Lutheran perspective, on the other hand, a real place of encounter is found, because here it is held that grace comes precisely when God *speaks* to the sinful person and by his Spirit gives the gift of hearing his Word. The tension between predestination and human responsibility cannot be rationalized away by appealing to some theological theory. Rather, it must be maintained that apart from the Spirit, the word is merely the letter, and that apart from the external word there is no encounter with the incarnate Christ.

The various understandings of the ministry of the church represented here can now be described on the basis of how the respective parties perceive the means of grace. Article 5 states that the ministry is instituted by God (explicitly only in the German text), and that its purpose is to bring the Word to people so that they may partake of the faith that justifies. First, the necessity for the ministry is affirmed. Second, according to the context, the ministry is clearly portrayed as a service to and for the congregation. It is directed toward people who in proclamation and the sacraments receive Christ as a gift through the Spirit.

This definition of the essence of the ministry corresponds with Luther's perception. His basic views had been clearly stated already in the writings of 1520, especially in *To the Christian Nobility* and *The Babylonian Captivity of the Church*. In the first of these treatises, Luther introduces his thoughts on the "priesthood of all believers." All Christians belong to the spiritual estate. The only differences between them are due to the differences of the various ministries. We become "spiritual" solely by Baptism, gospel, and faith. Therefore, it is not consecration by a bishop that makes a man a priest but the ministry which is laid upon him. Everyone belongs to the spiritual estate, but not everyone is intended for or called to the *ministry*. No one, therefore, should presume to do what we all have the same right to do unless he has been designated for that purpose.[16] The claim is often made that Luther placed great emphasis upon the idea of order. From the foregoing, however, it can be seen that the word *order* here means more than merely everything being done respectably. It is precisely the *special ministry* which makes it possible to preserve the priesthood of all believers. The intent is to guarantee that no one exalts himself above the others and assumes a self-appointed authority. The priesthood belongs to all, and therefore can be preserved only if the ministry of the Word is delegated to one designated by the congregation. Thus, Article 14 provides an important supplement to Article 5. Only one who has been properly called may exercise the ministry of the Word, because only such a one can act on behalf of the congregation. The self-appointed minister will always insist upon his own special qualities, thereby setting himself up against the priesthood of all believers. In this sense the ministry is necessary "for the sake of the Word." In *The Babylonian Captivity of the Church* the point of view is the same and it is even more expressly stated that the office of priest is the "ministry of the Word" (*ministerium verbi*), and also that the proclamation of the gospel is therefore the first duty of the priest.[17] From this it is clear that the necessity of the ministry is seriously upheld, for salvation itself depends upon the ministry of the Word.

It is not, therefore, with regard to the necessity of the ministry that the reformers parted company with Rome but in the definition of its

---

16. Clemen, 1:367, 35ff.; WA 6:408; *LW* 44 (Philadelphia: Fortress, 1966), p. 129.
17. Clemen 1:503, 22ff.; WA 6:566; *LW* 36 (Philadelphia: Fortress, 1959), p. 113.

nature or function. From the Roman Catholic perspective on the means of grace, priestly service is primarily sacerdotal (*sacerdotium*). Luther shows how the words "do this in remembrance of me" become the point of departure for the development of this view of the ministry.[18] The ministry is primarily viewed as a service to God inasmuch as the sacrifice of the Mass is the central element in worship and devotion. This is clearly demonstrated by the fact that the Mass can take place even if no one but the priest is present. Since ordination is a sacrament, and since the means of grace are instruments of the infusion of grace and the Spirit in and of themselves, it follows that ordination bestows a *character indelebilis* (an indelible character) which is a prerequisite for the ability to perform priestly duties. The validity of the means of grace depends upon the proper ordination of the sacrament's officiant. Here the ministry is not simply a function of the authority which belongs to the whole church (i.e., all Christians), but is a possession of a hierarchy upon whose existence alone, independently of the congregation, the mediation of grace depends. The call to ministry comes from God through the hierarchy, not through the congregation, which has no voice or influence whatsoever in such matters. The ministry stands over the people.

Exactly the same thing happens with Zwingli, but of course for completely different reasons. Due to his teaching about the Spirit working independently of, or—better said—with only accidental connection to the Word, he has difficulty in defending the ministry against the enthusiasts. He does it finally by giving consideration to the necessity of order in the congregation. The priest or prophet, however, as Zwingli typically enjoys pointing out, is not primarily the one by whom the means of grace come to the people. He is the Spirit-filled charismatic who holds himself above the people as guardian of their souls. He must oppose anything that is against God and build up whatever God wills. In this concept lies the basis for Zwingli's political activity. In *Fidei Ratio* he also refers to the idea that "the prophets" support the authorities.[19] It is true that Zwingli agrees in principle with the "priesthood of all believers." The pastor is to be chosen by the congregation.

---

18. Clemen 1:55, 25ff.; WA 6:563; *LW* 36:111.
19. *Bekenntnisschriften der reformierten Kirche*, pp. 92, 12ff.; ET, Reu, 2:176.

The congregation, however, needs the assistance of the experts, which in practice hands the decision over to the authorities. As the one who has been chosen to preach, the pastor must diligently study the Scriptures, preferably in the original languages. But just because of this he becomes the expert who knows God's Word and consequently ought to rule the congregation. In this way, the ministry receives an especially prominent place in the Zwinglian congregation, even though its actual basis seems to have been annulled by his peculiar doctrine of the means of grace.[20]

The primary focus of Article 5 is the place of the ministry in principle. The treatment of Articles 9–13, which deal with the functions of the ministry, will serve to deepen and clarify this principle. Finally, Article 14 will present an occasion for a renewed treatment of the ministry, although from a slightly different perspective.

---

20. Regarding Zwingli's understanding of the ministry, see R. Staehelin, *Huldreich Zwingli*, vol. 2 (1897), pp. 95ff.

Article 6

• THE NEW OBEDIENCE •

Text

Our churches also teach that this faith is bound to bring   1
forth good fruits and that it is necessary to do the good works
commanded by God.[1] We must do so because it is God's
will and not because we rely on such works to merit justification before God,[2] for forgiveness of sins and justification   2
are apprehended by faith,[3] as Christ himself also testifies,
"When you have done all these things, say, 'We are unprofitable servants' " (Luke 17:10). The same is also taught   3
by the Fathers of the ancient church,[4] for Ambrose says, "It
is ordained by God that whoever believes in Christ shall be
saved, not through works but through faith alone, and he
shall receive forgiveness of sins by grace."

After works have been denied any role in justification, they can be
assigned their rightful place. **Is bound to . . . is necessary to** (*debeat*

---

1. GT: ". . .Allerlei, so Gott geboten hat" (all. . .as God has commanded).
2. GT: "Gnad" (favor).
3. GT: "Glauben an Christus" (faith in Christ).
4. GT: "Die Väter" (the Fathers).

81

. . . *oporteat*): here, it seems, the idea of a duty incumbent upon the believer is introduced; this, of course, does not mean the abandonment of the Lutheran idea of works as the spontaneous result of faith. **Good works** must still be done. What is decisive is the motive: **because it is God's will**. Good works are those works enjoined by God's commandments: **commanded by God.** Next, works understood as merits with respect to being justified before God are rejected once again. According to Article 4, any trust in their meritorious character is illusory and is therefore also a false motivation for a person's actions. Once again, justification by faith is maintained. Luke 17:10 seems to be a somewhat incomplete scriptural proof, but its primary purpose is, of course, to emphasize the negative side, the rejection of merits. In previous articles the confessors have supported their teaching exclusively from the Bible and early church orthodoxy except for the one vague reference to *scriptores ecclesiastici* (the ancient Fathers) in Article 1. Here, the first direct use of a "proof from the Fathers" occurs. It is Ambrosiaster rather than Ambrose who is cited here (see *BK,* p. 60, note 4; *BC,* p. 37, n. 7). It must be admitted that the reference is extraordinarily apt. Taken out of context and set in the AC, it states exactly the same thing as Article 4.

Commentary

The question of the relationship between faith and works is so intimately related to the doctrine of justification by faith alone that any doubt about the answer disappears as soon as one has grasped the Lutheran teaching on justification. One might even say that if the question becomes a problem at all, it is evidence of a lack of understanding of what Luther means by faith. If the righteousness of faith is to give God the glory by being content with receiving all of his mercy in Christ, then the question about what I must do can never arise in relation to God. Before God, only Christ can accomplish anything. This truth applies not only for the beginning, but for the whole of Christian life. Article 6 is intended to establish two things: first, that the Lutheran doctrine of justification had not rendered works superfluous, as its opponents claimed; and second, that though the necessity of works is maintained, the motivation for them becomes completely different.

One who is familiar with the way Luther speaks about these things will be struck by the use of a particular word in Article 6: "faith *is bound to* (*debeat*) bring forth good fruits." Even though one must surely be careful about laying too much weight on this one formulation, it is certainly not incorrect to see here a faint suggestion of the difference between Luther and Melanchthon, which would become increasingly apparent in the years after 1530. In both the Schwabach and the Marburg Articles, the connection between faith and its fruits, works, is understood as an organic connection, something which follows as a matter of course. Precisely because faith is not a person's more or less well formulated ideas about God, but the Holy Spirit's gift through the Word, it is impossible for faith not to bear fruit.[5] With the Holy Spirit a new life of obedience ensues as well, for the Holy Spirit does not permit people to remain idle, as Luther says. It is simply impossible, therefore, that works should not follow faith. One cannot avoid the conclusion that the AC here offers an expression of the Lutheran teaching that is inferior to its predecessors.

Regarding the place of works in the Christian life, however, the AC is in complete agreement with Luther. Works are understood as the fruits of justification, that is, they are a consequence of justification, not a part of it. Understandably, the Council of Trent expressly condemns this understanding of the place of works, since to accept it would be to annul any notion of the increase of righteousness through works as humans cooperate with grace.[6] The disagreement with Rome, however, applies just as much to the kind of work as to its place. The good works which follow justification are the works which are *commanded by God* as opposed to self-conceived works invented by humans in order to please him.[7] This understanding of the place of works already

---

5. Luther often illustrates his view by expressly setting it in opposition to every "ought" ("is bound to"). See, e.g., WA 57, Gal. 105, 24ff.: "Sic tria et septem non debent esse decem, sed sunt decem. . . . Ita iustus non debet bene vivere et bene facere, sed bene vivit et bene facit" (Just as it is not the case that three plus seven ought to be ten, but that three plus seven are ten, . . . so it is not said that a just person ought to live well and do well, but that he actually lives well and does well [trans. J. Pierce]).

6. Session 6, canon 24.

7. For further elaboration on this, see Article 20, in which a series of these "useless" works is listed.

means that they cannot be motivated by the desire to obtain anything from God. By faith in Christ, a person is united with him. Now works occur on the basis of God's will, which the Christian is free to do precisely because he already has everything by faith. Therefore the idea that works should be meritorious is unthinkable. What this means, even though it is not directly stated, is that the object of the new obedience is not God but one's neighbor. "Behold, from faith thus flow forth love and joy in the Lord, and from love a joyful, willing, and free mind that serves one's neighbor willingly, and takes no account of gratitude or ingratitude, of praise or blame, of gain or loss."[8] These words from Luther's *The Freedom of a Christian* provide a capsule summary of the whole issue.

Although it affirms the basic principle of Article 6, the Confutation objects to the AC's incessant speaking of faith in connection with justification. Justification, according to the Confutation, falls under the categories of grace and love. Christ's word concerning the unworthy servant is intended to teach us that our works are never likened to divine wages. This is because faith and works are God's gifts, and to those who possess them eternal life is given by virtue of God's mercy. It can scarcely be stated better from the Roman side. In spite of this, however, Melanchthon protests powerfully in the Apology.[9] For the reformers, the doctrine of faith formed by love meant nothing less than the destruction of the gospel of the forgiveness of sin. As soon as love becomes the decisive thing, a person's thoughts are turned to works and away from dependence upon God's mercy which alone can save. The phrase "by faith alone" asserts that there is no other life in love than the life which God gives. Love originates in God's mercy. Without such love faith is not faith but merely an impotent idea.

Since both the Confutation and Melanchthon repeatedly deal with the concept of *fides caritate formata* (faith formed by love), and since it is of such great significance for understanding the reformers' perspective on the relationship between faith and love, it should be examined a bit more closely. Let us take as an example the formulation that has been considered up to now the classic in the Roman church,

---

8. Clemen 2:25, 17ff.; WA 7:36; *LW* 31 (Philadelphia: Fortress, 1957), p. 367.
9. Apology 4 §§107ff. (*BC*, pp. 122ff.).

that of Thomas Aquinas. In itself, faith is an act of the intellect, in which the intellect, moved by God, acknowledges the dogmas of the church as revealed truths. In this respect there is no difference between *fides informis* (unformed faith) and *fides caritate formata* (faith formed by love). The difference consists in the determination of the will. Seen from the side of the intellect, *fides informis* is just as complete as *fides formata*. Nevertheless, *fides informis* is a dead faith, because the will is not directed towards God. In *fides informis* the will is involved in the act of faith only as far as its assistance is necessary for the acceptance of revealed truths. That which perfects the will is love. Faith is the material, love is the form which gives faith its true character. As an intellectual act faith directs itself toward God as the first truth (*prima veritas*), but the act of the will, led by love, directs itself toward God himself. It is love, therefore, which is decisive in one's relationship to God. Faith, of course, must be there first, since the will cannot direct itself toward the good until the intellect has presented it to the will as the good. Because love forms faith, faith itself is not altered, but rather its subject, the person who now receives a new quality through the infusion of love and is lifted up to a supernatural life.

For Thomas there is no doubt that only *fides formata* justifies. The love spoken of here is completely beyond the capability of the natural human being. It is entirely God's gift. Once a person has received it, however, he really does become capable of loving God and thus of acquiring the merits necessary for salvation.[10] Behind this teaching lies the conviction that God can have fellowship only with those who are holy. Only when we partake of the nature of God through the infusion of love can we be united with him. Seen in this light Luther's "by faith alone" becomes a meaningless phrase, and "simultaneously righteous and sinner" an insult to the majesty of God.

We now turn to what Luther has to say about this. He makes short shrift of the concept of *fides informis*. Luther sees nothing but the delusion of Satan in the notion that faith, which is the gift of the Holy Spirit, can remain inactive and exist even in mortal sin. When God comes near, as he does in faith, something happens. *Fides informis*,

---

10. Re Thomas's concept of faith see *Summa Theologica* II-II, q. 1-6, and K. E. Skydsgaard, *Ja og nej* (Copenhagen, 1953), pp. 105ff.

therefore, is nothing but an imaginary faith.[11] He has just as little time for *fides formata,* however. If faith is invalid until love occurs, then human beings will quickly abandon faith in Christ, thinking that if faith does not justify, it is worthless, and that therefore the important thing is to emphasize love.[12] In Scholasticism's assertion of the significance of love for faith, Luther sees the intrusion of the law into the doctrine of justification, whereby Christ is pushed aside. Christ is not my work, he says, meaning that it is only Christ who can take away sin—and nothing we possess, whether it be infused by God or self-made.[13] One cannot grasp the work of Christ through love, however, but only by faith. In reality the discussion is about two completely different kinds of faith and two completely different kinds of love. Luther sees absolutely no value in *fides informis.* The idea that such a faith is "formed" by love (love being understood as a new supernatural quality), however, simply means for Luther that what had been a harmless and useless phenomenon becomes blasphemous. In this Luther sees a denial of God's mercy to *sinners.* For Luther, *fides caritate formata* is merely a "historical" faith, a *fides historica* which seeks to reach its goal by fulfilling the law, and thus is an expression of contempt for Christ. If one must speak of love in connection with faith, for Luther it is never *caritas* which seeks God as its "highest good" (*summum bonum*), but rather it is God's love which is revealed in the cross of Christ, and which through faith becomes active in the Christian's life as a love which loves God and neighbor without thought of gain. Here it is apparent how differently God's grace is understood. For Thomas, grace is a power by which human capability is strengthened so that a person can raise himself up to God. For Luther, grace is the fact that God in his mercy is present as the one who fights for sinners who have nothing to hold on to but the alien righteousness of Christ.

It should be clear by now that the real difference is about how the relationship to God itself is understood. The accusation of "works righteousness" which Luther directed against the theology of his time

---

11. *Lectures on Galatians,* 1535, WA 40/1:421f.; *LW* 26 (St. Louis: Concordia, 1963), p. 269.

12. WA 40/1:239, 18ff.; *LW* 26:136.

13. WA 40/1:240, 29ff.; *LW* 26:137.

thus attacks not only the view which holds that humans have the capability to do good works by their own power, but just as much strikes at Thomism, even though Thomas never forgets for a moment that human merits are God's gifts.[14] For, even though everything is set under grace, it is an absolutely essential premise for Thomism that a person must become worthy of eternal life *in himself*. Given this premise, therefore, it becomes completely unreasonable to say that faith is the fulfillment of the law. Faith is merely the necessary prerequisite. The law is fulfilled by works. Just as faith is merely the prerequisite, however, so Christ and his work, as necessary as he may be, is also merely a prerequisite. One could almost use Luther's own formulation, "Christ is not my work," but with a completely different meaning! Precisely because Christ is not my work, but merely the absolutely necessary prerequisite for my work, something else must be added. There must be an explanation of how my work can be completed on the basis of his, namely, by God's grace! Thus, works have retained their place in justification—by grace alone. But now the very thing that the emphasis on "faith alone" is intended to prevent in the Lutheran doctrine of justification has happened: righteousness is no longer equated with Christ's righteousness. In other words, the motivation for doing good works is no longer the good of the neighbor but the increase of righteousness. "Grace alone" here means that only by infused grace are humans capable of fulfilling the law, thereby raising themselves up to God. For Luther it means that in Christ, who is grasped by faith, the law *is* fulfilled, and therefore humans are free to love their neighbor without any thought for themselves or their own fulfillment of the law.

What is at stake here cannot be stated more clearly than Luther himself has done in his famous *Preface to the Epistle of St. Paul to the Romans:*

> Faith is not the human notion and dream that some people call faith. When they see that no improvement of life and no good works follow— although they can hear and say much about faith—they fall into the error of saying, "Faith is not enough; one must do works in order to be righteous and be saved." This is due to the fact that when they hear the gospel, they get busy and by their own powers create an idea in their

---

14. On the concept of merit, see the commentary on Article 20.

heart which says, "I believe"; they take this then to be a true faith. But, as it is a human figment and idea that never reaches the depths of the heart, nothing comes of it either, and no improvement follows.

Faith, however, is a divine work in us which changes us and makes us to be born anew of God, John 1[:12-13]. It kills the old Adam and makes us altogether different men, in heart and spirit and mind and powers; and it brings with it the Holy Spirit. O it is a living, busy, active, mighty thing, this faith. It is impossible for it not to be doing good works incessantly. It does not ask whether good works are to be done, but before the question is asked, it has already done them, and is constantly doing them. Whoever does not do such works, however, is an unbeliever. He gropes and looks around for faith and good works, but knows neither what faith is nor what good works are. Yet he talks and talks, with many words, about faith and good works.

Faith is a living, daring confidence in God's grace, so sure and certain that the believer would stake his life on it a thousand times. This knowledge of and confidence in God's grace makes men glad and bold and happy in dealing with God and with all creatures. And this is the work which the Holy Spirit performs in faith. Because of it, without compulsion, a person is ready and glad to do good to everyone, to serve everyone, to suffer everything, out of love and praise to God who has shown him this grace. Thus it is impossible to separate works from faith, quite as impossible as to separate heat and light from fire.[15]

---

15. WA, DB 7:9, 30—10, 23; *LW* 35 (Philadelphia: Fortress, 1960), pp. 370-371.

Article 7

• THE CHURCH •

Text

Our churches also teach that one holy church is to con- 1
tinue forever. The church is the assembly of saints in which
the Gospel is taught purely and the sacraments are administered rightly.[1] For the true unity of the church it is enough 2
to agree concerning the teaching of the Gospel[2] and the
administration of the sacraments.[3] It is not necessary that 3
human traditions or rites and ceremonies, instituted by men,
should be alike everywhere. It is as Paul says, "One faith, 4
one baptism, one God and Father of all," etc. (Eph. 4:5,6).

The article contains three statements: (1) the continuance of **one
holy church**; (2) the meaning of the word *ecclesia* (**church**); (3) the

---

1. GT: "Bei welchen das Evangelium rein gepredigt und die heiligen Sakrament
laut des Evangelii gereicht werden" (among whom the Gospel is preached in its purity
and the holy sacraments are administered according to the Gospel).

2. GT: "Da einträchtiglich nach reinem Verstand das Evangelium gepredigt (wird)"
(that the Gospel be preached in conformity with a pure understanding of it).

3. GT: "Und die Sakrament dem göttlichen Wort gemäss gereicht werden" (and
that the sacraments be administered in accordance with the divine Word).

basis of the **unity of the church**. **One holy church** (*una sancta ecclesia*): as the last part of the article demonstrates, *una* is strongly emphasized here. The AC represents no other church than the **one holy church**. **Is to continue forever**: this church will continue forever, i.e., as long as the earth remains. Next, it is stated what the church is— **the assembly of saints**. The expression reminds one of the Apostles' Creed: *communio sanctorum* ("the communion of saints"), from a Lutheran perspective. The use of *congregatio* (**assembly**) is no doubt meant to avoid the ambiguity that *communio* could have occasioned (see *BK,* p. 61, note 3). In order to make clear that this holy assembly is not every assembly which might decide to call itself "holy," it is more specifically defined by the relative clause **in which the Gospel,** etc. Purity of proclamation and right administration of the sacraments is the basis of this *congregatio* (cf. Article 5). The remainder of the article deals with what is necessary for the **unity of the church,** in other words, what belongs to the definition of the church. When next it is emphasized that uniformity in ceremonies is **not necessary,** the interest clearly lies in underscoring the claim that the evangelicals have not set themselves outside the one church by altering rites and ceremonies. **Human traditions**: everything that goes beyond proclamation and sacraments, such as church government, liturgy, etc. (cf. Articles 15 and 26).

Commentary

The two articles of the AC on the church give a clear account of the concept of the church which Luther attained from the year 1518 on. The groundwork was most likely laid much earlier, as in the case of the doctrine of justification.[4] However, it was not until the debate about the pope's divine authority, which erupted out of the indulgence controversy, that Luther began to draw out the consequences of the doctrine of justification which inevitably would lead to a new understanding of the nature of the church. This discussion quickly brought Luther to the point of asserting that the church is not bound to time, place, nor

---

4. See J. Vercruysse, *Fidelis Populis* (Wiesbaden: F. Steiner, 1968) and Scott H. Hendrix, *Ecclesia in via* (Leiden: Brill, 1974).

persons, and thus also not to Rome. The church is not a legal institution which rests upon the papacy, but rather it is the assembly of believers.[5] The first clear exposition of all the fundamental ideas in Luther's concept of the church appears in the treatise *On the Papacy in Rome* of 1520. The purpose of the treatise is to refute the notion that the pope's position as head of the church is derived from divine order. When Scripture speaks of Christendom, says Luther, it means the assembly of all believers on earth. It is not a physical assembly but rather a spiritual one, the unity of which is dependent neither on place nor time. Christ says, "My kingdom is not of this world," clearly indicating that the church is not bound to Rome, but is found wherever there is faith.[6] The physical and the spiritual unity are by no means identical. To belong to the Roman church makes no one a Christian, nor does one become a heretic by not belonging to it. One becomes a heretic only through false belief.[7] Thus, all earthly Christendom has no other head than Christ himself. The church cannot be numbered among secular societies any more than faith can be numbered among temporal blessings. As secular societies have physical, secular heads, the church has a spiritual head. Thus, it holds true that "the natural, real, true, and essential Christendom exists in the Spirit, and not in any external thing."[8]

Luther continues by declaring that Scripture recognizes no other way of speaking about Christendom. To use the word *Christendom* to refer to a "spiritual estate" is a misuse and there is not one word in Scripture to indicate that this "church" is instituted by God. This church is based on human laws. These two churches, therefore, must be called by two different names. We call the first a "spiritual, internal Christendom," the second, a "physical, external Christendom." This does not mean, Luther adds, that he wishes to separate the two "churches" from each

---

5. On the following discussion see Clemen 1:331-339 (WA 6:292-301; *LW* 39 [Philadelphia: Fortress, 1970], pp. 66-75).

6. ". . . Dass reich gottis . . . ist nit zu Rom/ auch nit an Rom gebunden/ wider hie nach da/ sodern wo da inwendig der glaub is . . ." (. . . The kingdom of God . . . is not in Rome, is not bound to Rome, and is neither here nor there. Rather, it is where there is inward faith); ibid., 331, 36f.; *LW* 39:66.

7. Ibid., 332, 20—333, 11; *LW* 39:67.

8. Ibid., 334, 21ff.; *LW* 39:69.

other; they belong together the same as soul and body.[9] Though the external church may be ruled by bishops, pope, etc., the true church has no earthly head, but is ruled by Christ alone in heaven.[10] Consequently, the papacy and bishops cannot be marks of the church since they merely govern the outer church according to human laws. Rather, the marks of the church are Baptism, the Lord's Supper, and the gospel, for where they are present there is no doubt that there are also saints present, even if they be nothing but infants in cradles.[11]

The AC corresponds completely to Luther's understanding when it begins with the assertion that there is "one holy church" which, by virtue of the means of grace, will "continue (*perpetuo*) forever." The Schwabach Articles read instead, "bis an der Welt Ende" (until the end of the world), which is of course also the sense here. The definition of the church which follows, "the assembly of saints," appears to have what Luther called "the spiritual, internal Christendom" in mind, i.e., the church which as the work of the Holy Spirit is an object of faith.[12] This does not mean, however, that it is pure "spirituality" which is referred to here, for the church is the assembly of saints "in which the Gospel is taught purely and the sacraments are administered rightly." By this qualification, the enthusiastic concept of the church as an association of kindred spirits is rejected. It is only in conjunction with the Word and the sacraments that such an association qualifies as a church, not because of the qualities of its members. It is precisely

---

9. Ibid., 334, 28—335, 23; *LW* 39:70.

10. Ibid., 336, 11ff.; *LW* 39:71.

11. "Die zeichenn/ da bey man eusserlich mercken kan/ wo die selb kirch in der Welt is/ sein die tauff/ sacrament und das Euangelium/ unnd nit Rom/ diss odder der ort. Dan wo die tauff und Euangelium ist/ da sol niemant zweyffeln es sein heyligen da/ und soltens gleich eytel kind in der wigen sein" (Not Rome, or this or that place, but baptism, the sacrament, and the gospel are the signs by which the existence of the church in the world can be noticed externally. Wherever there is baptism and the gospel no one should doubt the presence of the saints—even if they were only children in the cradle) (ibid., 339, 16ff; *LW* 39:75).

12. Cf. Luther's letter to Albrecht of Prussia of 1523, which clearly expresses his understanding: "Ecclesia est res in Spiritu et sancta, sicut dicimus: 'Credo ecclesiam sanctam catholicum.' Quod autem creditur, nec vidiri nec sentiri potest, Heb. 11 [v. 1]" (The church is in the Spirit and is holy in all things. As we say, "I believe in the holy catholic church." But the thing in which one believes cannot be seen or felt, because faith concerns things which are not seen [Hebrews 11 (:1)]); WA *Briefe* 3:210, 1ff.; *LW* 49 (Philadelphia: Fortress, 1972), pp. 61-62.

because faith is the way to salvation that the church is bound to the means of grace. Faith, after all, according to a Lutheran understanding, means that a person completely abandons himself to the Word and the sacraments (Article 5). If one seeks to divorce the church as *congregatio sanctorum* from its distinguishing marks, the Word and the sacraments, it shows that one has a completely different concept of faith, and thus a completely different doctrine of justification from the reformers. For when the church is divorced from the means of grace faith will inevitably be understood as a self-contained quality, while for the reformers it is of the very essence of faith and thus of the assembly of believers as well to be bound to external marks. Faith is the gift of the Spirit and as such is hidden. Consequently it cannot be known who truly belongs to the church. Faith, however, is also bound to the Word which can be heard and to the signs which can be seen.

It appears from Article 8 that, like Luther, the AC holds that the external church, the "assembly" which makes use of the sacraments, can be more extensive than "the assembly of saints." This qualification is necessitated by the fact that the church is bound to the means of grace, for although faith is hidden, the use of the means of grace is plain for all to see. Since this is true, one must allow for the possibility that even though faith is found only where the means of grace are used, the mere fact of their use is in itself no proof of the existence of faith. Stated differently, the assembly of saints does not exist apart from those who are gathered around the means of grace, but yet it does not necessarily include them all. The church as *congregatio sanctorum* ("the assembly of saints") and as the external church is thus organically united by Christ's ordinance in the Word and the sacraments.[13] Therefore, the sentence *extra ecclesiam nulla salus* (outside of the church there is no salvation) applies to the AC as well, though not on the basis of the episcopacy, as Cyprian held, but on the basis of proclamation and the sacraments. Furthermore, any hierarchical concept of the church is rejected in the definition of the church in the AC. The only thing which is absolutely necessary for the life of the church is the

---

13. Yet there are extreme cases in which this relationship can be altered; for instance, being barred from the sacrament cannot exclude a person from the true church if that person has true faith. See, e.g., Luther's *Sermon on the Virtue of Excommunication, 1518* (*LW* 39:3ff.).

existence of the means through which the Holy Spirit creates justifying faith.

Nothing more clearly reveals the double front of the Lutheran Reformation—against the enthusiasts and against Rome—than the concept of the church. Despite the deep chasm that separates the enthusiasts' and the Roman concepts of the church, there is much that binds them together in common opposition to the Lutheran concept. Both are characterized by the attempt to make the supernatural character of the church externally visible: in the one case, through an empirical possession of the Spirit which separates the church from the world; in the other, through a hierarchy which by virtue of its divine authority can ensure that the Holy Spirit speaks through the church. From the Lutheran perspective, both commit the same error: lack of faith in the incarnation. Both the enthusiasts and Rome deny that as God became man in Christ, he meets us now in the same manner under the form of human signs. The enthusiasts deny it by their very offense at the humanness of the signs. The Roman church denies it in that it permits the efficacy of these signs to be dependent on the cooperation of the hierarchy, denying their purely human nature. For the enthusiasts, the church becomes pure "spirituality," i.e., pure subjectivism. The Roman church, to be sure, achieves objectivity by understanding the church as an external-legal institution, but becomes subjectivistic through its teaching about human cooperation with grace, which makes it necessary to describe salvation as a psychological process. The definition of the church in the AC makes subjectivism in either sense impossible. One cannot speak first of the church as the assembly of saints and then afterwards speak of the Word and the sacraments, or vice versa. The church is the assembly of saints created in every respect by the Holy Spirit through proclamation and the sacraments. Where proclamation and the sacraments are present, there the assembly of saints is present as well. These two parts of the definition cannot be separated either logically or chronologically.

The definition of the church as the assembly of saints is severely criticized in the Confutation, which claims that the wicked are thereby excluded from the church. The concept of the church in the AC, in other words, is considered enthusiastic. In the Apology, Melanchthon answers the objection by referring to Article 8, which clearly demonstrates that this is not its meaning. However, he continues, the church as the body of Christ is not an institution, for the ungodly do not belong to Christ's body; only the *societas fidei et Spiritus sancti in human cordibus* (the association of faith and of the Holy Spirit in hearts) does. The phrase "the assembly of saints" is simply a clarification of what is meant when we confess in the Creed that we believe in the holy catholic church.[14] The church is catholic because it includes people from all over the earth. The wicked belong to the church in name only. Thus, it is necessary in defining the church to distinguish between what the church is in name and what it is in reality (*nomine et re*), for if it is simply defined according to its external form, people will not understand that Christ's kingdom is *iustitia cordis* (the righteousness of the heart) and *donatio Spiritus sancti* (the gift of the Holy Spirit). Then every distinction between the *populus legis* (people of the law), Israel, and the church would be abolished. The church is characterized precisely by the fact that the church and the people in the church are not identical, as they were in Israel. On the contrary, a sharp line is drawn through the external church, between the kingdom of Christ, which is identical with the *congregatio sanctorum,* and the kingdom of the devil, to which the ungodly belong. Of course, this will be apparent only when the kingdom of God is revealed. Nevertheless, that same line is in place even now, while the kingdom of Christ exists under the cross and is therefore hidden.[15] Since the Apology is directed towards the Roman theologians rather than the enthusiasts, Melanchthon primarily underscores in it that the church must be seen in relation to the individual.

The definition of the church is followed by a statement of what is necessary for the unity of the church. Agreement is required only in matters relating to Word and sacrament. Everything else is a matter of freedom. Naturally, the Confutation takes exception to this, stating that if it is "particular" rites that are thought of here (i.e., various local liturgies), the AC is commended; but if it is the "universal" rites which are common to the whole church which are meant, then it must be utterly rejected, since they should be observed by all and it must be

---

14. This understanding of *communio sanctorum* corresponds to Luther's customary interpretation of the Apostles' Creed. See specific references in *BK*, p. 61, note 3.

15. This summarizes the basic ideas of the Apology 7 and 8 §§1-22 (*BC*, pp. 168-172).

assumed that they stem from the apostles. Melanchthon meets this objection without evasion. He asks what his opponents mean by this distinction between "particular" and "universal" rites. "We are talking about true spiritual unity, without which there can be no faith in the heart nor righteousness in the heart before God." The righteousness of faith, however, is not dependent upon rites, whether they be universal or particular.[16] The issue is to establish what is necessary for salvation. Once it has been admitted that human traditions are not necessary, however, one is free to observe them willingly for the sake of peace.[17] Next, Melanchthon uses some passages in the New Testament to show how the apostles, to whom their opponents refer, resisted every inclination to make laws and ceremonies into requirements. In addition he cites a series of church usages which have been altered in the course of time which would, of course, have been completely unjustifiable if it was required to observe them on the basis of apostolic authority.[18] He closes by questioning whether the discussion is of any use at all when their opponents neither understand what is meant by the righteousness of faith nor by the kingdom of Christ.[19]

Melanchthon's explanations are thus clear enough. He says that the AC speaks of *spiritual* unity. Therefore he refuses to involve himself with the objections of the Confutation which concern an external, demonstrable unity. All that is needful for this spiritual unity to exist is proclamation and the sacraments. Everything else is understood as human traditions, which may vary without threatening the church. From this position Melanchthon can deny the validity of his opponents' concept of the church without denying the possibility that the church as *una sancta ecclesia* (the one holy church) exists also among them. Stated otherwise, the opponents' erroneous concept of the church, which causes them to set up false conditions for its unity, does not tempt Melanchthon to follow in their footsteps. He holds firmly to the formulation of Article 7, refusing thereby to understand the church in terms of confessions! There can be no doubt that the phrase *consentire de doctrina evangelii* (to agree concerning the teaching of the Gospel),

16. Ibid., §§30–32 (*BC*, pp. 173f.).
17. Ibid., §§33–34 (*BC*, pp. 174f.).
18. Ibid., §§35–44 (*BC*, pp. 175–177).
19. Ibid., §45 (*BC*, p. 177).

refers to proclamation, not to "correct doctrine" or something similar. This means that the AC had not yet drawn the consequences from the church schism which were later drawn by Lutheran Orthodoxy, namely, that pure doctrine in the sense of correct theology should be the criterion for the true church. The AC could very well be characterized as pre-confessionalistic, since it in no way envisions nor encompasses the idea of a confession as a line of demarcation of one denomination from another. Later it was to be different, but thus far the protest against the Roman concept of the church had not developed into an attempt to replace the hierarchy with anything else to guarantee the existence of the true church. The church lives solely by those divine acts by which God creates it through his Spirit.

Just as there is no room for confessionalism in the AC, so it is with the question of episcopacy and the true church. This too is excluded by the determination of what is necessary for the unity of the church. There is only one office necessary for the unity of the church, the ministry of the Word. The office of bishop can never be the church's foundation, any more than its absence can deprive the church of anything essential. The church can be the true church without it. The office of bishop belongs to the category of *traditiones humanae* (human traditions) which may be preserved as far as possible without thereby being necessary.[20]

While Luther's teaching about the church remained constant in its essentials, Melanchthon later modified his teaching in ways which Luther hardly would have accepted. It is generally known that the AC lacks the teaching about the universal priesthood of believers, which was a constitutive element in Luther's concept of the church. Even so, it cannot be claimed that the two articles conflict with this concept in any way. However, if one reads what Melanchthon has to say about the church later, in the last edition of the *Loci* (1559), for example, it becomes clear that he has no place for such a teaching. Here, despite the preservation of certain features of the concept of the church in the AC, the entire foundation for the clerical, institutional church of Orthodoxy has already been laid. Melanchthon likens the church to an "assembly of instruction" (*coetus scholasticus*) and emphasizes that

---

20. See further treatment of the office of bishop under Article 14 below.

there is a difference between "teachers" (*docentes*) and "learners" (auditores).[21] The church is defined in this manner: "The visible church is an assembly of those who embrace (*amplectentium*) the gospel of Christ and correctly use the sacraments, in which (assembly) God works through the ministry of the gospel and regenerates many to eternal life, but in which there are many unregenerate who nevertheless are in agreement concerning true doctrine."[22] Here the "gospel of Christ" has become identified with correct theology under the control of the clergy, with the result that the ministry is no longer simply serving the Word, but is in danger of becoming a new legal system superior to and ruling over the congregation.

The AC, as with the doctrine of the office of the ministry, lays down no hard and fast rules about church organization. Both the "established" (*folkekirkelig*) and "free-church" structures could be considered equally valid (in principle), on the basis of this view of the church. It avoids making binding things which according to the reformers belong to "human traditions." It is sufficient to agree on the gospel and the administration of the sacraments, for it is to these things that faith is bound, and it is faith alone that justifies. The connection between the Word and faith is being asserted here also. Therefore the concept of the church necessarily has two sides. No one can speak of faith apart from its bond to Christ's institution in Word and sacrament, for only here is found the faith which does not look at itself but to Christ alone. Conversely, it must never be forgotten that Christ's institution does not in itself save, but only as it creates faith in the heart of the individual.

---

21. *Werke*, 2, pp. 480, 28ff.
22. Ibid., p. 476, 12-17.

Article 8

• WHAT IS THE CHURCH? •

Text

Properly speaking, the church is the assembly of saints   1
and true believers. However, since in this life many hypocrites and evil persons are mingled with believers, it is allowable to use the sacraments even when they are administered by evil men, according to the saying of Christ, "The
scribes and Pharisees sit on Moses' seat," etc. (Matt. 23:2).
Both the sacraments and the Word are effectual by reason   2
of the institution and commandment of Christ even if they
are administered by evil men.[1]
Our churches condemn the Donatists and others like them   3
who have denied that the ministry of evil men may be used
in the church and who have thought the ministry of evil men
to be unprofitable and without effect.[2]

The purpose of this article is to make it impossible for anyone to

---

1. The GT is slightly different without altering the sense. It speaks of "false Christians, hypocrites," and adds "open sinners." The grounding of the efficacy of the
sacraments in the institution of Christ is omitted.

2. The GT is content with mentioning the Donatists and "others who hold contrary
views," without stating the Donatist understanding.

accuse the evangelicals of Donatism. The negotiators at the diet were well aware that fears of such an attack were not without grounds (see Article 7). **Properly speaking**: in its essence, the church is that which has been described in the previous article. The designation **true believers**, added here, contains nothing new, because, according to Articles 4 and 5, the word **saints** cannot mean anything else than **true believers.** The qualification which is immediately added, **however,** does not weaken the definition of the church, but is necessitated by the fact that the church exists in the world. The means of grace certainly constitute the church, as through them the Holy Spirit creates faith. Nevertheless, they do not visibly mark the boundaries of the church over against the rest of humanity. This makes the possibility of the existence of **hypocrites and evil persons** within the church unavoidable. The efficacy of the means of grace cannot be dependent on the spiritual quality of the one who administers them: **it is allowable to use the sacraments**, etc. Following a reference to Matt. 23:2, this understanding is developed more fully by indicating precisely what constitutes the efficacy of the means of grace: **are effectual by reason of the institution and commandment of Christ**. Where (i.e., when and where it pleases God) the means of grace are effectual, it is solely by the power of Christ's command. Any remaining doubt about their benefit due to questions about the worthiness of the priest is thereby eliminated.

The condemnation of **the Donatists and others** is natural, since the entire article is a treatment of the Donatist problem.

Commentary

The content of this article follows directly from the previous one. Since faith as the gift of the Holy Spirit is hidden, but nevertheless is bound to the means of grace, it is necessary to reckon with the possibility of the existence of pastors who do not belong to the true church. Therefore it is necessary to emphasize that the efficacy of the means of grace is not dependent on the personal qualities of the priest; otherwise, one could never be certain that the true church really existed at all. The church would not be bound exclusively to the free grace of God nor faith solely to the coming of Christ in Word and sacraments.

Only one thing determines the efficacy of the means of grace: the institution and command of Christ. The Confutation accepts this article without reservation. Thus, few words are needed in the Apology, although Melanchthon chooses to elaborate slightly. As the pastor administers the means of grace, he does not represent his own person, but rather Christ by virtue of the church's call, according to Christ's word, "He who hears you hears me" (Luke 10:16). Here the reformers stand together with the church of the papacy against the enthusiasts, all of whom were "Donatists."

The basis of the reformers' understanding, however, was completely different from that of the church of Rome. To hold that the means of grace are dependent solely on the command of Christ means that their efficacy cannot be bound to the priest's worthiness on the basis of his ordination any more than to his personal worthiness. The divine authority of the church has its basis in the Word of God alone. The reformers can affirm with great earnestness that the priest acts on behalf of Christ, but this function is not founded on the notion, held by the church of Rome, that ordination has bestowed a *character indelebilis* upon the priest which qualifies him for his office. Rather, it is founded upon the fact that the priest has been entrusted with the task of serving in the congregation with the Word, the efficacy of which is certain because it is *God's* Word—and for no other reason.

Article 8 goes no further than this, but the determination of the church as the assembly of saints and true believers seems to contain a warning against the attempt to make visible the division between the kingdom of Christ and the kingdom of the devil. It should be mentioned, however, that Luther occasionally did toy with the issue of the external form of the church, as in his *German Mass* of 1526. There he states that there are three ways to hold worship. The first two are public forms of worship, namely, the Latin and German masses. There is, however, a possibility which would be more in line with an evangelical institution. It would not be public. Rather, those who truly wished to be Christian should gather in a house for common prayer and reception of the sacraments. Here it would also be possible to maintain a healthy church discipline, teach the catechism, provide for the collection of alms, and so on. This could easily be instituted, Luther believes, if one only had the right kind of people to tend it. Since such persons are not to be found, however, Luther contents himself with the other two forms of worship for the time being.[3] These reflections demonstrate that Luther did not simply resign himself uncritically to the situation of an established (*folkekirkelig*) church. After the visitations, however, the development of the church's form in Electoral Saxony took a direction different from that which Luther apparently had envisioned. As church organizer Luther was not able to exert any decisive influence.[4]

---

3. Clemen 3:296, 37—297, 25; WA 19:75; *LW* 53 (Philadelphia: Fortress, 1965), p. 64.

4. Re church discipline see Articles 11 (Confession) and 12 (Repentance).

Article 9

• BAPTISM •

Text

[On Baptism][1] our churches teach that Baptism is nec- 1
essary for salvation, that the grace of God is offered through
Baptism, and that children should be baptized, for being 2
offered to God through Baptism they are received into his
grace.[2]

Our churches condemn the Anabaptists who reject the 3
Baptism of children and declare that children are saved without Baptism.[3]

The article makes three assertions. One, Baptism is **necessary for salvation**: there is no other way to the grace of God than the one commanded by Christ, namely, Baptism. Two, in Baptism **the grace**

---

1. See Article 1, note 1.

2. GT: "Gott . . . gefällig werden" (become acceptable to God); *recipiuntur in gratiam Dei:* it is a divine act which is being spoken of, a passage from condemnation to grace.

3. GT is more succinct: "welche lehren, dass die Kindertauf nicht recht sei" (who teach that infant Baptism is not right).

of God is offered: here the character of Baptism as a means of grace is upheld. Baptism is not merely an external sign, but brings grace. Three, it is maintained that **children should be baptized**. Here the confessors disassociate themselves from the Anabaptists, who are condemned in the second paragraph. The relative clause which follows should be understood in the same context. Its purpose is to reinforce the idea that the second assertion applies to small children as well.

The Anabaptists are condemned because of their wholesale dismissal of the third assertion and their refusal to accept the first with reference to children.

Commentary

Article 9 shows to an unusual degree the polemical restraint towards Rome which characterizes the entire AC. The Confutation approves the article and Melanchthon recognizes this approval in the Apology. This does not mean, however, that the two parties overlooked their serious differences which a differently worded article on Baptism would have exposed. Melanchthon's purpose is easily discerned. He intends to emphasize that the Lutherans have nothing in common with the Anabaptists. In this disassociation the papists are able to agree with him. On the other hand, one might very well ask if there were not grounds for the authors of the Confutation to inquire a bit more carefully about what the words "necessary for salvation" really meant. Likewise, there was good reason to ask about the nature of this grace which Baptism bestows. Since these questions were not in fact asked, however, we must look elsewhere to discover what issues, both then and now, stand between the church of Rome and the Lutheran church in the teaching on Baptism.

As soon as one examines the Schwabach and Marburg Articles it becomes clear that Article 9 is a completely new formulation. Article 9 of the Schwabach Articles maintains that Baptism consists of two parts: water and the Word of God. In contrast, the AC is framed in such vague terms that it never becomes clear what Baptism is in its essence. It seems strange that no mention whatsoever is made of faith. If there had been, it is certain that the verdict of the Confutation would have been different. Perhaps the reason behind this cautiousness was that Eck[4] in his 404 Articles had just recently labeled speaking of faith in connection with Baptism as heretical. Eck cites two of Luther's statements: that Baptism in itself profits nothing, but only faith in the word of promise to which Baptism is bound; and that Baptism does not profit an infant unless it have a faith of its own. In the Apology as well, Melanchthon has little to say about the relationship between Baptism and faith. Nonetheless, he speaks indirectly about the faith which follows *after* Baptism, adducing the fact that no Anabaptists have arisen among the Lutherans as an indication of how purely and carefully the gospel is taught. In addition, he asserts that it is the promise of salvation which is constitutive of Baptism, and this also concerns children. Since the promise, however, can be obtained only through Word and sacrament, it is necessary to baptize children in order for them to have a part in it. No account is given of the meaning of the relationship of faith to the use of the sacraments until Article 13.

Luther's first detailed exposition of his teaching on Baptism was set forth in his *Sermon on the Holy and Blessed Sacrament of Baptism* of 1519.[5] According to this treatise, the baptismal sign consists in the person being thrust into the water and then being lifted out again, which is why Luther believes that the older form of immersion really ought to be used instead of pouring. The significance of Baptism is dying to sin and the resurrection of the new person in the grace of God. This does not happen completely until bodily death occurs; thus all of life is a spiritual Baptism without ceasing until death. Sacramentally, a person is pure and innocent through the act of Baptism itself; yet the work of the sacrament remains to be completed—the resurrection at the Last Day. God, however, has already bound himself to the baptized person and has begun to recreate the person by training him all through life with many works and sufferings. Because of this re-creating activity God does not impute the sins which still remain after Baptism. Finally, the third thing in the sacrament is *faith* that Baptism really accomplishes all this and binds us to God. Faith is of all things the most necessary, for it is the ground of all comfort. Without faith a person must despair

---

4. Eck, Articles 215 and 227; Gussmann 2:128, 130; ET, Rcu, 2:109.

5. Clemen 1:185-195; WA 2:727-737; *LW* 35 (Philadelphia: Fortress, 1960), pp. 29-43.

of his sins. With faith, however, the person understands that our innocence in Baptism depends solely upon God's mercy. From this it is concluded that *penance* also has its foundation in Baptism. Through penance God administers once again the forgiveness he has promised in Baptism, which simply means that one's Baptism is operative again. It is not through works of satisfaction but by clinging to one's Baptism that a person is reinstated in the place that God in his mercy has promised. "Glaubst du, so hast du. Zweifelst du, so bist du verloren" ("Believe and you have it. Doubt, and you are lost").[6]

Luther's insistence on the importance of faith in connection with Baptism, of course, has to do with his conflict with Roman teaching about the sacraments being efficacious *ex opere operato*. One might just as well claim, however, that it is due to his zeal in stressing that Baptism is entirely God's work. The emphasis on faith does not mean that Luther's view is a midpoint between the Roman and the Anabaptist views on Baptism. On the contrary, the emphasis on faith is necessary precisely because Baptism is not a human work but an act of God. On this point, as on several others, the section on Baptism in *The Babylonian Captivity of the Church* provides an excellent supplement to the *Sermon*.[7] Here Luther distinguishes between the "parts" of Baptism in a slightly different manner. The first thing which ought to be considered is the divine promise which is bound to Baptism and upon which our entire salvation depends. Therefore we ought to exercise our faith in the promise, for without faith Baptism profits us nothing. The point is simply to take God at his Word. Thus, no sin can condemn one who has been baptized—except unbelief, which refuses to trust that God has spoken the truth. This does not mean, however, that faith is understood as a condition for the validity of the sacrament. Faith is, rather, a confidence in God's promise which depends on the power of Baptism precisely because it is God's own work. Therefore, Luther indignantly opposes the Roman church's setting penance up as a replacement for Baptism, in effect making penance into a kind of second Baptism. Sin cannot destroy Baptism, and therefore to do penance is

---

6. Clemen 1:192, 1f.; *LW* 35:38.
7. Ibid., 459-478; WA 6:526-543; *LW* 36 (Philadelphia: Fortress, 1959), pp. 57-81.

nothing else than to return to one's Baptism, which means once again to hear the word of promise in faith.

The second part of Baptism, according to *The Babylonian Captivity*, is the sign, the sacramental act itself. Here Luther attacks the central point in the medieval understanding of the sacrament, namely, the claim that the sacraments are *efficacia signa gratiae* (efficacious signs of grace) which means that they, as opposed to the "sacraments" of the old covenant, are efficacious simply by virtue of the performance of the sign (*ex opere operato*) as long as "the door is not barred" (by mortal sin). Luther denies that there is any such difference between the old and new covenants. On the contrary, the decisive thing in both cases is the word of promise, which requires faith, not works. *Non sacramentum, sed fides sacramenti justificat* (Not the sacrament, but the faith of the sacrament justifies).[8] It is faith in the word of promise which fulfills what Baptism signifies. "The sacraments . . . are not fulfilled when they are taking place, but when they are being believed."[9] To say that the sacrament contains the power to effect justification in itself is to make it into a work. "For if the sacrament confers grace on me because I receive it, then indeed I receive grace by virtue of my work, and not by faith."[10] After this Luther turns to the question of what Baptism signifies, namely, death and resurrection. The thoughts expressed here correspond completely to the *Sermon* of 1519.

It might appear as if this understanding of Baptism implies a spiritualizing of the sacrament—and so it has often been construed. However, one must understand Luther's position within the context of the polemical situation. His concern was to deal with the medieval understanding of the sacraments. If one examines the details of the conflict more closely, the decisive elements in Luther's view of Baptism will emerge.

1. In Luther's emphasis upon the sacramental word as the *word of promise* there is a completely different understanding compared with that of the Middle Ages. Here the sacramental word is no longer conceived of merely as the words of consecration (the "form" of the

---

8. Ibid., 466, 26f.; *LW* 36:66.
9. Ibid., 467, 11a.; *LW* 36:66.
10. Ibid., 467, 22ff.; *LW* 36:67.

sacrament, according to medieval terminology), but as identical with the gracious Word of God, the word of Christ, i.e., the gospel. When the word of promise becomes the decisive thing in the sacrament it becomes obvious that faith is necessary. If the grace conferred by the sacrament is a word from God in which he binds himself to the person, then that grace can be received only by faith. Any notion of the sacrament being efficacious *ex opere operato* is thereby precluded.

2. This does not mean, as has often been erroneously suggested, that Luther, confronted by a massive sacramentalism, substitutes a more "spiritual" understanding of Baptism, or, stated differently, that over against Scholasticism's "objective" understanding he holds to a more personal-subjective view. At issue here is not the opposition between the spiritual and the material, but rather the opposition between the righteousness of faith and the righteousness of works. Where faith ceases to be decisive, works soon fill the vacuum. Undeniably, the teaching that the sacraments are efficacious *ex opere operato* emphasizes grace to a high degree, but it is a completely different kind of grace. It is not the kind of grace which consists in God binding himself to humans through his promise. Rather, it is a grace by virtue of which a person is enabled to merit his own salvation, and thereby a grace which places justification under the category of law and works. Therefore it is the doctrine of justification itself which Luther sees threatened by the idea of the sacraments as *signa efficacia*. Only in the indissoluble bond between the Word and faith is it possible to maintain that Baptism is God's own work.

3. The final proof that Luther's understanding of Baptism is not spiritualistic, however, is given in what he has to say about the sign, the baptismal act itself. He warns against making a distinction in Baptism between something inner which is ascribed to God and something outer which is ascribed to man. Any separation of the Word from the sign is incorrect. Both should be ascribed to God. It is God himself who baptizes with his own hands, through the pastor as his instrument, and who through the voice of a human being promises the forgiveness of sins.[11] As God's own work, the sign can never become useless unless a person turns away from it.[12] This means further that the sign is not

---

11. Ibid., 464, 13ff.; *LW* 36:62.
12. Ibid., 469, 19ff.; *LW* 36:69.

merely a "symbol" for an inner reality independent of the sign. "This death and resurrection we call the new creation, regeneration, and spiritual birth. This should not be understood only allegorically as the death of sin and the life of grace, as many understand it, but as actual death and resurrection."[13] The sign is God's work because through it he begins his re-creation of the person. The sign has not been relegated to something unessential here, but with the Word has also been given a completely different place from the one it held in the medieval sacramental understanding, where it was seen as the sacrament's substance.

4. This brings us to the last point in Luther's opposition to the scholastic doctrine of Baptism. Due to his understanding of Word and sign as two sides of the same act of God, Luther, as suggested above, had to oppose speaking of penance as a sort of replacement for Baptism. In *The Babylonian Captivity* he says, "You will likewise see how perilous, indeed, how false it is to suppose that penance is 'the second plank after shipwreck' . . . ."[14] One must beware of those who reduce the power of Baptism by saying that grace is poured in through Baptism, but that later it is poured out again by sin.[15] In scholastic teaching Baptism becomes merely the first step in a series of sacramental acts in which each has its place in the quantitative distribution of "grace." This system severely limits the significance of Baptism. Baptism is indispensable because it is and must remain the *first* step, but after Baptism, as soon as the first mortal sin has been committed, the sacrament of penance assumes the role which Baptism once held. By contrast, Luther understands Baptism as encompassing the entire life of the Christian. What God has begun in Baptism is not completed until bodily death and resurrection. Thus Baptism is understood from a radically eschatological perspective. In Baptism through the gracious promise of God a person is made completely pure and innocent in the sense that the person's sin is not imputed even though it has not yet disappeared. In faith one possesses all of the benefits of Baptism, but we are still in the flesh. Therefore we should always be baptized by faith until death.

---

13. Ibid., 468, 11ff.; *LW* 36:68.
14. Ibid., 463, 1a.; *LW* 36:61; cf. 460, 14ff.; *LW* 36:58.
15. Ibid., 469, 10ff.; *LW* 36:69.

Luther's baptismal teaching shows clearly his understanding of the continuance of justification, which is customarily called sanctification. Sanctification is not an empirically demonstrable progress in an ethical sense, but the continuous dying and rising again with Christ by faith until bodily death. Since Luther refuses to understand grace as a power which gradually cleanses and elevates nature, it is impossible for him to understand the continuance of justification in any other way. Thus renewal becomes precisely a renewal: "The sinner does not so much need to be washed as he needs to die, in order to be wholly renewed and made another creature, and to be conformed to the death and resurrection of Christ, with whom he dies and rises again through Baptism."[16]

While the treatises of 1519 and 1520 are determined by the conflict with Scholasticism, the baptismal teaching of the Catechisms is marked to a greater degree by the conflict with the Anabaptists, which had emerged in the meantime. The effect of this was a change in emphasis, but not an essential alteration of his position. The Anabaptist position was determined by the enthusiastic understanding of the Holy Spirit discussed previously. Despite the disregard for the sacraments which followed from this, the Anabaptists, because of their biblicism, maintained the necessity of Baptism. Baptism, however, should not be performed until the subjective conditions had been met independently of Word and sacraments. Baptism became "the baptism of the Spirit," and thus the primary mark of identification of those who were "filled with the Spirit" and thereby belonged to the true church. According to this view, of course, infant Baptism was considered invalid.[17] This compelled Luther to speak of Baptism in a slightly different manner. The issue turned partly on the concept of "external things," and partly on the relationship between faith and Baptism. Against the spiritualism of the Anabaptists Luther was forced to emphasize the sign more strongly than before. This he does in the Large Catechism in a series of points: (1) Baptism is instituted by God's command and ordinance. (2) Baptism is performed in God's name, which means that it is God's own work. (3) The external part of Baptism, water, is of course a small

---

16. Ibid., 468, 31ff.; *LW* 36:68.
17. See, e.g., G. H. Williams, *The Radical Reformation* (Philadelphia: Westminster, 1962).

thing in itself, but the decisive thing is that it is bound together with and hallowed by God's Word, which cannot and must not be separated from the water. (4) On these grounds, therefore, it is false to separate faith from "the thing," as the Anabaptists do. Faith must have something upon which to cling. That something must be something external which can be grasped by the senses, just as the entire gospel is an external, oral proclamation. "Summa, was Gott in uns tuet und wirket, will er durch solch äusserliche Ordnung wirken" (In short, whatever God effects in us he does through such external ordinances).[18] By this Luther believed that the polemic against "äusserlich Ding" (external things) had been refuted. It is still necessary, however, to elaborate on the relationship of faith to Baptism. While Luther maintains that Baptism is of no use without faith, he also emphasizes that Baptism stands secure independent of faith: "For my faith does not constitute Baptism but receives it."[19] Baptism is no less a proper Baptism because it has been improperly received, for it is God's ordinance which cannot be altered by humans. That would be the same as arguing, "If I have no faith, then Christ is nothing."[20] Luther's reason for putting so much emphasis on faith is precisely to assert thereby that Baptism is God's work.

There is very little about all this in the AC. We learn nothing further about what it means to say that Baptism is necessary for salvation. From Luther's perspective the explanation would be simple: in the promise of Baptism the forgiveness of sins is declared, as God binds himself with the person in the battle against sin, which is not overcome completely until death. Baptism is the sacrament of justification, without which a person remains in the power of sin and the devil.[21] This

---

18. *BK*, p. 167, §30; LC 4 §30 (*BC*, p. 440, §30).

19. LC 4 §53 (*BC*, p. 443).

20. LC 4 §58 (*BC*, p. 444).

21. Even though the actual clash between Luther and Zwingli occurred over the issues of Christology and eucharistic doctrine, it is not surprising that there are also clear differences in their respective teachings on Baptism. This would be inevitable, given Zwingli's teaching on the relationship between the Holy Spirit and the means of grace. In the negotiations at Marburg, Zwingli consented to call Baptism a work of God whereby we are reborn. In *Fidei Ratio*, however, where he did not need to consider the politics of Saxony, he speaks entirely out of the other side of his mouth. Here he states directly that the sacraments neither give nor convey grace. Baptism therefore presupposes grace. Zwingli would retain infant Baptism because those infants whose parents are Christian are regarded as members of the church (*Bekenntnisschriften der reformierten Kirche*, pp. 86f.; ET, H. E. Jacobs, 2:168f.).

makes it clear what sort of grace it is that Baptism confers. It is not a habitual grace, but God's graciousness toward the sinner through which his life is renewed.

The last point addressed by Article 9 is the necessity of infant Baptism. It is well known how Luther, as a consequence of his view of the relationship between faith and the efficacy of Baptism, attempted to demonstrate that even infants can believe. It is not possible to examine Luther's concept of infant faith any more closely here.[22] Suffice it to say that when Luther speaks in this manner it is simply one more piece of evidence that he did not understand faith as a subjective quality. The idea is that faith is bestowed upon the infant in Baptism. When the AC maintains that children should be baptized and that through Baptism they are received into God's grace, it requires no other basis than this: Baptism as it is expressly developed in the Large Catechism is in itself an act of God through which God initiates salvation. That Baptism then requires faith in order to "profit" a person is a presupposition of the doctrine of justification, even though it is not mentioned here.

When Zwingli wanted to clarify his position on Baptism he proceeded by comparing his views with those of the church fathers and Scholasticism, arriving at the conclusion that all had been in error since the apostles.[23] Thereby he destroyed any continuity he might have had with church history. This corresponds very well to his concept of the church, in which every connection with the external, visible church and the company of the elect is abolished. As typical as this statement is for Zwingli, Luther's statement about Baptism in *The Babylonian Captivity* is just as characteristic for him as he praises God who, according to the riches of his mercy, has protected the sacrament of Baptism from being ruined by human fabrication.[24] For Luther, nothing human can destroy the work of God in Baptism. Of course, some have succeeded in causing people to doubt the power of their Baptism through the teaching of penance as "the second plank after shipwreck," but this can never render Baptism itself any less valid.

---

22. For further discussion see R. Seeberg, *Lehrbuch der Dogmengeschichte*, 4/1: 395f., and K. Brinkel, *Die Lehre Luthers von der* fides infantium *bei der Kindertaufe* (Berlin, 1958).

23. See Plitt, 2:265f.

24. Clemen 1:459, 37ff.; *LW* 36:57.

Article 10

• LORD'S SUPPER •

Text

[On the Lord's Supper][1] our churches teach that the body   1
and blood[2] of Christ are truly present and are distributed to
those who eat in the Supper[3] of the Lord. They disapprove[4]   2
of those who teach otherwise.

The interpretation of the text depends entirely upon the meaning of the words **are truly present and are distributed.** The word **truly** excludes any symbolic understanding and affirms the real presence without giving any further explanation as to how this real presence is to be understood. That which is given in the Supper is really Christ's body and blood. The phrase **to those who eat in the Supper** joins the real presence to the sacramental act (eating and drinking). Despite the intentional ambiguity of the whole article, its formulation points to the conviction that the nature of the Supper is communion. Clearly, the entire article is concerned with the worship of the congregation.

---

1. *Coena:* the Roman term for the principal meal of the day.
2. GT: "Wahrer Leib und Blut Christi wahrhaftiglich . . ." (the true body and blood of Christ are really . . .).
3. GT: "Unter der Gestalt des Brots und Weins im Abendmahl . . ." (in the Supper of our Lord under the form of bread and wine).
4. *Improbant:* a very mild rejection which is used only in this article.

Commentary

The main concern of Article 10 seems to be to avoid giving offense. Its formulation rejects the views of Zwingli and the enthusiasts. While transubstantiation is not mentioned, neither is it precluded. The German text reads, "unter der Gestalt des Brots und Weins" (under the form of bread and wine). "Gestalt" would be *species* in Latin, making the German text a very close approximation of the formula employed by the Fourth Lateran Council of 1215: *sub speciebus panis et vini* (under the forms of bread and wine).[5] The German text expresses itself more sharply on other points as well. While the Latin merely states that the body and blood of Christ are "truly present" and distributed "in the supper," the German text attaches the word "true" (*wahr*) directly to "the body and blood of Christ," precluding any possibility of understanding Christ's presence as a "spiritual" presence.

While the German text thereby eliminates any doubt about its intention to affirm the real presence, the *vere* ("truly") of the Latin text came under discussion since it was criticized as ambiguous. The criticism was rejected on the grounds that since there were no Zwinglians among the signatories, there could be no doubt about its meaning.[6] It is thus established that the Latin text can be legitimately understood only if *vere* is understood to mean the real presence. Even beginning with this premise, however, the two texts are very different. In the Latin text, the location of Christ's presence is *in coena Domini* ("in the Supper of the Lord"), since it is the distribution and reception to which it refers. The German text, on the other hand, reads "unter der Gestalt des Brots und weins" (under the form of bread and wine), after

---

5. *Concilium Lateranense IV* 1215, "De fide catholica," Denzinger, 802: "*Una vero est fidelium universalis Ecclesia,* extra quam nullus omnino salvatur, in qua idem ipse sacerdos est sacrificium Iesus Christus, cuius corpus et sanguis in *sacramento altaris* sub speciebus panis et vini veraciter continentur, transsubstantiatis pane in corpus et vino in sanguinem potestate divina . . ." (The universal church of the faithful is truly one, outside of which no one at all is saved, within which the very same Jesus Christ is priest and sacrifice, whose body and blood are truly contained under the forms of bread and wine, by divine power bread transubstantiated into the body, and wine transubstantiated into the blood [trans. Justin Pierce]).

6. See W. Maurer, *Zum geschichtlichen Verständnis der Abendmahlsartikel in der Confessio Augustana;* Festschrift für Gerhard Ritter (1950), pp. 208f. Cf. *BK,* p. 64, note 3.

which the distribution and reception are added. In other words, the German text implies that it is at least possible to regard the Supper as being more than and other than Communion. The Latin text, of course, does not explicitly deny this, but a natural reading suggests that the Supper here is considered to be identical with Communion.

It is also noteworthy that here the rejection of those who teach differently is the only place in the AC which uses neither the word *damnant* (condemn) nor the word *reiiciunt* (reject). Instead, the milder *improbant* (disapprove) is used. Again, the German differs from the Latin in retaining the customary *verwerfen* (reject). Nevertheless, in this passage we find a trace of the intentions which came to expression in the Marburg Colloquy of 1529 initiated by Landgrave Philip of Hesse. The landgrave continued to base his policy on the idea of a federation of all the evangelical powers against Hapsburg, for which reason he sought to the end to avoid a eucharistic teaching which would exclude the Zwinglians and Strasbourg. He was forced, however, to yield to Saxony. The use of the word *improbant* in the AC is the single clear expression of any consideration for Philip's policies. Even so, the door is thereby held open for further negotiations, and the contrast between the two sides is reduced as far as possible. Because the Saxons are after the best possible result with respect to the emperor, however, consideration for the left wing of the Reformation could not extend any further than to this *improbant*.[7]

Even though Article 10 avoids all polemics against Rome, this does not mean that the AC leaves us in doubt about the Lutheran position over against the Roman church (as well as over against Zwingli). This critique is simply left to other articles. Of major importance in this connection is Article 13, which clearly rejects both the spiritualistic and the scholastic understanding of the sacraments, congruent with the understanding of Word and sacraments set forth in Article 5. Article 22 defends the distribution of both kinds in the Supper, referring to the testimony of Scripture and early church practice. Article 24 treats the Mass, attacking the idea of the Mass as sacrifice and thus also the private Mass. Article 10 can be understood rightly only in the context of these other articles.

---

7. See Maurer, pp. 186ff.

The Confutation shows clear evidence that its authors feel somewhat uncertain about Article 10. They can find no objection to the words, although they would have preferred to see an explicit affirmation of the church's faith that a change in the substance of the elements occurs. Moreover, the only premise upon which the article can be accepted is that it be understood that the entire Christ is present under each form, so that the blood of Christ *per concomitantiam* (by concomitance) is no less present under the form of bread than it is under the form of wine. Finally, the article is criticized for not closing with an explicit condemnation of those who deny the real presence. Such comments, in spite of their cautious form, could easily have given Melanchthon occasion to elaborate on the Reformation position. Typically, however, he makes no use of the occasion in the Apology, but merely notes that this article is approved by the Confutation. By making this statement, he actually gives tacit approval to the Confutation's interpretation of the article. He reinforces this impression when next he approvingly states that the Roman and Greek churches agree in teaching the bodily presence of Christ. In the examples he uses to substantiate the claim that the Greek Church also teaches this way, the verb *mutare* (changes) appears twice, the same word which the authors of the Confutation employ in their demand that the reformers explicitly acknowledge the teaching of the Lateran Council of 1215. Here it is obvious that Melanchthon's efforts at being conciliatory have been carried to the point of consciously obscuring the differences, rather than merely suppressing them.[8]

---

8. There seems to be general agreement on this judgment. Maurer interprets the German text with its sharp anti-Zwinglian formulation as an expression of Saxon political policy. The expression "unter der Gestalt," etc., he thinks was occasioned by a writing of Luther's opponent Wimpina directed against the Schwabach Articles, which were already rejected by the emperor (Maurer, pp. 196ff.). Maurer believes he has found the basis for the Latin text in one of Melanchthon's collections of citations from the church fathers on the Lord's Supper from March 1530. In the preface he writes that the fathers, like the Lutherans, held that "videlicet corpus et sanguinem Domini vere adesse in coena dominica" (one may understand the body and blood of the Lord to be truly present in the Lord's Supper). This cautious formulation in the Latin text, according to Maurer, can be explained by the fact that Melanchthon foresaw the possibility of a disputation, to which indeed Eck had issued a challenge with his 404 Articles. Therefore he deemed it necessary to have a basis which would make tactical maneuvering possible (Maurer, pp. 195f.). Maurer's investigations shed light

This means that the AC's article on the Supper, like the article on Baptism, is a new formulation. The Schwabach Articles contain the characteristically Lutheran affirmation of two parts: first, the sacrament itself (Christ's body and blood in the bread and wine); second, faith. There is not one word in Article 10 about faith. As in Article 9, Article 13 must be taken into consideration here. Thus faith is excluded from the definition of the sacrament and enters the discussion only in connection with its use. While distinguishing in this manner between the essence of the sacrament and its use is certainly not typical of Luther (apart from the Catechisms), the question is whether Luther's insistence on the word of promise as that which alone constitutes the sacrament does not in fact make Melanchthon's division quite reasonable. Faith does not belong to the essence of the sacraments in the same manner as in Reformed sacramental teaching. Article 13 makes clear that even though the formulation of the article on the Lord's Supper can conceivably be harmonized with Roman teaching, the AC's teaching is nevertheless recognizably Lutheran. Article 10 itself asserts only one thing, the real presence, because this was one point where expression could be given to something held in common. On the other hand, the paths separate as soon as the discussion begins to focus on what is at stake in maintaining the real presence, and in this respect Article 13 is as clear as one could ask.

Melanchthon later sought to develop his eucharistic teaching in a manner which would open the possibility for reaching agreement with the Reformed churches. In the Augustana Variata the words *vere adsint et distribuantur* ("truly present and are distributed") are replaced by

---

on a number of details in connection with Article 10. These are not sufficient, however, to remove the impression that pragmatic considerations prevailed in the question of the Lord's Supper.

Wilhelm H. Neuser, *Die Abendmahlslehre Melanchthons in ihrer geschichtlichen Entwicklung* (1968), has a different interpretation (see pp. 414-473). He believes that a theological conflict accounts for the two diverging formulations. We find Melanchthon's teaching in the Latin text, while the German expresses a more "Lutheran" teaching on the Supper. Neuser speculates that Agricola inserted the Lutheran formula "unter Brot und Wein" in the German text in order to stress the real presence. Melanchthon then is supposed to have inserted the Roman expression "unter der Gestalt" in order to refute Eck's accusation that the Lutherans taught that *in Eucharistia manet substantia panis et vini* (in the Eucharist, the substance of bread and wine remains).

vere exhibeantur ("truly exhibited").[9] While Article 10 in the AC is open to no other understanding than that all who receive bread and wine receive Christ's body and blood, this new formulation leaves room for an understanding which would concede that all who partake in communion are invited to partake of Christ's body and blood, but that the unbelievers, i.e., those who do not receive this invitation, partake only of bread and wine. As opposed to this Melanchthonian obliqueness, Luther, in the Smalcald Articles, totally rejects any compromise with the Reformed perspective; there it is stated that the true body and blood of Christ are not only given and received by the godly but also by the ungodly, clearly emphasizing the teaching of *manducatio indignorum* (reception of the body and blood by the unworthy) and thus reaffirming the AC's position.[10]

Luther's eucharistic teaching is set forth for the first time in *Ein Sermon von dem hoch würdigen Sakrament des heiligen wahren Leichnams Christi und von den Bruderschaften* (a sermon on *The Blessed Sacrament of the Holy and True Body of Christ, and the Brotherhoods*) of 1519.[11] It is developed in exactly the same manner as the sermon on Baptism, which was written during the same time. It is necessary to know three things: the sign, its significance, and faith, which binds the first two together and makes use of them. The doctrine of transubstantiation does not come under attack yet, but it is recommended that one avoid all subtleties and simply know that Christ's body and blood are really present in the sign. Of this Luther still uses the expression *Gestalt* (form). The significance of the sacrament is the fellowship of the saints; the one who receives the sacrament is united with Christ and all his saints and shares in all their blessings. Also, all suffering and sin become a common possession in accordance with Paul's word that the members of Christ's body share everything with one another. The Lord's Supper is the sacrament of love; there we are given a sure sign that Christ and his saints intercede for us with God that our sin may not be reckoned to us; and therefore we must also be willing to share every evil with each other. The sacrament is of no benefit to

9. See *BK* pp. 65, 45f.
10. SA 3.6; *BC*, p. 311.
11. Clemen 1, 196-212; WA 2, 742-758; *LW* 35 (Philadelphia: Fortress, 1960) pp. 49-73.

self-sufficient people. It is more important to esteem Christ's spiritual body, which is precisely this fellowship, than his natural body; the sign is useless apart from what it signifies. Just as in the sermon on Baptism, faith is emphasized as the decisive thing. Luther thus already here opposes speaking of the sacrament as an *opus gratum opere operato* (a work acceptable by [virtue of] the work [having been] performed). This notion creates a false security, while faith perishes. "All this comes from the fact that they pay more attention in this sacrament to Christ's natural body than to the fellowship, the spiritual body." [12] In opposition to this false understanding of the external sacrament, the sign, Luther refers repeatedly to the fact that it is given in order to nourish and strengthen faith. Finally, it should be mentioned that Luther cautiously draws attention to his preference that the cup be given to the laity, even though he does not believe that the cup in and of itself would mean anything with respect to the validity of the sacrament.

While the sermon of 1519 presents Luther's own perspective in a nonpolemical manner, in the following year he goes on the attack, first in *Ein Sermon von dem neuen Testament, d.i. von der heiligen Messe (A Treatise on the New Testament, that is, the Holy Mass)*,[13] and then even more strongly in *De captivitate babylonica (The Babylonian Captivity of the Church)*.[14] In the first of these writings Luther asserts even more strongly than in 1519 that it is the word of promise giving us the forgiveness of sins and eternal life which is the true gift in the sacrament. But because we poor humans live in our five senses and therefore must have an external sign to which to cling, along with the words, God has given us the bread and wine under which we receive the true body and blood of Christ.[15] Moreover, Luther now openly attacks the idea of the Mass as a sacrifice, something which he had not discussed in 1519. We shall return to this later. By the time of *The Babylonian Captivity*, Luther was ready to deal with Roman eucharistic teaching as a whole. The sacrament of the altar is held under three captivities. The first is the denial of the cup to the laity. The second is the assertion

12. Clemen 1, 206, 13ff.; WA 2, 752; *LW* 35:63.

13. Clemen 1, 299-322; WA 6, 353-378; *LW* 35:75-112.

14. The section on the Lord's Supper: Clemen 1, 427-459; WA 6, 498-526; *LW* 36 (Philadelphia: Fortress, 1959), pp. 19-57.

15. Clemen 1, 305, 1ff.; WA 6, 359; *LW* 35:86.

of transubstantiation as an article of faith. The third captivity is the sacrifice of the Mass and the idea of the Mass as a good work. The Mass is rather Christ's testament which consists in the promise of the forgiveness of sins. Before the inheritance can be passed on, however, the testator must die. Thus the incarnation of Christ and his death are both comprehended in the same testament. The Mass is completely God's work, and its power consists in Christ's word of the forgiveness of sins, for which reason both promise (*promissio*) and faith (*fides*) must be present. Accordingly, Luther maintains that of the sacraments' two parts, word and sign, it is the word which is decisive. Thus Luther's eucharistic teaching, as one might expect, corresponds completely to the general perspective on the sacraments which he had developed in connection with Baptism. Central to both sacraments is the word of promise, God's efficatious word which can only be received by faith. Opposition to the doctrine of transubstantiation is not yet a cardinal point for Luther, but he does present some ideas on this issue which reveal a growing understanding of what is decisive for this question as well. What is true in regard to Christ, he says, is also true in regard to the sacraments. It was not necessary, however, for the human nature to be transubstantiated in order for the divine nature to be present under "the accidents of the human nature." [16] However, this decisive argument which roots eucharistic teaching in Christology is not pursued. [17] Luther's only concern is to oppose the doctrine of transubstantiation as dogma. Apart from this, he maintains the real presence without being concerned about developing a theory about how this can be so. Not until the battle against the spiritualists did he find occasion to deal with this question more closely.

In the beginning of the 1520s Carlstadt taught that the sacrament is a remembrance of Jesus' death. It does not involve the Spirit in any way except for the fact that this remembrance is possible only for one who has received the Spirit. In this way, the Supper becomes an external act from which only those who are especially filled with the

---

16. Clemen 1, 442, 30ff.; WA 6, 511; *LW* 36:35.

17. Luther deals very forcefully with the same question in a treatise against Henry VIII of England. Here Luther cites the argument in favor of a doctrine of transubstantiation which states that human substance is unworthy to be united with the divine. Luther answers that such reasoning jeopardizes salvation itself, for then God has not become man, and then human beings are all too unworthy to receive God's Spirit.

Spirit can derive any benefit.[18] Luther's response, *Wider die himmlischen Propheten (Against the Heavenly Prophets)*, 1525, marked the beginning of the eucharistic controversy, which, especially through Zwingli's participation, was to have such far-reaching significance for the Reformation. We cannot deal adequately with the controversy here, but must be content to emphasize what was at stake for Luther, without going into details. Even in the controversy with Carlstadt, the main point at issue was the real presence, and so it remained after Zwingli became Luther's principal opponent. In his *Sermon von Sakrament des Leibs und Bluts Christi, wider die Schwarmgeister (The Sacrament of the Body and Blood of Christ—Against the Fanatics)* of 1526, Luther still gives no explanation of the real presence.[19] In this treatise he states that with respect to the sacrament there are two things to be known and proclaimed. The first is *what* one is to believe (*objectum fidei*). The second is the faith itself, or one's use of that in which one believes. The first is something external, namely, the sacrament itself, concerning which we believe that Christ's body and blood are in the bread and wine. The second is in the heart: how the heart is to relate to the external sacrament. "Until now," says Luther, "I have not preached very much about the first part, but since it has been brought into question, it must be spoken of." Luther then seeks to demonstrate through an exposition of the words of institution that Scripture teaches the real presence, even though we do not understand how this comes about. In his next treatise, in the controversy which was directed against Oecolampadius, and which appeared in the spring of 1527—approximately the same time as Zwingli's first contribution (*Amica exegesis*)—Luther went further. In *Dass diese Worte Christi, 'dass ist mein Leib etc.,'' noch feststehen, wider die Schwarmgeister (That These Words of Christ, "This Is My Body," etc., Still Stand Firm against the Fanatics)*,[20] he develops his doctrine of ubiquity as an explanation of how Christ participates in the divine attributes and consequently can be present everywhere. This claim serves to refute the opponents' argument that Christ as man "sits at God's right hand" and therefore cannot be in the Supper. Neither in this treatise nor in his last contribution,

---

18. See R. J. Sider, *Andreas Bodenstein von Karlstadt* (Leiden: Brill, 1974).

19. WA 19, 482-523; *LW* 36:329-362.

20. WA 23, 64-283; *LW* 37 (Philadelphia: Fortress, 1961), pp. 3-150.

Vom Abendmahl Christi: Bekenntnis (Confession Concerning Christ's Supper) of 1528 does Luther attempt to explain the nature of the real presence. The explanations in which Luther employs certain of the scholastic definitions which he had learned from his youth are without exception determined by the polemical situation. Therefore one cannot simply isolate the elements in Luther's argumentation which smack of metaphysical speculation, and on that basis accuse him of departing from the view which he had set forth on the Supper in 1519 and 1520. Also in the eucharistic controversy Luther affirms the union of promise and faith to be decisive. What is actually at stake for him in eucharistic teaching is nothing less than the incarnation. It is therefore no accident that important elements in his Christology are to be found here. Before any final conclusions are drawn, however, it would be helpful briefly to examine Zwingli's teaching.

In *Fidei Ratio* Zwingli presents a careful account of his eucharistic teaching. In the supper of thanksgiving, he says, the true body of Christ is present by the contemplation of faith (*fidei contemplatione*), which means that those who thank the Lord for the benefits shown in the Son acknowledge that Christ truly assumed flesh, suffered, and washed away our sins with his blood, and that all this is present now through the contemplation of faith. But that the body of Christ in essence and in reality is present in the Supper, as the papists and certain others who look back to the fleshpots of Egypt assert, Zwingli denies, maintaining that it is false teaching, and that he will prove it to be so. Next, a series of scriptural references is cited in support of his claim. The body of Christ is in heaven until the second coming. Against the *maducatio oralis* (oral eating), he cites John 6:63, "The flesh is of no avail," and John 3:6, "That which is born of flesh is flesh." Consequently, spirit can only be attested by spirit and not by anything corporeal. "This is my body" must therefore be understood symbolically. The Lord's Supper is a memorial festival in which the symbol takes the name of the thing it commemorates. Partaking in the Supper does not give the forgiveness of sins, for if that were the case Christ died in vain, since the Supper occurred before the crucifixion.[21] This eucharistic teaching

---

21. *Bekenntnisschriften der reformierten Kirche*, pp. 87ff.; ET, H. E. Jacobs, 2:170ff.

must be seen against the background of Zwingli's understanding of the relationship between the Word and the Spirit. For Luther, the assertion of faith's independence from Word and sacraments was a denial of the incarnation. The manner in which Zwingli understands John 6:63 makes the incarnation an impossibility, which means that salvation itself is lost as well. Behind Zwingli's understanding lies a philosophy which maintains a metaphysical opposition between the divine and the human which is in turn identified with the biblical opposition between "spirit" and "flesh." For Luther the concepts "spirit/flesh" are parallel with "faith/unbelief." Indeed, it is a presupposition for his entire understanding of the incarnation and justification that this opposition is the only thing which drives a wedge between God and humanity. Salvation depends completely upon Christ's humanity, which meets us precisely in Word and sacraments. It is this which establishes the necessity of maintaining the real presence. At the same time this means that Luther must reject the doctrine of transubstantiation as well as every spiritualistic understanding of the Supper's reception, for in both cases the issue is not merely differing opinions on minor nuances, but the understanding of the incarnation itself.

The eucharistic theories of Luther's opponents make him accuse them of what one could call "offense at Christ's humble form." In addition, however, he must attack them in a more comprehensive manner. Through their understanding of the incarnation the opponents on both sides make the Supper into a work. This happens from the spiritualistic understanding due to their teaching that Christ's presence in the Supper is not God's work which is accomplished independently of humans, but that it is created by humans themselves by virtue of the quality of their faith. With respect to the Roman understanding Luther finds the same thing in the teaching about the sacrament's efficacy *ex opere operato*, in the idea of the Mass as a sacrifice, and in the idea of the Mass as a good work. The first point is dealt with in connection with Baptism. Regarding the others, limitations of space make it necessary to confine ourselves to a brief account of the main points of Article 24 in the AC. First, the false accusation that the Mass has been abolished in Lutheran congregations is rejected. On the contrary, it is held in the highest honor. That the Mass is an act of the congregation is emphasized through the assertion that the most important purpose of the various ceremonies is to instruct the people. Most of the article is devoted to the abuses of the Mass which have been discarded in the Lutheran congregations. From a purely practical standpoint the subject is the so-called mercenary masses which had made the reading of Masses a commercial matter. From the perspective of dogma, the idea of the Mass as a sacrifice stands in the center. The article summarizes the idea as follows: Christ had by his passion made satisfaction for original sin and had instituted the Mass as an offering (*oblatio*) for daily sins, both mortal and venial. This has given rise to the understanding of the Mass as a work which removes the sins of the living and the dead *ex opere operato*.[22] This teaching leads to the private Masses and also to the mercenary exploitation of the Mass. Article 24 proceeds to refute this teaching as follows: (1) The suffering of Christ is the only offering for all our sins. The notion that humans should supplement Christ's work is "eine unerhorte Neuigkeit" (an unprecedented novelty). (2) Holy Scripture teaches us that we are justified by faith in Christ, but if the Mass takes away the sins of the living and the dead *ex opere operato,* then justification comes from the work of the Mass and not from faith. (3) The Mass was instituted in order to strengthen faith and to comfort consciences by the administration of the sacrament.[23] Article 24 goes on to point out that the essence of the Mass is Communion and therefore an act of worship in the assembled congregation.[24] Even though the criticism is moderate in its tone (the German text expresses itself more strongly throughout), it does contain the essentials of the Lutheran rejection of the offering of the Mass. To understand the Mass as an offering is to turn everything upside down. The Mass then becomes a human work given to God instead of God's gracious promise, confirmed by the sign of bread and wine, under which Christ himself is offered to us with all his gifts. The reformers yield no quarter to the idea of the Mass as a sacrifice, for here the understanding of the incarnation and justification itself is at stake.

---

22. §§21–23. As previously stated, the Confutation protests against this characterization by pointing out that it is not the Mass, but penitence, which removes sin. The Mass, on the other hand, removes the punishment for sin, supplements the works of satisfaction, and brings an increase of grace.

23. §§24–33.

24. §§34–39.

At the Council of Trent (Session XIII) the Roman church established its eucharistic teaching and condemned the various deviations. The first section on the real presence is developed in a manner which the Lutherans would have been able to endorse.[25] However, the real presence is defined further in terms of transubstantiation and those who reject this are condemned (canon 2).[26] Moreover, the theory of concomitance is dogmatized in defense of the distribution of the bread alone (chap. 3), and the permanence of transubstantiation apart from communion is defended as well—and consequently the veneration and adoration of the host (chap. 3, canons 6 and 7). Luther's assertion that faith alone is sufficient preparation for the reception of the sacrament is condemned (canon 11). All in all, the decree simply acknowledges long-standing church tradition adding the necessary distinctions over against the reformers. A special session (XXI) is devoted to the remaining question about Communion under both kinds, at which the reformation objection is rejected. Session XXII deals with the sacrifice of the Mass and confirms that the criticism advanced by the AC and especially by Luther strikes a central issue. We are instructed here that the sacrifice (*sacrificium*) in the Mass is truly (*vere*) propitiatory (*propitiatorium*), and that by it we obtain mercy and grace from God, if we come contritely and penitently to God with an upright heart and right faith. We please God by this sacrifice, which is the same sacrifice as that on the cross; only the manner of offering is different. It can be

---

25. Introduction to chap. 1: "Principio docet sancta Synodes et aperte ac simpliciter profitetur, in almo sanctae Eucharistiae sacramento post panis et vini consecrationem Dominum nostrum Iesum Christum verum Deum atque hominem *vere, realiter ac substantialiter* sub specie illarum rerum sensibilium contineri" (First of all, the holy council teaches and openly and plainly professes that after the consecration of bread and wine, our Lord Jesus Christ, true God and true man is *truly, really, and substantially* contained in the august sacrament of the Holy Eucharist under the appearance of those sensible things) (Denzinger, 1636).

26. Chapter 4: ". . . Nunc denuo sancta haec Synodus declarat, per consecrationem panis et vini *conversionem* fieri *totius substantiae panis* in substantiam corporis Christi Domini nostri, et *totius substantiae vini* in substantiam saguinis eius. Quae conversio convenienter et proprie a sancta Ecclesia *transsubstantiatio* est appellata" (. . . this holy council now declares it anew, that by the consecration of the bread and wine a *change* is brought about *of the whole substance of the bread* into the substance of the body of Christ our Lord, and *of the whole substance of the wine* into the substance of his blood. This change the holy Church properly and appropriately calls *transubstantiation*) (Denzinger, 1642).

offered for the sins, punishments, satisfactions, and other necessities of the faithful who are living, and also for those who have died in Christ (chap. 2). Regarding private Masses, it is stated that the council would indeed prefer that every single Mass include the reception of the sacrament by the faithful. Nevertheless, it commends the Masses in which the priest alone receives the sacrament. The Masses are celebrated by a public minister of the church, not only for himself, but for all the faithful who belong to the body of Christ (chap. 6). Hereby the keynotes for the functions of the priest have been struck: he performs a service to God by celebrating the Mass, while in Lutheranism the officiant serves as the instrument of God's self-giving to us in Christ in Communion.

The two-front battle which the reformers fought finds expression within the AC in Article 13. Here, on the one hand, the spiritualistic understanding is rejected and, on the other, the teaching that the sacrament is efficacious *ex opere operato*. The reason the reformers can maintain that the word of Christ alone constitutes the sacrament and at the same time oppose the teaching of *ex opere operato* is that the latter teaching (as mentioned previously) is based on a concept of grace which the reformers do not endorse. It has meaning only if grace is understood as a divine power which is infused in humans variously in the various sacraments. For the reformers, grace is one. In the proclamation of the gospel and the sacraments, they know of only one grace, that promise which sacramental words embody. It is precisely this promise which is the gift of the sacrament. To state that God's promise retains its power regardless of human attitude is not to teach that the sacraments work *ex opere operato;* not even because it has pleased God in the Supper to bind this promise to Christ's bodily presence in the bread and wine. If it is true that salvation is God's work alone, then the promise must not be dependent upon humanity. Just as the proclamation of the gospel is a proclamation of salvation for one who believes, and one of judgment for one who does not believe, so the sacrament, in this case the Lord's Supper, by the very fact of its administration, works either salvation or judgment. Maintaining the real presence, therefore, does not mean—as has been claimed—that Luther has fallen back on Scholasticism and teaches "magic," but simply expresses the fact that in the sacrament the promise is bound to a sign about whose efficacy there can be no doubt, since the sign is given precisely in order to strengthen that faith which alone can receive the promise.

Article 11

• CONFESSION •

Text

[On confession] our churches teach that private absolution   1
should be retained in the churches.[1] However, in confession
an enumeration of all sins is not necessary, for this is not   2
possible according to the Psalm, "Who can discern his errors?" (Ps. 19:12).

Two things are stated here. Private confession **should be retained**,
with **absolution** being given to the individual following confession. It
is not necessary as a condition for absolution to enumerate every sin
committed. As grounds for this the AC refers to its impossibility,
consciously opposing the Fourth Lateran Council of 1215, which had
specifically demanded the recounting of all sins.

Commentary

After dealing with Baptism and the Lord's Supper, the AC proceeds
to treat in Articles 11 and 12 problems concerning the Sacrament of

---

1. The GT is slightly stronger: "dass man in der Kirchen *privatam absolutionem*
erhalten und nicht fallen lassen soll" (that private absolution should be retained in the
church and not be allowed to fall into disuse).

Penance. Even though it is not directly stated, the placement of this subject between the article on the Lord's Supper and the article on the use of the sacraments makes it natural to assume that the AC considers Penance to be one of the sacraments. It is well known that the reformers' position on this question was a vacillating one. The usage in which only Baptism and the Supper were called sacraments eventually prevailed because Penance lacked the sign, but this did not mean that the reformers considered it of any less significance. One might say, therefore, that the placement of the articles on Penance in the AC has no bearing upon whether one would call Penance a sacrament. Penance, in any case, held an important place in the theology of the reformers.

"Confession" is the title not only of Article 11 but also of Article 25, which functions almost as a commentary on Article 11. Such a commentary is doubtless needed, since Article 11 takes up only one point in the evangelical critique of medieval confessional practice, namely, that it is not necessary to enumerate all sins. In addition, it is stated without further clarification that private absolution should be retained. Article 25 refers to the fact that in the Lutheran churches confession is practiced prior to communing. It is the absolution, however, that is decisive, being defined so that it becomes a proclamation of the gospel, emphasizing primarily the comfort which it gives to the conscience. Thus, the absolution is the voice of God which promises the forgiveness of sins. Clearly the AC's interpretation of the absolution involves a complete change in the basis of penance.

Before investigating this change, however, the place of confession in the church must be examined more closely. While the AC never expresses itself definitely, except with reference to confession preceding the Supper, the Marburg and Schwabach Articles clearly assert that confession cannot be coerced. The vagueness of the AC gives the Confutation occasion to demand explicit adherence to the Fourth Lateran Council of 1215, which requires confession at least once annually.[2] Confronted directly by this demand, Melanchthon answers in the Apology that the ancient canons and fathers do not speak of any definite time for confession (Apol. 11 §5), so that adherence to annual confession may be characterized as a human tradition (11 §8). Melanchthon's reference to the requirement of confession prior to communion

---

2. *Concilium Lateranense* 4, Cap. 21 (Denzinger, 812).

is reemphasized in *Instructions for the Visitors*,[3] among other writings. This arrangement, especially promoted by Bugenhagen,[4] had eventually won out. Originally, the other perspective—that everything was free—had been the dominating one.

In the struggle against the prevailing confessional practice, Luther had fought with great zeal against coercion. In The 95 Theses Luther denies that Jesus' word "Do penance" can be understood as sacramental penance, and in his *Explanations of the Ninety-five Theses,* he asserts that sacramental penance had been instituted by the popes and the church without being commanded by Christ. It is only the inner penance that is commanded by God.[5] In *The Babylonian Captivity* he explains that even though private confession is not commanded by God, since it cannot be proven from Scripture, it is still useful, even necessary, since it is the only means of comfort for distressed consciences. He does not oppose confession, but confessional tyranny. Therefore he also opposes the so-called reservation, according to which absolution could be given only by the pope in certain cases. He asserts further that the right to absolve is given to every Christian and thus is not reserved to priests.[6] During his stay at the Wartburg, Luther developed these ideas further in his treatise *Von der Beichte, ob die der Papst Macht habe zu gebieten (On Confession, Whether the Pope Has Power to Command It).*[7] Here Luther again rejects the notion that forced confession can be proven from Scripture. A confession obtained by force is never pleasing to God, because, for one who does not really want to confess, it would be best to stay away. Luther reiterates that the Office of the Keys belongs to the entire congregation, according to Matthew 18. Despite the fact that coercion is undesirable, there are

---

3. "Man sol auch niemand zum heiligen Sacrament gehen lassen, er sey denn von seinem Pfarher ynn sonderheit verhört, ob er zum heiligen Sacrament zu gehen geschickt sey" (No one should be allowed to go to communion who has not been individually examined by his pastor to see if he is prepared to go to the holy sacrament), *Werke* 1:245; *LW* 40 (Philadelphia: Fortress, 1958), p. 296.

4. See Plitt, 2:331.

5. Thesis 2, Clemen 1:24, 4ff.; WA 1, 331; *LW* 31 (Philadelphia: Fortress, 1957), p. 85.

6. Clemen 1:482-483; WA 6, 546-547; *LW* 36 (Philadelphia: Fortress, 1959), pp. 86-89.

7. WA 8:138-185 (no English translation available).

two good grounds for confession: (1) shame, the cross of humiliation, and (2) the precious promise of God which comforts the conscience when the absolution is spoken. Here, as always when he speaks of confession, Luther maintains that the word of forgiveness in the absolution is the most important part.

It is from this perspective on confession that the reorganization of the church in Saxony developed. During Luther's absence, Carlstadt had opposed the practice of confession and tried to abolish it completely as unnecessary. When Luther returned to Wittenberg, however, he quickly turned against Carlstadt on this point, as well as on many others.[8] The next stage was Bugenhagen's introduction in 1523 of the practice of going to confession before communing. At this point, however, it was still no more than an invitation. It was not until the visitations that this invitation took on the character of a general regulation.[9] Despite the fact that coercion is still rejected in principle, Luther's position in the Large Catechism has changed from what it was seven or eight years earlier. Everything is of course free, but one who does not willingly come to confession for the sake of the absolution is not a Christian and must not partake in the sacrament. Contempt for confession is a clear indication of contempt for the gospel itself.[10] While in the early treatises the tendency was clearly to let confession be free, in the sense that as a Christian one might use it or let it be, the freedom referred to here is of a more civil character. One should not force anyone to go to confession, because one should not force anyone to be Christian.

The rejection in Article 11 of the demand for a full enumeration of sins is developed further in Article 25. While Article 11 simply declares that it is impossible, Article 25, following Luther's example, indicates that this demand has the effect of disturbing consciences which would never find rest if it were true that only sins which are enumerated were forgiven. A few citations of canon law are introduced in support of this position. The Confutation counters that it is required only that those sins be confessed which are remembered, and demands that the

---

8. See R. J. Sider, *Andreas Bodenstein von Karlstadt* (Leiden: Brill, 1974).

9. Plitt, 2:335f.

10. LC, Brief Exhortation, §§28ff. (*BK*, p. 732, 1ff.; *BC*, p. 460).

Lutherans instruct their people accordingly. In the Apology Melanchthon answers that he does not dispute at all that some sins must be enumerated in confession. At issue is the demand that *all* sins must be confessed. This demand, as the demand for annual confession before the parish priest, stems from the Fourth Lateran Council of 1215. Melanchthon states that this requirement has caused great suffering for consciences. The thinking of the reformers is clear. For them the primary issue is the absolution, for it is there that the forgiveness of sins is promised to the individual. If conditions are imposed regarding the enumeration of individual sins, etc., confession becomes a hazardous thing instead of what it should be, the comfort of the gospel for the penitent sinner.

There is sufficient data in what has already been presented to define the point of contention with Rome on this matter more precisely. In their differing attitudes toward the question of the enumeration of sin, they reveal their differing views on the purpose of confession, on the nature of sin, etc. Instead of drawing our conclusions from the discussions surrounding the AC, however, we will contrast the two perspectives as they are presented by Luther in the Large Catechism and by the Council of Trent respectively. Luther begins on the basis of his own experience by saying that the demand of enumerating all mortal sins had tortured consciences to the point that no one was able to confess enough. Worst of all, however, was the fact that no one knew what the purpose of confession was or how great a comfort it held. He then speaks of two kinds of persons. First, there are those who have used the removal of papal tyranny as license to live as they wish. They ought to be returned to subjection under the pope, since they will not obey the gospel. To others, however, who hear it gladly, one must always preach, so they may be persuaded not to fail to obtain something so precious. In addition to confession proper, there are two other kinds of confession which also belong to the Christian life. Before God our prayer is a confession since in it we acknowledge that we are sinners and pray for God's grace, and before the neighbor each must admit his or her guilt and ask for forgiveness. Both of these confessions are expressed in the Lord's Prayer: "Forgive us our sins, as we forgive those who sin against us." These two types of confession are public, daily, and necessary. There also exists the secret confession, which takes place privately before a single brother or sister. Its purpose is to help us against those things which especially distress us and trouble our consciences, by seeking advice and comfort from a brother or sister as often as we will. This type of confession is not included in any commandment like the other two, but is free for everyone to use as needed. Christ himself has given us the absolution in order that one who is distressed may be loosed and absolved from sins by God through a human being. In this context it is emphasized that the absolution which is God's work has until now been made to be dependent upon our work of lamenting our sin, thereby transforming the gift into a burden. In opposition to this we must consider our work as of little value and magnify God's Word highly, for we do not come to confession to give but to receive. Then follows the strict admonition, previously noted, to make use of confession in the present. Luther closes his exhortation with the following words:

Therefore, when I urge you to go to confession, I am simply urging you to be a Christian. If I bring you to this point, I have also brought you to confession. Those who really want to be good Christians, free from their sins, and happy in their conscience, already have the true hunger and thirst. They snatch at the bread just like a hunted hart, burning with heat and thirst, as Ps. 42:2 says, "As a hart longs for flowing streams, so longs my soul for thee, O God." . . . In this way, you see, confession would be rightly taught, and such a desire and love for it would be aroused that people would come running after us to get it, more than we would like. We shall let the papists torment and torture themselves and other people who ignore such a treasure and bar themselves from it. As for ourselves, however, let us lift our hands in praise and thanks to God that we have attained to this blessed knowledge of confession.[11]

It is clear that for Luther confession is an unmistakable blessing precisely because he understands it as the gospel, the declaration of the forgiveness of sins. Over against this understanding, however, the Roman church maintains its view and sets it forth clearly and sharply in the Council of Trent. In the chapter entitled "De Confessione" (Confession), the council begins by asserting that the church has always

---

11. LC, Brief Exhortation, §§32–35. (*BK*, p. 732, 40ff.; *BC*, pp. 460-461.

understood that the Lord prescribed a complete confession of sins for all who have fallen after Baptism. The reason given for this is that priests are instated as *judges,* and they cannot exercise their office as judge if they are not aware of all mortal sins. The council's attitude is different toward venial sins, since these do not exclude a person from the grace of God and moreover can be expiated by other means. It is explained more precisely how the priest, in order to be able to make an accurate judgment on the character of the trespass, must also know the circumstances surrounding it. The council next takes a position in direct opposition to the reformers' contention that a complete enumeration is impossible, referring again to the fact that one is only required to disclose what one remembers, leaving the rest to be included in the general confession. Finally, secret sacramental confession is defended as a usage of the church from its beginning, which usage is endorsed by the decisions of the Lateran Council.[12] The reformation critique of these things is also condemned in the canons appended to the decree.[13]

It is impossible to summarize the reformation understanding of confession and Penance apart from Article 12. On the basis of the problems connected with Article 11, however, one can perceive the intimate relationship between justification and Penance, which has the effect of making the controversy over the Sacrament of Penance an extremely sharp one. Here we enter an area which stands in the most intimate connection both with the experiences which were decisive in the development of Luther's doctrine of justification, and with the events which drove him openly to attack the church's practice regarding indulgences.

---

12. Session XIV, chap. 5 (Denzinger, 1679-83; ET, Schroeder, pp. 92-94). H. N. Clausen, *Den Augsburgske Confession* (Copenhagen, 1851), pp. 154f., points out the inner contradiction which lies in the Council of Trent's demand for a complete enumeration of all mortal sins as the presupposition of the priest's activity as judge, while admitting that some may be forgotten even after a painstaking search of the conscience.

13. Canons 6, 7, and 8.

Article 12

• REPENTANCE •

Text

[On repentance] our churches teach that those who have   1
fallen after Baptism can receive forgiveness of sins whenever they are converted, and that the church ought to impart   2
absolution to those who return to repentance. Properly   3
speaking, repentance consists of these two parts: one is   4
contrition, that is, terror smiting the conscience with a knowledge of sin, and the other is faith, which is born of the Gospel,   5
or of absolution, believes that sins are forgiven for Christ's
sake, comforts the conscience, and delivers it from terror.[1]
Then good works, which are the fruits of repentance, are   6
bound to follow.[2]

Our churches condemn the Anabaptists who deny that   7
those who have once been justified can lose the Holy Spirit,
and also those who contend that some may attain such   8
perfection in this life that they cannot sin.[3] Also condemned   9
are the Novatians who were unwilling to absolve those who
had fallen after Baptism although they returned to repent-

---

1. GT: "Welcher Glaub wiederum das Herz tröstet und zufrieden macht" (this faith will comfort the heart and again set it at rest).
2. GT: "Danach soll auch Besserung folgen, und dass man von Sünden lasse" (Amendment of life and the forsaking of sin should then follow); a reference to Matt. 3:8 follows.
3. GT does not mention the doctrine of perfection.

ance. Rejected also are those who do not teach that remis-   10
sion of sins comes through faith but command us to merit
grace through satisfactions of our own.

First it is affirmed that **repentance** is possible. Next the two parts
of repentance, according to a Lutheran understanding, are presented.
The first sentences are "anti-Novatian" (cf. the second part in the
condemnation). It is not only possible to obtain the **forgiveness of sin**
after the fall, but such forgiveness can be received **whenever**; i.e.,
this possibility is limited neither by time nor number. It always exists
for one who has fallen. There is one "condition," however: **whenever
they are converted**. What is meant by this is explained in the following
sentence: to be converted is to **return to repentance**. Upon the fulfillment of this "condition," the church **must** (*debeat*) impart absolution.

Repentance consists of **contrition** and **faith**. The customary se-
quence of *contritio* (contrition), *confessio* (confession), *absolutio* (absolution), *satisfactio* (satisfaction) is not even mentioned. In medieval
terminology, *contritio* designated perfect contrition which originates
in sorrow over sin and is supported by the resolve to sin no more, as
opposed to *attritio* (attrition), contrition born of fear. At first glance,
the expression **terror smiting the conscience** (*terrores incussi con-
scientiae*), might seem to refer most closely to the concept of attrition.
Since, however, it is the conscience which is being discussed, it involves more than merely fear of punishment; it involves also an acceptance of the judgment upon sin. The words **that is** (*seu*), by which
this clause is tied to *contritio*, also indicate that the two designations
are to be considered parallel expressions.

The second part of repentance is **faith, which is born of the Gospel,
or of absolution**. It is evident here that the absolution is understood
as proclamation. It is identical with the gospel. The content of faith
must consequently be identical with the justifying faith which **believes
that sins are forgiven for Christ's sake**. By such faith the conscience
is comforted and delivered from its fear. No mention is made of works
of satisfaction, but rather of **good works, which are the fruits of
repentance** (cf. Article 6). **Are bound to**: faith and works are again
joined by this phrase (as in Article 6).

The negative section initially rejects **the Anabaptists** who deny that the Holy Spirit, once received, can be lost. **Once been justified** must refer here to those who claim to have received the "baptism of the Spirit." Thus the AC rejects the idea that the indwelling of the Holy Spirit can be understood as an indelible quality in a person. The entire anthropological perspective of the reformers clearly impels them to reject the notion of the sinlessness of the justified. **The Novatians** are condemned because they deny that repentance is possible. The confessors undoubtedly had more real interest in the last sentence. At issue here was the battle against the concept of **merit** in connection with works of satisfaction, a subject which is brought up time and again (e.g., Articles 15, 20, 26, 27, and 28).

Commentary

Because of the teaching about Penance as "the second plank after shipwreck," this sacrament inevitably came to occupy an extremely important place in medieval church life. As previously stated, it eventually supplanted the place of Baptism, and therefore it is not surprising that the scholastic doctrine of justification within various schools was determined by the perspective on Penance. If justification is thought of as a psychological process, then in practice it must be defined in close conjunction with the Sacrament of Penance. Early in the Middle Ages it became common to divide the sacrament into three parts, and in the Council of Florence, Pope Eugenius V decreed that it consisted of the heart's contrition (*cordis contritio*), the mouth's confession (*oris confessio*), and satisfaction for sins (*satisfactio pro peccatis*) according to the judgment of the priest.[4]

Thus the three-part division became the universal teaching of the church, and the Confutation was compelled to react against the AC's division of repentance into contrition and faith. It attributes the three-part division of repentance to the days of the Apostles and contends that the church fathers taught the same. Reference is also made to Leo X's bull *Exurge Domine* of June 15, 1520, which condemns Luther's statement that the three-part division is founded neither in Scripture

---

4. The bull *Exultate Deo*, 22 Nov. 1439 (Denzinger, 1323).

nor in the fathers.[5] Luther had expressed this view in *Eyn Sermon von dem Ablass und Gnade (A Sermon on Indulgence and Grace)* of April, 1518, among other places.[6] The same critique of the three-part division is found in the *Instructions for the Visitors,* which, identically to the AC, teaches that repentance consists of contrition and faith.[7] More important than the critique of the formal division of repentance is, of course, the change in the understanding of its nature, which compelled the reformers to adopt a different structural analysis.

The introductory sentence in Article 12, which affirms the possibility, through the absolution of the church, of forgiveness after a fall, is unhesitatingly acknowledged by the Confutation (§§1–2). The AC has stated its position in such general terms here that every rejoinder is preempted. Such is not the case, however, with the statement regarding what constitutes repentance. In addition to its rejection of the AC's division, the Confutation criticized the introduction of faith as a part of repentance. It also protests against the rejection of works of satisfaction by which the AC, according to the Confutation's authors, places itself in opposition to the gospel, the apostles, and fathers, the councils, and the whole Catholic church. One cannot object, therefore, that its authors have overlooked the differences.

Before we examine the text of the AC more closely, it would be appropriate to review the most important elements in Luther's treatment of these matters. Ockhamistic theology, in which Luther was trained, taught that the contrition which precedes the reception of the sacrament of Penance must be *contritio,* true brokenheartedness over sin, and that this contrition is attainable by means of a person's natural powers. This is precisely the teaching which brought Luther to the brink of despair in the monastery, because it made the efficacy of the Sacrament of Penance dependent upon the person's being rightly prepared. Since everything depended upon one's being truly freed from sin and restored to grace in Penance, it followed that a person's disposition became the decisive factor in his relationship to God. Staupitz helped Luther by

---

5. Sentence 5 (Denzinger, 1455; *LW* 32 [Philadelphia: Fortress, 1958], p. 32): "There is no basis in Scripture or in the holy teachers of ancient times for the doctrine that penance has three parts: contrition, confession, and satisfaction."

6. Clemen 1:11, 27ff. (WA 1, 243).

7. Mel. W. 1:245, 11ff.; *LW* 40 (Philadelphia: Fortress, 1958), pp. 295-296.

pointing out that love to God is not the goal of repentance, but its beginning, thereby leading him toward dependence on God's prevenient grace instead of his own disposition. Luther never did overcome his difficulties, however, until he broke through to a new understanding of justification through his own studies, which occurred during his work on *Lectures on the Psalms* in 1513–1515. Together with his new perspective on original sin and the righteousness of God came a new understanding of repentance as well. Luther, therefore, was well prepared when the indulgence controversy drove him to discuss these problems.

The position taken by Luther in The 95 Theses on indulgences was not a revolutionary breakthrough as such. Throughout the late Middle Ages the notion of inner repentance being the presupposition behind outer repentance had gained more and more prominence. The understanding of all of life as a continuous act of penance marked much of the religious life of the time, endangering the significance of the Sacrament of Penance. Luther's theology, with its emphasis on the cross, mortification, etc., was deeply influenced by this line of thinking.[8] Repentance is simply a human's situation on the way from sin to righteousness, and stretches from the womb to the grave. This perspective is clearly articulated in the famous first thesis: "When our Lord and Master Jesus Christ said, 'Repent,' he willed the entire life of believers to be one of repentance." Right repentance is thus a life under the cross, in hatred of self, and under continuous mortification of the flesh. God alone can forgive the guilt of sin. The pope only can declare it forgiven (§§6 and 38). By true contrition sin is already forgiven by God (§36). When Luther nevertheless wishes to uphold the necessity of the Sacrament of Penance, he does so by referring to the fact that God only forgives one who will humble himself before his parish priest (§7). Submission to the Sacrament of Penance thus belongs to the posture of penitence. As previously mentioned, most of this was already familiar ground. What made it revolutionary was the intensity and relentlessness with which the consequences of this perspective were pursued. Though it was to be stated more plainly later, The 95 Theses

---

8. See R. Seeberg, *Lehrbuch der Dogmengeschichte* (Erlangen and Leipzig, 1895-1898), 4/1:158ff.

contains the two fundamental ideas which are determinative of the AC's doctrine of repentance as well: (1) *contrition* for sin, which receives forgiveness from God alone through the declaration of the priest (i.e., absolution); and (2) *faith,* which consists in precisely the repentant posture which, for life in its entirety, throws the person upon God's grace. It would not be long before Luther himself expressed this teaching in absolutely unmistakable terms.

In the short *Sermo de poenitentia* (Sermon on Penance) of 1518,[9] Luther is especially concerned with the issue of how the penitent obtains forgiveness. He unhesitatingly answers that it is not contrition but only a firm faith in God's graciousness in Christ which makes us a recipient of forgiveness and righteous before God. Faith is tied to Christ's promise: "Whatever you loose on earth," etc. Without this faith, neither contrition nor the reception of the sacraments is of any use. The following year, the same year in which the two previously mentioned treatises on Baptism and the Lord's Supper appeared, Luther offered a more detailed explanation of penance in *Ein Sermon von dem Sakrament der Busse (A Sermon on the Sacrament of Penance).*[10] There is only one true way to the forgiveness of guilt, and that is the Sacrament of Penance. Indulgences and works are of no use. God gave the Sacrament of Penance for the comfort of all sinners when he gave Peter the keys on behalf of the whole church. As in the Latin sermon, the word in the power of the keys is understood as a gracious word of "joy and blessedness of heart. . .against all despair." The sacrament consists of three things. The first is absolution, through which forgiveness is proclaimed by virtue of the word of Christ. The second is grace, the forgiveness of sins. The third is faith, without which the sacrament accomplishes nothing. From this it follows that forgiveness is not obtained on account of one's worthiness, but on account of faith. Therefore, one should not rely upon one's contrition or one's works, but upon the word of Christ. Already here the content of Penance has been completely transformed. The duty of the priest now consists in proclaiming God's gracious word of forgiveness by means of the Office of the Keys. Next, Luther maintains that forgiveness is not within the

---

9. WA 1:319-324.

10. Clemen 1:174-184; WA 2:713-724; *LW* 35 (Philadelphia: Fortress, 1960), pp. 9-22.

province of the pope or any priest but depends upon "the word of Christ and your own faith" alone, for Christ will not have our salvation be based on anything human but only upon himself. The Office of the Keys, in fact, is not an authority given to priests at all, but a service which they are to render others. If no priest is present, any Christian can take the priest's place. Luther does here refer also to the traditional three-part division of Penance, but abolishes its meaning by saying that where faith is present, contrition, confession, and satisfaction come easily, but where it is absent, none of these parts is adequate. From the beginning Luther was uneasy regarding satisfaction, because he feared it opened the door to works-righteousness. In the sermon, regarding satisfaction he says that the best satisfaction is to sin no more and to do all possible good toward one's neighbor. This is in effect to drop works of satisfaction altogether and to replace them with works of faith. Regarding contrition, which had given Luther so much trouble in the monastery because he never could be certain whether he was sufficiently contrite, he now says that no person can be sufficiently contrite no matter how hard he tries. God's Word, on the other hand, is sufficient and certain. As is apparent from this account, Luther has succeeded in interpreting Penance along the same line as Baptism and the Lord's Supper, making justification by faith its content as well. Sacramental Penance has lost the place it held in the Roman church, since the Christian life, as we have seen, is a life in Baptism. Penance is no longer a juridical act, in which the priest renders his opinion as judge in place of God, but a divine promise which is grasped by faith. The priest, therefore, is not a lord, but a servant of God's gracious word of the forgiveness of sins. Hereby every condition for receiving absolution is eliminated, because the priest *truly* stands in God's place, i.e., he is merely an instrument through which God acts toward humans. Contrition is no longer a condition for obtaining grace, but a fruit of faith in the threats and promises of God.[11] Satisfaction is no longer compensation for previous sins. Rather, the only true satisfaction consists in a new life. Thus all that remains of the sacramental act (regardless of whether one now wishes to use the word *sacrament* or not)

---

11. Cf. *The Babylonian Captivity*, whose section on penance could not be included because of space limitations (Clemen 1:480, 26ff.; WA 6:545; *LW* 36:81-90).

is confession and absolution. We have seen how Luther viewed this. Repentance, however, is not abolished, for it is simply the Christian way of life.

Returning now to the AC, we find that Article 12 basically recapitulates the thoughts reported here. Apart from the occurrence of the word *absolution*, there is nothing in the first part of the article which requires that Penance be understood as a specific act. The section could just as well carry the title "Human Beings under Law and Gospel." Seen from this perspective, the degree to which Penance is understood as God's work becomes clear. Repentance is God's strange work which is meant to drive people to God's proper work (*opus proprium*). Thus, the contrition spoken of here is not a performance, but the exposure of sin inherent in the gospel. The Christian's life as repentance is nothing else than a life in faith which gives God alone the glory. This line of thinking is expressed admirably in the Smalcald Articles, where Luther, after speaking about the office of the law, says that the New Testament retains this office, since each person stands accused of sin. He continues (German text): "Dies ist nicht *activa contritio*, eine gemachte Reu, sondern *passiva contritio*, das recht Herzeleid, Leiden und Fuhlen des Todes" (This is not *activa contritio* [artificial remorse], but *passiva contritio* [true sorrow of the heart, suffering, and pain of death]).[12] Thus contrition becomes the way through which God draws humans to himself. Because humans continuously live in sin, however, they must always be brought from the law to the gospel anew, i.e., live in repentance.

In the Apology Melanchthon answers with uncommon vehemence, yet with great care. Although it is impossible here to account even somewhat fully for the content of the lengthy section on repentance, some individual thoughts must be mentioned. Since we are passing over the very detailed critique of the Roman understanding of Penance, we will confine ourselves to giving an account of the AC's teaching. Regarding contrition, Melanchthon makes absolutely clear that it is not a result of human striving. It comes into being as the Word of God denounces sin, for the sum of the gospel is to denounce sin and to offer the forgiveness of sins and righteousness for Christ's sake. Contrition, in other words, is the work of the law (12 §29). The second

12. SA 3, 3 §2 (BK, p. 437; *BC*, p. 304).

part of repentance is faith in Christ which raises up again and enlivens (12 §§35ff.). This can be summed up in the Word of Christ, "Repent, and believe in the gospel." In the first part he denounces sin; in the second he comforts us and shows us the forgiveness of sins (12 §45). Reference is also made to Paul's word about the Christian's death and resurrection with Christ, which likewise demonstrates that contrition and faith stand side by side (12 §46). Thus, Melanchthon understands repentance as being identical with life under God's Word, the law and the gospel, which makes it identical with justification. Therefore, repentance is entirely God's work in both of its parts.

The position of the Apology on absolution ought also to be mentioned. Absolution may properly be called the Sacrament of Penance, according to Melanchthon (§§41f.). Like Luther, he defines it as being identical with the gospel.[13] Together with the confession of sin which precedes it, absolution constitutes all that remains of Penance as a specific act or, if one will, as a sacrament. This has been made clear in connection with Article 11. As can be seen, however, it in no way follows that Penance loses its significance thereby. On the contrary, it becomes the sum of the Christian life.

The second part of the article begins by opposing the Anabaptists' doctrine of perfection, which renders repentance superfluous. Among the better-known enthusiasts, Denck taught that the new person does not sin. For him, resistance to and triumph over temptation will always prevail. Similar points of view are held by other Anabaptists. Schwenckfeld was somewhat less decisive, although he considers those who have been reborn as "wesentlich gerecht" (essentially righteous). Franck, on the other hand, seems to have been more careful on this point.[14] Clearly, the reformers wished to renounce every connection with such teachings, even though there actually was no danger of their being mistakenly suspected of entertaining such opinions. The condemnation of the Novatians seems somewhat irrelevant. It is most likely taken from Luther's *Confession* of 1528.[15] Similar phenomena, however, may also be observed in certain enthusiasts.[16]

---

13. The repetition alone demonstrates how important it has been for Melanchthon to establish this point: §§39, 61, and 105.

14. See Plitt 2:355, and BK, p. 67, note 2.

15. Clemen 3:512, 39f. WA 26:507; *LW* 37 (Philadelphia: Fortress, 1961), p. 368.

16. See Plitt 2:355, according to whom Urbanus Rhegius is supposed to have labeled the Anabaptists as neo-Novatians.

The rejection of works of satisfaction, which the Confutation naturally enough complains about, is easily understood on the basis of the new perspective on repentance. In the Apology, Melanchthon spends a number of pages addressing this question. He painstakingly refutes the attempt of the authors of the Confutation to establish a Scriptural proof, attacks the teaching about works of supererogation, and contends that the historical origin of satisfaction as an external discipline is rooted in the practice of public penitence. Melanchthon undermines the foundations for satisfaction in the Sacrament of Penance, first by rejecting the distinction between the remission of guilt and the remission of punishment, and then, like Luther, by referring to good works as the fruits of repentance. As soon as repentance is perceived as the Christian life in its entirety, the teaching of works of satisfaction becomes unnecessary, in fact downright dangerous.

Finally we will review briefly the teaching of the Council of Trent on Penance, which naturally is to a great extent negatively determined by the reformers' teaching. It is, of course, important for the Council of Trent to establish the divine institution of Penance for the reconciliation with the church of those who have fallen after Baptism. The passage from John 20:22-23 ("Receive the Holy Spirit. If you forgive the sins of any, they are forgiven; if you retain the sins of any, they are retained") is interpreted to mean that the power of forgiving and retaining sins (*potestatem remittendi et retinendi peccata*) is transferred here to the apostles and their successors. This understanding is explicitly set in opposition to that of the reformers, according to whom the passage is about the power to proclaim God's Word (chap. 1). Because of the relationship of Penance to Baptism, it is also necessary to define the difference between the two sacraments. Besides their external forms, the differences consist in the following: (1) In Baptism the acting priest is not a judge, since the church cannot exercise its juridical authority over those who have not already entered it. It is different for those who have fallen after Baptism, who are of the "household of faith." (2) There is a distinction between the fruit of Baptism and the fruit of Penance. In Baptism we put on Christ (Gal. 3:27) and become a new creation, since we obtain full forgiveness of all sins. In Penance we do not arrive at this renewal without great labor on our part, which God's righteousness demands. Penance, therefore, may rightly be called *laboriosus quidam baptismus* (a laborious kind of Baptism). It is necessary for the salvation of those who have fallen, as Baptism is for those who have not been born anew (chap. 2).

The council goes on to give an account of the components of Penance, using the traditional division and setting it in opposition to that of the reformers. The section on confession was dealt with under Article 11. Regarding contrition, the council states that it is the soul's sorrow over and detestation for sin combined with the resolve to sin no more. The traditional distinction is made between perfect contrition (*contritio perfecta*), which includes love, and attrition (*attritio*). The latter is also an acceptable disposition for the obtaining of grace, according to the council (chap. 4).

As might have been expected, the opposition to the reformers emerges most sharply in the section on absolution. First, the idea that the Office of the Keys can be exercised by anyone other than priests and bishops is rejected. Then, regarding the absolution itself, it is stated that "it is not a bare ministry only [*nudum ministerium*], either of proclaiming the Gospel or of declaring that sins are forgiven, but it is after the manner of a judicial act, by which sentence is pronounced by him [i.e., the priest] as by a judge" (chap. 6). After this, the council defends the practice of the "reservation" of certain cases for the decision of a higher court, where the confessor has no jurisdiction (chap. 7). This is logical, of course, given the premise that the absolution is a juridical act. The last two sections in the decree are devoted to satisfaction (chaps. 8 and 9). Over against the reformation position that the guilt of sin is never forgiven apart from the elimination of the whole punishment, the council maintains the distinction between the two, which is essential for the preservation of the idea of satisfaction.

In comparing the council's teaching on Penance with that of the AC, it becomes obvious that the differences encountered are not merely incidental but are based on radically different understandings of the gospel itself. Nowhere does the degree to which Roman Catholicism was determined by a legal, and thus for the reformers a law-oriented, perspective emerge more clearly. While it is true that the Catholicism of Trent is a reformed Catholicism in relation to the late Middle Ages, the penitential system which presents itself to one who deals with Trent is still essentially the same teaching which Luther fought against, convinced as he was that it abolished the gospel by replacing it with the law.

Article 13

• THE USE OF THE • SACRAMENTS

Text

[On the use of the sacraments] our churches teach that   1
the sacraments were instituted not merely to be marks of
profession among men[1] but especially to be signs and testimonies of the will of God toward us, intended to awaken
and confirm faith in those who use them. Consequently the   2
sacraments should be so used that faith,[2] which believes
the promises that are set forth and offered, is added.

[Our churches therefore condemn those who teach that   3
the sacraments justify by the outward act and who do not
teach that faith, which believes that sins are forgiven, is
required in the use of the sacraments.][3]

---

1. GT: "Zeichen seien, dabei man äusserlich die Christen kennen muge" (signs by
which people might be identified outwardly as Christians).

2. GT: "Derhalben sie auch Glauben fordern und dann recht gebraucht werden, so
man's im Glauben empfähet und den Glauben dadurch stärket" (For this reason they
require faith, and they are rightly used when they are received in faith and for the
purpose of strengthening faith). The GT of Article 13 ends here, and thus lacks the
mention of the promises.

3. This condemnation was added later to the text of the AC (in the so-called *editio
princeps*) and was included in brackets in *BC* (trans.).

145

One senses a hidden polemic in the statement on the purpose of the sacraments. The words **not merely to be**, etc., are obviously addressed to someone specific. The expression **marks of profession among men** virtually functions as a quotation. As we shall see, it is, in fact, a very precise summary of Zwingli's sacramental perspective. This is followed by the AC's own teaching: the sacraments are **to be signs and testimonies of the will of God** (cf. the comments on Articles 9 and 10). **To waken and confirm faith**: because the sacraments are testimonies of God's will toward us, they serve to awaken and confirm faith. **Consequently**: since this is the meaning of the sacraments, it is clear that they are to be used in such a manner that faith puts its trust in God's promises. Without faith, the sacraments cannot be what they are intended to be, **signs . . . of the will of God toward us**, which will is expressed precisely in **the promises that are set forth and offered** in the sacraments.

Commentary

In the treatment of the articles on Baptism and the Lord's Supper, it was already necessary to involve Article 13. Even though the AC's distinction between the sacraments' essence and their use may seem commendable for the sake of clarity, it is only permissible if the one is always kept in mind while the other is under discussion. Moreover, Article 13 does have something to say about the essence of the sacraments, since it speaks of their purpose. Taken in isolation, both Article 9 and Article 10 permit widely varying interpretations. Seen in light of Article 13, however, the possibilities are drastically limited. Since the characteristic elements in the Lutheran sacramental perspective have already been set forth in the preceding articles, nothing really new can be said here. We will seek to account for certain problems which arise naturally from the text of the article and also by means of it to define more precisely the various positions held.

The purpose behind the institution of the sacraments is stated clearly. They are "intended to awaken and confirm faith in those who use them," since they are to be "signs and testimonies of the will of God toward us." Set in opposition to this is the understanding of the sacraments which holds them "merely to be marks of profession among men.'' This rejection is undoubtedly directed primarily toward Zwingli. We have seen how, on the basis of Zwingli's position, the sacraments completely lose their character as means of grace, since he denies that God's Spirit can be mediated through anything bodily. In *Fidei Ratio* he expresses himself with unmistakable clarity. The sacraments neither convey nor dispense grace. Rather, they are given as a public testimony of that grace which is previously present in every individual.[4] In opposition to this position, which makes the disposition of the person receiving the sacrament decisive, the AC points out that the sacraments are divine acts, in which the promises of salvation are "set forth and offered." Thus it certainly follows that they are to be "so used that faith . . . is added" (i.e., to the eating and drinking), for, as we have seen, only by faith can it be maintained that the sacrament is completely God's work.

While it is thus affirmed that the sacraments demand faith, it is stated at the same time that they are given "to awaken and confirm faith." The circle in which we find ourselves hereby serves to preclude every possibility of localizing the coming of grace apart from the meeting of Word (in proclamation and sacrament) and faith. Lutheran sacramental teaching, therefore, rejects both Zwingli's spiritualistic view and the Roman *ex opere operato* with equal intensity. Against Zwingli, according to whom a person must *first* be endowed with the Spirit and *only then* is able to understand the Word and make use of it, a protest must be lodged. Likewise, a protest must be lodged against Rome, which *first* demands that the person have the right disposition and *only then* allows grace to be given through the sacrament. Lutheran teaching on the Word and faith presupposes a specific understanding of the incarnation, which expressly forbids the offense against bodiliness which is inherent in Zwingli's sacramental view, but which just as

---

4. "Credo, imo scio omnia sacramenta, tam abesse ut gratiam conferant, ut ne adferant quidem aut dispensent . . ." (I believe, yea I know, that all the sacraments are so far from conferring grace that they do not even convey or distribute it . . .) (*Bekenntnisschriften der reformierten Kirche*, p. 86, 8f.; ET, H. E. Jacobs, 2:168). "Ex quibus colligitur (quod in re sacramentaria volens ac libens admitto) sacramenta dari in Testimonium publicum eius gratiae, quae cuique privato adest" (From this it is inferred—as I willingly and gladly admit in regard to the subject of the sacraments— that the sacraments are given as a public testimony of that grace which is previously present to every individual) (ibid., p. 86, 46f.; ET, p. 169).

expressly rejects the "materialization" of grace which is characteristic of Roman teaching. Both Rome and Zwingli make it possible to locate grace apart from the meeting of Word and faith, which for the reformers means apart from the incarnate Christ. For Zwingli's part this is clear, since he holds the Spirit's coming to be entirely unmediated. This applies equally to Rome, however. Here the presence of grace is guaranteed as an objective quantity, precisely because the sacraments are only apparently earthly things. (The most striking illustration of this is the doctrine of transubstantiation.)

In the first printed edition of the AC an explicit condemnation of the teaching about the sacraments' efficacy *ex opere operato* was added. This is superfluous, however, since the manner in which faith is spoken of is in itself an attack on this teaching. Strangely enough, the condemnation was included in the older edition (Müller's) of the confessional writings.[5] Even a cursory reading of the Confutation makes it obvious that it could not have been in the original manuscript, in view of the fact that the Confutation's authors approve the article.

Even without the condemnation, the Confutation's approval is strange, since one might have expected that the indirect attack would have been noticed. It contents itself with the request that the teaching on the sacraments should specifically name the *seven* sacraments. The Apology makes a somewhat evasive answer. Regarding confirmation and extreme unction, it states clearly that these rites do not have the command of God, and the church has never viewed them as being necessary for salvation (13 §6). If the sacraments are those rites which have God's command and to which is tied the promise of grace, then there are three true sacraments: Baptism, the Lord's Supper, and absolution (which is the Sacrament of Penance). Ordination could well be called a sacrament if the ministry be understood as the ministry of the Word (*ministerium verbi*), since it is commanded by God and has great promises. Similar principles apply in the case of marriage which, however, if it is to be called a sacrament must be distinguished from the "signs of the New Testament." In addition, Melanchthon thinks that several other things might be called sacraments, for example, prayer. He closes by saying that no intelligent person would quibble

---

5. See note 3.

about number. What is most important is that everything which is commanded by God and has God's promise is kept (13 §17). This last remark must certainly be said to cover the reformers' opinion on this issue very well. It was impossible, in any case, for them to consent to seven sacraments, since some of them lacked a divine command.

Thereupon Melanchthon switches from defense to the attack, saying that it is more important to know how to use the sacraments. Without faith the promise is useless. But since the sacraments are signs of the promises, it follows that there must be faith (13 §§18–22). Regarding the teaching about *opus operatum* no support can be found in the fathers. Melanchthon closes by citing the famous statement of Augustine: "Faith in the sacrament, not the sacrament, justifies" (12 §23).

Since the Word is the means of grace, both in proclamation and in the sacraments, it is clear, as Melanchthon says in the Apology (13 §5), that they have "the same effect." There can be no other conclusion when grace is understood as a personal relationship and not as something else. It is impossible, on this basis, to create any sort of sacramental "order of precedence." The grace which is given through the sacraments is none other than that which is brought by the spoken Word. The difference consists in that the Word in the sacraments is accompanied by a sign, which is not the case in proclamation. Since, however—in the sacraments also—grace is given in the meeting between the Word and faith, the sign cannot be understood as a *signum efficax* (efficacious sign). Therefore, Melanchthon emphasizes that when he speaks of the faith which receives the promise, he means a *fides specialis* (personal faith), which accepts the promise as a present reality, not merely a faith which believes in general that God exists (13 §21). One cannot distinguish the Roman and the Lutheran sacramental teachings from each other by saying that, while the Roman teaching merely requires a purely negative disposition, that one not "bar the door," the Lutheran teaching requires much more, namely, a true faith. In Roman teaching the primary issue is indeed a proper disposition; when that is present, the sacrament works *ex opere operato*. The Lutheran demand for *fides specialis*, however, is not a demand for a disposition—perhaps a better or finer one. If that were the case, one could as well have preserved the expression *ex opere operato*, simply explaining *what* is required to make the sacrament into a *signum efficax*. No, the demand for *fides specialis* means that the sacraments' "benefit" (*Nutzen*), to use Luther's expression, depends upon whether the sign, the sacramental act, is received as a "sign and testimony of the will of God toward us." By "the will of God toward us" the AC naturally means nothing else than that which is the content of the gospel: that God is gracious to us. The sacramental act is a testimony to the grace which consists in that God himself comes to meet human beings. If the sign were efficacious by virtue of being performed, it would mean, according to the Lutheran view, that a person would be able to receive grace without meeting God himself. The grace which the sacrament—the sign—conveys, however, is precisely Christ himself, crucified and risen for us. Therefore it cannot be received without *fides specialis* which believes the present promise. From the beginning, Lutheran sacramental understanding centered on *fides et promissio* (faith and promise), specifically in direct contrast with the teaching of *ex opere operato*.

This does not mean, however, that the realistic understanding of the sacraments has been abandoned in any way. If the sign is really a sign of God's grace, as the promise claims, then of course it cannot be understood "symbolically," for in that case it would only become the sign when the person understood it as such. The validity of the sign is completely independent of human attitude or opinion. Therefore, every spiritualistic understanding of the sacrament must be rejected. Its "benefit," however, presupposes faith. Thus the Roman teaching about the sacrament as *signum efficax* must also be rejected.

Naturally enough, the Council of Trent found occasion to express itself on the sacraments in general. This is done in a series of canons, most of which are directed against the Lutheran reformers. The Council maintains that there are seven—and only seven—sacraments, and that they are all instituted by Christ (canon 1). In addition, the council anathematizes those who deny that grace is given to all who do not "bar the door" (canon 6), and those who say that the sacraments do not confer grace *ex opere operato,* but that faith alone in the divine promise is sufficient to obtain grace (canon 8). As the teaching on the individual sacraments also demonstrates, the Council of Trent holds firm on precisely those points in scholastic teaching which the reformers opposed most vehemently. In other words, for those who adhere to the Lutheran position, the Council of Trent provides no occasion for any significant revision of the reformation polemic.

Article 14

• ECCLESIASTICAL • ORDER

Text

[On ecclesiastical order][1] our churches teach that nobody should preach publicly in the church or administer the sacraments unless he is regularly[2] called.[3]

The issue is the right to teach **publicly.** It is well known that the Lutheran reformation had strongly enjoined heads of households to instruct their children and servants (the Small Catechism). In the public worship service, however, only one who is **regularly called** can teach or administer the sacraments. The interpretation of the article hinges entirely upon how the phrase **regularly called** (*rite vocatus*) is understood. See the commentary.

---

1. GT: "Von Kirchenregiment" (order in the Church). The concept *ordo* means "order" or "estate." In medieval terminology it also refers to church ordinance. As the GT demonstrates, the reference here is to the church's rule and authority.

2. *Rite* is an adverb whose root is *ritu,* the ablative of *ritus.* It means "legally," "lawfully," "according to custom and usage."

3. GT: "Ohn ordentlichen Beruf" (without a regular call).

Commentary

On the basis of Article 5 we have seen the Lutheran understanding of the function of the ministry of the church. The ministry is necessitated by the doctrine of justification. Since the faith which justifies comes from hearing the Word, the church cannot exist without proclamation. In Article 5 the issue is the nature and necessity of the ministry. Here, however, the issue is the conditions which must be fulfilled for the ministry to be legitimate. Since Article 14 deals with only one issue, all our attention must be directed toward what is meant by the phrase "regularly called" (*rite vocatus*). The Confutation approves the article with the understanding that "regularly called" means "called in accordance with ecclesiastical ordinances." A comparison is made with Old Testament order. One who is regularly called is one who is called as Aaron was, and not according to a "Jeroboamic call." This reservation on the part of the Confutation compels Melanchthon to express himself more clearly in the Apology. There he states that the Lutherans, as they have often testified, desire that the existing church polity, including the hierarchy, be maintained in accordance with the ancient canons. If this is to be possible, however, the bishops must cease persecuting the church and oppressing the gospel. It is the bishops themselves who are to blame for the disintegration of canonical polity. It is they who must answer to God for the disruption in the church which they have brought about with their raging against true teaching. Melanchthon assures his readers that the Lutherans have clear consciences in this matter, for "we know that the church is present among those who rightly teach the Word of God and rightly administer the sacraments. It is not present among those who seek to destroy the Word of God with their edicts, who even butcher anyone who teaches what is right and true . . ." (14 §4; BC, pp. 214f.). The perspective applied here to the division in the church is worthy of note, because it was the perspective of the reformers as a whole. True, the formulation of the AC is shaped by the church-political situation in 1530 in many ways, but its general aim—to demonstrate that the Lutheran Reformation has nothing to do with the formation of a new church, but is the result of the hierarchy's falling away—has nothing to do with church-political tactics. It is a conviction which lays the whole responsibility for the division in the church upon the pope and the bishops.

Article 14 has no parallels in the Schwabach or Marburg Articles and is most likely occasioned by Eck's attack in the 404 Articles. Eck listed the rejection of the sacrament of ordination and the teaching of the universal priesthood of believers among the Lutheran heresies.[4] The impression that the Lutherans were opponents of the ministry, therefore, had to be countered. As the attitude of the Confutation demonstrates, the attempt to find a formulation, the wording of which could not be labeled heretical, was successful. The deciding factor is, of course, the precise meaning of the phrase *rite vocatus* (regularly called). The corresponding German text reads "ohn ordentlichen Beruf" (without a regular call). It guards against overemphasizing the word *rite* in the sense of "according to canonical usage." The issue is first and foremost the call. By avoiding any mention of the teaching of the priesthood of all believers, the AC has suppressed an important premise in Luther's perspective on the ministry. It is precisely on the basis of this idea that Luther, in *To the Christian Nobility,* justifies the congregation's right to intervene when confronted by the failure of the ministry. On the basis of the priesthood of all believers, "ordentlich Beruf" (a regular call) is not dependent upon the participation of the bishops. In an emergency situation, what is truly necessary for the ministry becomes clear. Luther's famous example might be called to mind here: If a small group of Christians found themselves in the middle of a desert without an episcopally ordained priest, and they then agreed to choose one of themselves to exercise the priestly duties, he would be as truly a priest as if all the bishops and popes had ordained him.[5] He would have been called to this office, and that is the only thing which is absolutely necessary. In an emergency situation the congregation, by virtue of its right as an assembly of priests, must intervene. It would be erroneous, however, to assume from this that Luther considered the election of priests by the congregation to be the only proper method. The doctrine of the priesthood of all believers has nothing to do with democracy. It is not a matter of necessity that the right to call be exercised by the congregation itself, but it is certainly to be assumed that the congregation must approve the choice.[6] The decisive point in

---

4. Articles 267 and 268, Gussmann, 2:134; ET, Reu, 2:112.
5. Clemen 1:367, 17ff.; WA 6:407; *LW* 44 (Philadelphia: Fortress, 1966), p. 128.
6. See Karl Holl, *Luther,* pp. 337f., 378.

Luther's thinking here is not that the doctrine of the priesthood of all believers automatically changes the circumstances under which the right of call is exercised. Rather, his point is that the congregation as an assembly of priests has the unimpeachable right to intervene if the gospel is oppressed either by the authorities who possess the right to call or by the congregation's priest. In the first instance, it has the right to assume the authority to call; in the second, to depose its priest.[7] There is every reason to believe that Luther considered it desirable for the bishop to exercise the right to call as the representative of the calling church. This would cause no conflict with the doctrine of the priesthood of all believers, because the bishop would not function as a superior who exercised this authority by virtue of his ordination, but as a servant upon whom has been laid the duty of exercising the church's right to call.[8]

Ecclesiastical developments in the 1520s, however, rendered such a polity impossible. The bishops opposed the proclamation of the gospel. Therefore the congregations were forced to intervene and assume the authority to call which the bishops had abused. It also became necessary to ordain priests.[9] In *To the Christian Nobility,* Luther, as previously noted, had rejected the absolute necessity of ordination. The call alone is indispensable for the ministry. Ordination, he continues, is the same as though the bishop, acting on the behalf of all, selects one and commands him to exercise the authority which all possess in equal measure on behalf of all the others.[10] In other words, ordination is the same thing as exercising the right to call. In *The Babylonian Captivity* Luther develops this view by means of a direct critique of the sacrament of ordination. As he did in the treatise to the nobility,

7. Cf. Luther's treatise, *That a Christian Assembly or Congregation Has the Right and Power to Judge All Teaching and to Call, Appoint, and Dismiss Teachers, Established and Proven by Scripture,* 1523 (Clemen 2:395-403; WA 11:408-416; *LW* 39 [Philadelphia: Fortress, 1970], pp. 301-314). Here also the congregation's right to intervene when the bishops have fallen away is maintained (cf. Apology).

8. This attitude toward the bishops follows directly from Luther's willingness to entrust them with ordination, if they will serve the gospel. For further discussion of ordination, see the following paragraph.

9. Actually, ordinations were not performed until 1535. Until then installation into the office was considered sufficient. See BK, p. 458, note 2.

10. Clemen 1:367, 11ff.; WA 6:407; *LW* 44:128.

here too he denies the existence of a special spiritual estate and rejects the idea that a priest is different from other Christians in any way except his ministry (i.e., the service he performs). No one is a priest or bishop unless he preaches the Word, having been called to do so by the church.[11] Ordination is not a sacrament, but a particular rite by which the church chooses and calls its pastors.[12] From this it follows that nothing other than the call itself imparts ordination. The notion that ordination imparts an "indelible character" (*character indelebilis*) is pure invention. One who no longer exercises the ministry of the Word becomes a layperson again.[13] Here it is emphasized that to be a priest is not to be a member of an estate, but to exercise an office. Luther's attack on ordination as a sacrament does not undermine the office of ministry as commanded by God and necessary for the church, but is a consequence of the understanding of the ministry which is determined by the doctrine of justification. Luther also desired that ordination by the bishops, understood as the churchly form for assuming the office, be retained. Throughout his life, however, he persisted in maintaining that whether this would be possible would depend on the attitude of the bishops. If one seeks to understand Article 14 against the background of Melanchthon's interpretation in the Apology, the phrase *rite vocatus* must be given the same meaning: no one ought to exercise the functions of the church's ministry without being publicly called to that ministry in the name of the whole church (or the congregation). It is not crucial who exercises the right to call, as long as it is done on behalf of the congregation. As far as is possible, it ought to be done in accordance with ecclesiastical polity, but an emergency situation may demand that certain regulations be abandoned, without rendering the call any less valid. Understood in this way, Article 14 says the same thing as Luther in the Smalcald Articles, where he declares that for the sake of love and unity he is prepared to let bishops

---

11. Clemen 1:501, 34f.; WA 6:564; *LW* 36 (Philadelphia: Fortress, 1959), p. 113; "Ministerium verbi facit sacerdotum et Episcopum" (It is the ministry of the Word that makes the priest and the bishop) (Clemen 1:503, 27f.; WA 6:566; *LW* 36:115).

12. "Quendam ritum Ecclesiasticum" (a certain churchly rite) (ibid., 498, 34f.; WA 6:561; *LW* 36:108); "ritus quidam eligendi Concionatoris in Ecclesia" (a certain rite by which preachers are appointed in the church) (ibid., 501, 36f.; WA 564; *LW* 36:113).

13. Ibid., 500, 8ff.; 505, 1ff.; WA 6:562; 567; *LW* 36:109, 117.

be in charge of ordination and confirmation. This is not a matter of necessity, however, for even without regular bishops the ordination of new priests can and must take place.[14] This whole understanding, which reveals the uncertainty of the time, does not go beyond the state of emergency which existed. In this connection the different directions taken in Wittenberg and Geneva should be noted. The Lutheran reformers refrained completely from any dogmatization of the measures which circumstances forced them to take. In Geneva, on the other hand, these questions were tackled with the conviction of being sure of exactly what a biblical understanding demanded. From a political perspective, the Lutheran uncertainty may have been a great liability, but at the same time it has been a beneficial reminder that the church also existed before 1517. Every "dogmatization" of the arrangements which the reformers made during the "state of emergency" would be in conflict with the AC.[15]

Here, where the requirements for the ministry of the church are set forth, it is logical to call attention to Article 23, which, in accordance with the Lutheran perspective on the ministry, rejects celibacy as a general requirement for priests. It is impossible here to rehearse the whole article and the ideas it builds on. Suffice it to say that the abolition of compulsory celibacy is a natural consequence of the change in the pastoral office from being a sacerdotal ministry to being a ministry of the Word in the congregation. Since Article 14 directly broaches the question of bishops, however, it is necessary to make a further study of the Lutheran view on that subject. We must confine ourselves to dealing with the AC's account in Article 28, "Ecclesiastical Power." The main points in the article, which amounts to a small treatise, are as follows:

1. Ecclesiastical and secular power must not be confused (§§1–4). If bishops have secular power, it is not as bishops, but as secular officials (§§18–19).[16]

---

14. SA 3,10 (*BK* 457; *BC*, p. 314). Luther's willingness is, of course, purely hypothetical, for he immediately asserts that they neither are nor will be true bishops.

15. Cf. H. Asmussen, *Warum noch lutherische Kirche?* (1949), who also deals with the relationship between the Lutheran and the Reformed churches. What he says about the ministry is characterized more by his personal views than by history. See pp. 89, 92ff.

16. For further development of this point, see Article 16.

2. The power of bishops, according to the gospel, is God's command to preach the gospel, to remit and retain sins, and to administer the sacraments. This is a purely spiritual authority, which is exercised by the Word alone. Secular power, which deals with bodily matters and is exercised by the sword, is something else. The two do not concern each other (§§5–17).

3. With respect to the jurisdiction of bishops, it consists in forgiving sins, rejecting false teaching, and excluding open sinners from the church, all through the Word alone without the use of human power. In these things the congregations are bound by necessity and divine law to show them obedience (§§20–22). If the bishops have any other jurisdiction, such as with regard to matrimony, tithes, etc., they have this jurisdiction only by human right (§29).

4. If bishops command anything which conflicts with the gospel, the churches must oppose it (§§23–28).

5. Bishops and pastors are permitted to make regulations so that what is done in the church may be done in good order (§§53–54), and churches ought to comply with such regulations for the sake of love and peace (§55).

6. The question of the scope of this right is dealt with in great detail. The main principle is that bishops do not have the right to ordain anything against the gospel or to impose regulations by means of which grace or justification are to be gained. To impose such commandments as necessary is to oppress consciences as is forbidden in Scripture (§§30 52, 56–68).

7. Bishops could easily retain the obedience of the church if they would give up those traditions which cannot be observed without sin. If they will not, the Lutheran churches must follow the apostolic rule to obey God rather than humans. The article closes by stating exactly what the issue is. The intention is not to take control away from the bishops, but simply to admonish them to permit the gospel to be taught in its purity and to give up those regulations which cannot be kept without sin. If they refuse to do this, they must themselves consider how they will answer to God for provoking division in the church by their obstinacy (§§69–78).

Precisely because the Lutheran reformers do not consider themselves church founders, it is logical that the AC regards the office of bishop as being normal in the church. The office of bishop is also a *ministerium verbi* (ministry of the Word), however, which means that a bishop is not a true bishop by virtue of his ordination alone. If he does not exercise the ministry of the Word, he is not to be obeyed. The church does not stand or fall by the office of bishop. The only thing necessary is the ministry of the Word, which is the true task of the bishop as well. The fate of the office of bishop, therefore, must depend on whether or not it serves the Gospel.[17]

---

17. As opposed to Lutheran openness regarding the office of bishop, it is characteristic of both the Roman and the Reformed churches that they hold extremely rigid positions, considering the office indispensable and absolutely unjustifiable, respectively.

Article 15

• ECCLESIASTICAL RITES •

Text

[On ecclesiastical rites][1] our churches teach that those 1
rites should be observed which can be observed without sin
and which contribute to peace and good order in the church.
Such are certain holy days, festivals, and the like.

Nevertheless, men are admonished not to burden con- 2
sciences with such things, as if observances of this kind
were necessary for salvation. They are also admonished 3
that human traditions which are instituted to propitiate God,
merit grace, and make satisfaction for sins[2] are opposed to
the Gospel and the teaching about faith.[3] Wherefore vows 4
and traditions about foods and days, etc., instituted to merit
grace and make satisfaction for sins, are useless and contrary to the Gospel.

---

1. GT: "Von Kirchenordnungen, von Menschen gemacht" (with regard to church
usages that have been established by men). *BC* does not include the words enclosed
with brackets.

2. GT: "Dass man dadurch Gott versuhne und Gnad verdiene" (for the purpose of
propitiating God and earning grace).

3. GT: "Der Lehre vom Glauben an Christum entgegen" (contrary to the teaching
about faith in Christ).

The article is divided into three parts. The first part maintains that the existing rites should be retained insofar as they (1) do not, as mentioned in the previous article, conflict with the gospel, in which case, of course, they cannot be kept **without sin**; and (2) **contribute to peace and good order in the church. Holy days and the like** are mentioned as examples.

The second part consists of an admonition not to **burden consciences.** This happens when traditional rites of the church are considered **necessary for salvation.** To the question of what, then, is necessary for salvation, the answer must be identical to that which is necessary for the unity of the church (cf. Article 7). Ceremonies and church rituals are not among these essentials.

The last part of the article is a rejection of traditions which stand in conflict with what has been established up to this point. Specifically the statement targets **vows** (i.e., monastic vows), and **traditions about foods and days** (i.e., regulations on fasting). Concerning these things it is stated that they are **opposed to the Gospel**, not by virtue of their mere existence, but because their purpose, according to the AC, is to merit grace and make satisfaction for sin. Therefore they are also **useless** because all merit and satisfaction occurs for the sake of Christ alone.

Commentary

Here the AC continues its treatment of the shape of life in the church which was introduced by the previous article. Article 16 completes the discussion about secular existence. Article 15 contains nothing that does not follow naturally from the doctrine of justification and those forms of worship which correspond to it. From the preceding discussion of Article 14, it has become apparent that the Lutheran reformers did not desire any revolution in church life. This conclusion is corroborated by the historical events in Saxony from 1520 on. The intention of the reformers was precisely to reform, that is, to change only that which had to be changed. This perspective, set forth in the first part of the article, includes both the reformers' fundamental understanding and their actions in the reorganization of the church in Saxony. It is important, however, to note that the AC does represent a certain shift of emphasis in relation to Luther's understanding. Luther's view is set forth in the Schwabach Articles, where it is maintained that in the case of ceremonies which do not conflict with God's Word, one is free to use them or not, but under the rule of love, so that needless offense not be given nor the general peace unnecessarily disturbed. The position of the Marburg Articles is similar. The AC does not mention the freedom which the other articles allow under the rule of love. The difference need not be considered a fundamental one, however, and can no doubt be accounted for by the whole tone of the AC.

The second part puts these church rituals in their proper place by the statement that they must not burden consciences by being regarded as necessary for salvation. In the Apology, Melanchthon explains more precisely what their purpose is: from the example of the church fathers we learn that they are useful for the instruction of the common people. Their purpose is purely pedagogical. Thus the church calendar, which is mentioned as an example in the first part of the article, serves to teach people when to assemble. In addition, rites and traditions are necessary so that everything might be done decently and in good order (Apol. 15 §§20–21).

In the third part, the AC deals with those traditions which, according to the Schwabach Articles, are contrary to God's Word and must be eliminated. As examples, monastic vows and fasting are mentioned. This last theme is repeated in Article 26, "The Distinction of Foods." What the AC attacks as being contrary to the gospel is (1) making the church's regulations on fasting into law, (2) works-righteousness stemming from the Sacrament of Penance (works of satisfaction), and (3) the whole ascetic perspective of life as an expression of the highest way of life for a Christian (monasticism). Article 26 advances three main arguments against considering human traditions useful for meriting grace and making satisfaction for sins: (1) The doctrine of grace and justification by faith is obscured (§4). (2) Traditions have displaced the commands of God (§§8ff.). (3) Consciences are placed in great danger because of human inability to comply with all the regulations which were considered necessary (§§12ff.). To elaborate further on the first point would be superfluous. It is obvious that the assertion that works are necessary for salvation is contrary to the doctrine of justification by faith. The second objection, however, deserves further elaboration. In its entirety it reads:

> In the second place, these precepts obscured the commands of God, for traditions were exalted far above the commands of God. Christianity was thought to consist wholly in the observance of certain holy days, rites, fasts, and vestments. Such observances claimed for themselves the glamorous title of comprising the spiritual life and the perfect life. Meanwhile the commands of God pertaining to callings were without honor—for example, that a father should bring up his children, that a mother should bear children, that a prince should govern his country. These things were regarded as secular and imperfect works, far inferior to those glittering observances. This error greatly tormented the consciences of devout people who grieved that they were bound to an imperfect kind of life—in marriage, the magistracy, or in other civil occupations—and admired the monks and others like them, falsely imagining that the observances of such men were more pleasing to God (AC 26 §§8–11; *BC,* p. 65).

Here the basic elements in the ethical reappraisal which justification brings about are briefly, but especially clearly, outlined. The works which God commands do not lead away from life in one's earthly calling but have their place precisely there. It is characteristic that the further development of the article on church life given by Article 26 necessarily touches on that which is the theme of Article 16 on secular existence, for life cannot be separated into two parts, a higher, spiritual part, and a lower, secular one. The doctrine of justification and the ethics of vocation therefore also lead to the rejection of monastic life as a higher Christian sphere of existence. In Article 27, "On Monastic Vows," the AC elaborates on this position more fully.[4]

With respect to the third point in the critique, various examples are offered to demonstrate how the false understanding of church traditions had proliferated. With almost monotonous consistency, the doctrine of justification by faith is affirmed once again. Moreover, Article 26 rejects the charge that church discipline and mortification of the flesh

---

4. This article follows the same line of thought as Luther's treatise *De votis monasticis (On Monastic Vows)* of 1521.

are forbidden by the reformers. On the contrary, the evangelical side has always taught concerning the cross that Christians must bear affliction with patience. This is the true mortification, to be exercised by afflictions and crucified with Christ (26 §§30ff.). Thus the AC clearly emphasizes that the cross in the life of the Christian is not a self-chosen cross for the purpose of acquiring merit, but that cross which meets the Christian in his calling apart from any desire on his part. These ideas stand in the closest proximity with the idea of the Christian life as a continous penance, in which God exercises the person's faith and constantly puts to death the Old Adam through earthly trials.

The Confutation naturally approves the language about retaining those rites which can be retained without sin, and urges princes and cities to see to it that they are observed or reinstituted if they have been abolished. The last part of the article, on the other hand, is utterly rejected as false. The response to Article 26 is more detailed, but actually does nothing more than reject the various arguments one by one. It also reaffirms the power of the ecclesiastical authorities to establish laws for the church.

Besides what has been discussed previously, mention should be made of Melanchthon's claim in the Apology that the Lutheran churches keep the canonical regulations better than their opponents. He refers to the fact that the Lord's Supper is frequently administered and received by many, after prior confession. This stands in contrast to the opponents' abuse of the Mass for the sake of profit. Great care is given to the Christian instruction of children, in contrast to the negligence of the opponents. In many regions among the opponents, no sermons are preached during the whole year except during Lent. Moreover, when they do preach, the subject is human traditions, the worship of saints, and other insignificant things, instead of repentance, the fear of God, faith in Christ, etc. (Apol. 15 §§38ff.). In addition, the most important points of AC Article 26 are repeated: bishops do not have the authority to institute anything as necessary for justification (Apol. 15 §31); of course there must be good order in the church (15 §22), but it is only for the sake of instruction, not salvation (15 §§20f.), that such rites and traditions are to be kept.

In this context it is logical to touch upon the question of the worship service. Luther's reserve on this point is well known. The only direct consequence of the Reformation was the abolition of private Masses[5] and the excision of those sections of the canon of the Mass which presuppose the Mass as a sacrifice. Luther's writings on the worship service are purely of an advisory nature.[6] He did not desire to prescribe anything. Apart from those changes which he considered essential on doctrinal grounds, the most important innovation was the introduction of the German language in the *Deutsche Messe (The German Mass)* of 1526. The principle behind Luther's work on liturgical questions, therefore, was identical to that of the AC: as far as possible to retain the tradition, but not by necessity. In both of his proposals for the worship service, Luther warns against making such things into law.[7] Typically, Lutheranism fights a double front here, as in other places— against Rome and against the Zwinglian reformation. In both cases Christian freedom is threatened. The one would make the liturgical tradition into law, the other would legalize its abolition. But where Christian freedom is threatened, one's very relationship to God is threatened, for thereby one's works provide the way to God, and faith is obscured. It is obvious to Luther that worship life must assume a form of some kind, but, as he states in *An Order of Mass,* this necessity is

---

5. Cf. Luther's *De abroganda missa privata* and *Vom Missbrauch der Messen* (both translated under the title *The Misuse of the Mass*) of 1521.

6. The pertinent treatises here are *Von Ordnung Gottesdiensts in der Gemeine (Concerning the Order of Public Worship),* 1523; *Formula missae et communionis (An Order of Mass and Communion),* 1523; *and Deutsche Messe (The German Mass),* 1526. All are in *LW* 53.

7. "In quibus omnibus cauendum, ne legem ex libertate faciamus, aut peccare cogamus eos, qui aliter fecerint, vel quaedem omiserint . . ." (But in all these matters we will want to beware lest we make binding what should be free, or make sinners of those who may do some things differently or omit others . . .) (Clemen 2:434, 26ff. WA 12:216; *Formula missae; LW* 53 [Philadelphia: Fortress, 1965], p. 30; *An Order of Mass and Communion).* "Vor allen dingen wil ich gar freundlich gebeten haben / auch umb Gottis willen / alle die ienigen / so diese unser ordnunge ym Gottis dienst sehen / odder nach folgen wollen / das sie ia keyn nöttig gesetz draus machen / noch yemands gewissen damit verstricken odder fahen / sondern der Christlichen Freyheit nach / yhres gefallen brauchen / wie / wo / wenn und wie lange es die sachen schicken und foddern" (In the first place I would kindly and for God's sake request all those who see this order or desire to follow it: Do not make it a rigid law to bind or entangle anyone's conscience, but use it in Christian liberty if, where, how, and as long as you find it to be practical and useful) (Clemen 3:294, 2ff.; WA 19:72, *Deutsche Messe; LW* 53:61, *The German Mass).*

of the same character as the necessity for food and drink. We cannot do without them, but they do not commend us to God. It is only faith and love which do so.[8] It is necessary that the Word be proclaimed and the sacraments administered, for this is commanded by God, and it is necessary that the worship service assume some kind of form, but it is also necessary that the form not be *made* necessary. Despite its different emphasis, this is in reality also the intention of Article 15. This attitude means that it is not only an overemphasis on liturgical forms, but also certain ways of opposing liturgical efforts, which very easily assume the character of law. To be offended by the form of the worship service is not a sign that Christian freedom is being maintained. On the contrary, just as with high church adherence to the "canonical" forms, it is evidence that the law has taken over.

Even though Luther's proclamation of Christian freedom was clear enough in principle, its practical results were not always very encouraging. Too often, contempt for every regulation issued came to be the consequence of the Reformation. One might think, for example, of the tumultuous conditions that forced Luther to leave the Wartburg, against the elector's will, to restore order in Wittenberg. He rightly perceived a new slavery to the law in Carlstadt's violent behavior. Against this background and the activity of other enthusiasts, the emphasis in the AC that it was not order as such that should be opposed, but a false understanding of church traditions, is understandable. Because the chief importance of church traditions was their pedagogical value, it was natural to retain these traditions to as great a degree as possible. It is incontestable that Luther also preferred to adhere to church tradition wherever it could be justified, but he categorically refused to act as lawgiver for the church.

---

8. Clemen 2:435ff.; WA 12:214; *LW* 53:31.

Article 16

• CIVIL AFFAIRS •

Text

[On civil affairs][1] our churches teach that lawful civil or-   1
dinances are good works of God[2] and that it is right for   2
Christians to hold civil office,[3] to sit as judges,[4] to decide
matters by the imperial and other existing laws, to award
just punishments,[5] to engage in just wars, to serve as soldiers, to make legal contracts,[6] to hold property, to swear
oaths when required by magistrates, to marry, to be given
in marriage.

Our churches condemn the Anabaptists who forbid Chris-   3
tians to engage in these civil functions. They also condemn   4
those who place the perfection of the Gospel not in the fear

---

1. GT: "Von der Polizei und weltlichen Regiment" (On police and worldly rule).

2. GT: "Dass alle Obrigkeit in der Welt und geordnete Regiment und Gesetz gute Ordnung, von Gottgeschaffen seind . . ." (that all government in the world and all established rule and laws were instituted and ordained by God for the sake of good order).

3. *Magistratus:* "ministry of state," "place of authority." Everything that belongs to the administration of the state, princes, or leaders and their representatives, is referred to under this term.

4. GT: "Dass Christen mögen in Oberkeit, Fürsten- und Richter-Amt ohne Sünde sein" (that Christians may . . . occupy civil offices or serve as princes and judges). *Exercere iudicia* means "to direct or lead legal investigations," i.e., to be a judge.

5. *Supplicia:* "punishment"; GT implies that capital punishment is being referred to. *Supplicium* is also often employed especially in this sense.

6. GT: "Kaufen und verkaufen" (buy and sell).

of God and in faith but in forsaking civil duties.[7] The Gospel teaches an eternal righteousness of the heart,[8] but [meanwhile][9] it does not destroy the state or the family. On the contrary, it especially requires their preservation as ordinances of God and the exercise of love in these ordinances.[10] Therefore Christians are necessarily bound to obey their magistrates and laws except when commanded to sin, for then they ought to obey God rather than men (Acts 5:29).

5

6

First, it is affirmed that **lawful civil ordinances** are in harmony with God's will, indeed part of God's work. Next, a series of examples is presented in order to demonstrate that a Christian can hold any honest civil occupation. The validity for Christians of imperial law and the law of individual territories is affirmed. Then, such matters as the waging of war, military service, trade, ownership of property, and matrimony are mentioned, to demonstrate that the AC takes a positive attitude toward secular existence in its entirety.

The negative section first opposes the Anabaptists' criticism of Christian participation in the things mentioned, and then, more generally, opposes every flight from the world in the name of the gospel. It is simply impossible that Christian perfection should consist in such a flight, because **the gospel teaches an eternal righteousness of the heart.** This means that such external things have nothing to do with the gospel. The gospel concerns the heart alone. The gospel does not

---

7. GT: "Haus und Hof, Weib und Kind leiblich verlassen und sich der beruhrten Stucke äussern" (forsaking of house and home, wife and child, and the renunciation of such activities as are mentioned above).

8. GT: "Lehrt nicht ein äusserlich, zeitlich, sondern innerlich, ewig Wesen und Gerechtigkeit des Herzen" (does not teach an outward and temporal but an eternal mode of existence and righteousness of the heart).

9. *Interim:* "during the interim," "meanwhile"; it can also mean "however," i.e., "yet," "but," "nevertheless." The last sense is no doubt the most natural here, but this does not foreclose the possibility that the former could also apply. (While *BC*'s translation opts for the second interpretation, the first has been included in brackets to make the full range of meaning available to the reader [trans.]).

10. GT adds "ein jeder nach seinem Beruf" (each according to his own calling).

dissolve **the state or the family**: *politia,* organized society or the state; *oeconomia,* the more restricted society, the family and members of the household. The gospel strengthens these orders. It is precisely in them that love is practiced. The duty of obedience to the authorities and their laws is limited by only one circumstance, when the demands of God and the authorities come into conflict with each other. Then the apostolic rule, that one must obey God rather than men, applies.

Commentary

After treating matters concerning church life in Articles 14 and 15, the AC now turns to civil existence. Article 16 has two basic aims. First, together with the two previous articles, it seeks to prove that the Reformation will not subvert either religious or secular structures. Therefore it disassociates itself from the revolutionary tendencies of the enthusiasts. In addition, the article seeks to provide an evangelical interpretation of civil existence. In the 404 Articles, Eck had collected a series of Lutheran statements under the title "Against Obedience and Princes." It was comprised of various sentences from the teachings on Christian freedom, which Eck presented as being directed against secular authority.[11] This attack posed a real danger, since it coupled the Lutheran reformation together with those groups which, in the name of the gospel, had turned against the authorities.

In previous years following the Peasants' War, the negative attitude of these groups, especially the Anabaptist movement, had become clear. In Wittenberg there were still vivid memories of Carlstadt and Thomas Müntzer. In *Wider die himmlischen Propheten (Against the Heavenly Prophets),* Luther had lumped them together without concerning himself with the various disagreements between them. He saw "the rebellious spirit," not only in Thomas Müntzer's "revolutionary theology," which eventually called directly for battle against the authorities, but also in Carlstadt's spiritualism. In Article 16, however, it is plain that it was not these views, but rather the attitude of the Anabaptists that necessitated a rejoinder in the AC. In the first place, there were no visible tendencies toward the use of force on the part of

---

11. Eck, Articles 332–341 (Gussmann, 2:142ff.; ET, Reu 2:116).

the Anabaptists. On the contrary, they wanted to disassociate themselves completely from the use of force. They acknowledged, from such passages as Romans 13, that the authorities did have the right to use the sword, but only against the wicked. The community of God (i.e., the Anabaptist brotherhood) was to have nothing to do with the world at all. They were simply to wait for the coming of God's kingdom and until then hold themselves aloof from all public duties. It was clear that this could not be done without provoking the authorities to intervene. The Anabaptists' practice of adult Baptism was considered rebaptism by both Lutherans and Catholics, and it was blasphemy, as far as the authorities were concerned. The negative attitude toward society had to be considered rebellion. From the very beginning, the Anabaptists were persecuted almost everywhere, but they persevered in the belief that one should patiently bear the sufferings which accompanied renouncing the world. The problem which this created regarding love for one's neighbor was solved by regarding only those individuals as neighbors who belonged to one's own group. This made it easy to turn one's back, not only on society's institutions, but also its people.[12]

In opposition to the Anabaptists, who are condemned, the first part of Article 16 asserts that legitimate civil ordinances are good works of God. The German text elaborates somewhat: "All government in the world and all established rule and laws were instituted and ordained by God for the sake of good order." Directly from this follows the second statement of this first part, that Christians are permitted to participate in all of these things. Most of the examples listed of such civil occupations are self-evident. A couple of them, however, require further comment. The article speaks of "engaging in just wars." What is meant by this? Neither the AC nor the Apology gives any help in defining the just war as over against an unjust one. If one considers the attitude of the elector of Saxony as late as 1530, *iure bellare* (just war) is primarily to be understood as opposed to rebellion. It is known that Luther denied every right to rebel against an unrighteous prince. He based this position on the fact that God says, "Vengeance is mine,

---

12. On the Anabaptists' perception of the world, see G. H. Williams, *The Radical Reformation* (Philadelphia: Westminster, 1962).

I will repay." Moreover, there are many other admonitions in Scripture to obey the authorities. To set oneself up as judge by revolting against the authorities clearly violates God's ordinance and commandment and also opposes all natural law and equity.[13] What would become of the world, asks Luther, if everyone had the right to punish injustice?[14] The fact that there are unjust public officials does not at all undermine the ordinance which gives the authorities alone the right to punish in God's place.[15] Luther is under no illusions regarding the moral quality of the authorities. On the contrary, he believes that the greatest number of princes are godless tyrants.[16] This, however, changes nothing regarding the authorities' *office*. It is people who are evil. The ordinance is God's and therefore good, and no one is to rise up against it without a special command from God. A rebellion, therefore, can never be a just war. Everything points to the conclusion that Luther could consider a war just only if it were waged to stop an invading enemy or a rebellion, and undoubtedly Article 16 is to be understood in a similar vein.

A second question which held Luther's interest was trade. Here the article's *lege contrahere* (make legal contracts) corresponds to the German text's "buy and sell." In this context it is appropriate to note Luther's battle against usury and unfair profit. Aversion to interest was asserted even in the Middle Ages. Luther's concern is to point to the Christian's responsibility in these relationships. In addition, he also

---

13. *Ob Kriegsleute auch in seligem Stande sein können (Whether Soldiers, Too, Can Be Saved)*, 1526; Clemen 3:328, 28ff.; WA 19: 641; *LW* 46 (Philadelphia: Fortress, 1967), pp. 87ff.

14. Ibid., 333, 24f.; WA 19: 641; *LW* 46:114.

15. "Denn es sind zwey ding / unrecht sein / und unrecht straffen / Jus et executio Juris / iustitia et administratio iustitie / Recht und unrecht haben ist yderman gemein / Aber Recht und unrecht geben und austeylen / das ist des / der uber recht und unrecht herr ist / wilcher ist Gott alleine / der es der oberkeit an seine stat befehlt / Drumb sol sichs niemand unterwinden / er sey denn gewis / das ers von Gott odder von seiner dienerynn / der oberkeit / befehl habe" (For two completely different things are involved in being unjust and condemning injustice, in law and the execution of the law, in justice and the administration of justice. However, God alone is lord over justice and injustice, and God alone passes judgment and administers justice. It is God who commits this responsibility to rulers to act in his stead in these matters. Let no one presume to do this, unless he is sure that he has a command from God, or from God's servants, the rulers) (ibid., 333, 17ff.; WA 19: 641; *LW* 46:114).

16. Ibid., 334, 25f.; WA 19: 643; *LW* 46:115.

attempts to offer practical suggestions about national economic problems. Luther dealt with these problems whenever he discussed the Seventh Commandment, and also wrote special treatises about them.[17] It is therefore probably correct to interpret *lege* (legal) as a warning against profiteering and charging interest.

The last section of the article contains a condemnation of those who believe that the perfection of the gospel consists in renouncing the world, followed by some remarks on an evangelical perspective on civil life. The final statement makes it clear that obeying the authorities must be on the condition that this can be done without sin. The condemnation is directed in part against the "passive" Anabaptists, previously mentioned, and partly against monasticism. The theological background of this section is the Lutheran doctrine of the two kingdoms and the corresponding two ruling orders. The condemnation of the false understanding of evangelical perfection and the positive view of secular life both spring from the distinction between the spiritual and secular ruling orders and presuppose that these two areas can be kept distinct from one another. The last remark about the limit of the duty of obedience, however, suggests that it is impossible completely to prevent conflict between the spiritual and secular orders. Even though the doctrine of the two kingdoms is determinative for the whole section, this is not stated so directly that the Confutation found any reason to comment. The Confutation concludes that the article is in harmony with civil as well as canon law, and it praises the princes because they condemn the Anabaptists. In the Apology, therefore, Melanchthon can be brief. He nevertheless takes the opportunity to point out that the pivotal point here is the distinction between Christ's kingdom, which is spiritual and therefore belongs to the heart, consisting of faith and the fear of God, and "a political kingdom," which is something external, consisting of lawful ordinances. The gospel introduces no new laws about the civil estate, but commands us to obey the existing laws, regardless of who has formulated them. He rebukes Carlstadt and the monks who have obscured the gospel and the spiritual kingdom by

---

17. Two sermons: *Von dem Wucher (Usury; LW* 45 [Philadelphia: Fortress, 1962], pp. 273ff.), 1519 and 1520. *Von Kaufshandlung und Wucher (Trade and Usury; LW* 45:231ff.), 1524. *An die Pfarrherrn, wider den Wucher zu predigen,* 1540 (no ET available).

their contempt for the existing ordinances. As a result they forget wherein Christian perfection truly lies. To seek perfection in ordinances which are to replace existing ones is to make perfection into something external, whose content is works of law and not the righteousness of faith. Viewed through these considerations, the political and social conservatism of the Reformation cannot be blamed on blind adherence to the status quo. Here too the issue is justification. The attempt to form a Christian society is not only hopelessly utopian, which the Lutheran reformers, having no false illusions about the world, realized; it is also in error, because Christ's kingdom is created by the Holy Spirit and not by laws and commands, no matter how "Christian" they might be. Instead of conclusions drawn from the sparse material in the Apology, however, a review of Luther's perspective on these matters would be helpful.

As early as 1520, Luther, in the treatise *To the Christian Nobility*, had made his first attack on the traditional understanding. In the same manner as he rejected the existence of a special spiritual estate, he liberated secular authority as well. Spiritual and secular were no longer distinctions between estates of different rank, but between two distinct offices, the office of the Word and the office of the sword. Just as the ministry of the Word is extended to all Christendom, so also is the ministry of the sword, for which reason ecclesiastical authority is never superior to secular authority.[18] With these ideas the foundation was laid, and the development of the doctrine of the two kingdoms in the following years was simply its logical consequence.[19] In the treatise *On Whether Soldiers, Too, Can Be Saved,* Luther himself briefly summarizes the doctrine of the two kingdoms:

> For God has established two kinds of government among men. The one is spiritual; it has no sword, but it has the word, by means of which men are to become good and righteous, so that with this righteousness they may attain eternal life. He administers this righteousness through the

18. Clemen 1: 366-370; WA 6: 407-411; *LW* 44 (Philadelphia: Fortress, 1966), pp. 126-133, the attack on "the first wall."

19. The account which follows is based primarily on the treatises *Von weltlicher Oberkeit (On Secular Authority),* 1523, and *Ob Kriegsleute,* etc. *(Whether Soldiers, Too . . .),* 1526, in addition to the relevant secondary literature, esp. Gustaf Wingren, *Luther on Vocation,* trans. C. C. Rasmussen (Philadelphia: Fortress, 1957).

word, which he has committed to preachers. The other kind is worldly government, which works through the sword so that those who do not want to be good and righteous to eternal life may be forced to become good and righteous in the eyes of the world. He administers this righteousness through the sword. And although God will not reward this kind of righteousness with eternal life, he still wishes peace to be maintained among men and rewards them with temporal blessings.[20]

Both kingdoms belong to God, the one for salvation, the other for the preservation of the world. The spiritual kingdom is most easily delimited. It consists solely in the proclamation of the gospel, and it rules only over those who have received the Word in faith. Since the two kingdoms together comprise God's rule over the whole earth, it is clear that the secular kingdom not only includes the state, but also all bodily, earthly, external existence. Luther, as does Article 16, usually divides the secular kingdom into *politia* (the authorities) and *oeconomia* (the household, i.e., the family). These two, together with *ecclesia* (the church), which is the spiritual kingdom's only province, constitute the three "estates" or "hierarchies."[21] The secular kingdom, therefore, comprises all of social existence, and apart from faith's relationship to God, Luther cannot conceive of a person's being in a situation in which he or she is not related to other people. It is to the secular kingdom that works—and therefore the law—belong. There is no doubt that Luther holds that what makes the secular kingdom necessary is sin. Without external coercion, which forces us to exercise a degree of outward righteousness, the world cannot be preserved. Thus it is precisely the task of the secular kingdom to restrain evil and to enforce good. This does not mean, however, that its character is purely negative. It is in the secular kingdom, in one's calling, that one is crucified, made subject to the law, and forced to do good works for one's neighbor. The secular kingdom is also an expression of God's love. Though each kingdom has its own particular task to perform, they both work toward the same end, the Christian's death and resurrection with Christ. Through the secular kingdom the cross is laid

---

20. Clemen 3:323, 4ff. (WA 19: 629; *LW* 46:99-100).
21. See, e.g., Luther's *Confession* of 1528 (Clemen 3:510, 17ff.; WA 26: 504; *LW* 37 [Philadelphia: Fortress, 1961], p. 364).

upon the person in his or her calling; through the spiritual kingdom the resurrection is proclaimed and made effective by the gospel.

Both kingdoms are God's work, God's weapons in the battle against the devil and sin. Therefore there is close connection between them. This connection, however, is destroyed if they are mixed together, which is what happens if the freedom of the gospel is suppressed by the law, or conversely, if the freedom of the gospel is made applicable in the secular realm. There is no sword in the spiritual kingdom; that is, the law and the authorities have no role to play there. When coercion is introduced there, it has been forgotten that Christ's kingdom is spiritual, founded on the Word and the righteousness of faith. In the secular kingdom, on the other hand, the law must reign. If one abolishes the law there, all the powers of evil break loose. This understanding, therefore, rejects all attempts at theocracy. Such attempts are expressions of a failure to appreciate the essence of Christ's kingdom, and thus in the final analysis also of God's good ordinance, the secular kingdom. The world cannot be ruled by Christianity, for the gospel never uses force.

The place where the two kingdoms are held together is the calling. If the kingdoms are mixed together, the consequence which inevitably follows is that the calling is disregarded. If one—for example, the pope—attempts to make the law applicable in the spiritual kingdom, it means that works are turned upwards toward God instead of being directed toward one's neighbor in service of one's calling. Thus, one shows contempt for the works demanded by one's earthly existence. If, on the other hand, one attempts, as did the rebellious peasants, to forsake obedience, claiming the right to do so on the basis of Christian freedom, the consequences are the same. The calling and its task are disregarded. The right distinction between the spiritual and the secular is maintained precisely in the person's calling. For the love which the Christian receives from God through the gospel expresses itself nowhere other than in the works demanded by earthly existence. Thus, keeping the two kingdoms distinct from each other is the prerequisite for maintaining the right connection between them. Luther has been criticized for turning Christendom into a bourgeois church through the doctrine of the two kingdoms. One should not forget, however, that his thoughts about these things are determined completely eschatologically: ordinances are transitory, perishable, because they belong to the world of sin. Perhaps this is suggested in the last paragraph of Article 16, where the gospel's proclamation of the "eternal righteousness of the heart" is clearly separated from civil life, when it is further stated: "Meanwhile [during the interim], it does not destroy the state or the family." The language of the Schwabach Articles is clearer still: "Until the Lord comes in judgment and all power and authority are abolished, one is to honor worldly authority and rulers." The entire doctrine of the two kingdoms must be seen from such a perspective.

Although Luther began his reflections on these matters while attacking the theocratic tendencies of the Catholic church, and within a few years was forced to deal with the enthusiasts' political use of the gospel in support of the peasant revolt, it was the danger of the encroachment of the state and its interference in the spiritual kingdom which became his greatest practical concern. The proviso of the AC regarding obedience to the authorities was a central concern for Luther, in part of course because of the Catholic princes' opposition to the Reformation, but also because of church-political developments in Saxony. This concern was already prominent in Luther's most famous treatise on secular authority, as the title clearly indicates: *Temporal Authority: To What Extent It Should Be Obeyed.* Luther's basic position follows directly from the doctrine of the two kingdoms. The secular kingdom has nothing to do with the soul, for God permits no one to rule over it besides himself.[22] Faith is the work of the Holy Spirit and therefore cannot be coerced by commands.[23] If the princes act against

---

22. "Das weltlich regiment hatt gesetz / die sich nicht weytter strecken / denn uber leyb und gutt / und was eusserlich ist auff erden. Denn uber die seele kan und will Gott niemant lassen regirn / denn sich selbs alleyne. Darum wo welltlich gewallt sich vermisst / der seelen gesetz zu geben / do greyfft sie Gott ynn seyn regiment / und verfuret und verderbet nur die seelen . . ." (The temporal government has laws which extend no further than to life and property and external affairs on earth, for God cannot and will not permit anyone but himself to rule over the soul. Therefore, where temporal authority presumes to prescribe laws for the soul, it encroaches upon God's government and only misleads souls and destroys them . . .) (Clemen 2: 377, 5ff.; WA 11: 262; *LW* 45:105).

23. "Denn es ist eyn frey werck umb den glauben / datzu man niemandt kan zwingen. Ya es ist eyn gottlich werck ym geyst / schweyg denn / das es eusserliche gewallt sollt erzwingen und schaffen" (For faith is a free act, to which no one can be forced. Indeed it is a work of God in the spirit, not something which outward authority should compel or create) (ibid., 379, 15ff.; WA 11: 264; *LW* 45:108).

this, they should not be obeyed even if they then deprive a person of life and property. It is typical of Luther that he characterizes princely injustice as the normal state of affairs: "A wise prince is a mighty rare bird, and an upright prince even rarer."[24] One should not be surprised at this, for the world is God's enemy and must oppose God. If it resorts to violent persecution, one is not to oppose it but to suffer. It is simply logical, then, for Luther to oppose the persecution of heretics. Heretics must be refuted by the Word and not by force, for "thoughts are tax-free."[25]

Luther had the opportunity to express his ideas at the time of the reordering of the church in Saxony. The elector, as is well known, came to play a significant role, which was to have decisive historical consequences. When Luther appeals to the authorities in matters concerning the faith, it is not on the basis of their duty as governing authority, but on the basis of the obligation of a *Christian* lord. He does not ask for the exercise of the office, but for the performance of a service of love. Before long, however, other ideas were to encroach upon this perspective. In the elector's instructions to the visitors of 1527, it is stated that the elector is responsible for the spiritual as well as the temporal well-being of his subjects. There is no indication that it is not the elector who is in charge of the proceedings. In his preface to the articles of visitation of 1528, Luther undeniably speaks a different language. He emphasizes that this is an emergency situation. In reality the bishops ought to be doing the visiting, but because of their desertion, the church must help itself. Consequently the elector is asked to help as a Christian brother. As elector he must expel those who will not yield to the ordering of the church, for the state cannot tolerate dissension. Regarding the visitations, Luther consistently maintains that the bishops ought to carry them out, and that the service of the nobility is of a temporary nature. Melanchthon, of course, had a somewhat different understanding, as he was apt to concede the princes the right to attend to issues of concern to the church. Regarding the further

---

24. Ibid., 382, 21f. (WA 11: 267; *LW* 45:113).
25. Ibid., 379, 24f. (WA: 11, 264; *LW* 45:108).

development of the relationship between church and state in the Lutheran lands, especially in Germany, one must concede that Luther's basic viewpoints did not prevail in actual practice. Princely rule over church government emerged victorious over all efforts to hold the spiritual and secular kingdoms apart from each other.[26]

---

26. Regarding the doctrine of the two kingdoms, see also my comments in *Thomas Müntzer und Martin Luther* (Bauernkriegs-Studien, Schr. des Vereins für Reformationsgeschichte 189 [1975], pp. 69-97).

Article 17

• THE RETURN OF •
CHRIST
FOR JUDGMENT

Text

Our churches also teach that at the consummation of the   1
world Christ will appear for judgment and will raise up all
the dead. To the godly and elect he will give eternal life and   2
endless joy, but ungodly men and devils he will condemn to   3
be tormented without end.

Our churches condemn the Anabaptists who think that   4
there will be an end to the punishments of condemned men
and devils. They also condemn others who are now spread-   5
ing Jewish opinions to the effect that before the resurrection
of the dead the godly will take possession of the kingdom
of the world, the ungodly being suppressed everywhere.

The German text contains no significant variants.

The article consists of three parts: (1) an affirmation of the belief
in Christ's return for final judgment over all people; (2) the rejection

of anything which is suggestive of the doctrine of apocatastasis; and (3) the rejection of the notion of an earthly millenial reign.

Commentary

To the extent that it is possible to detect any definite "structure" in the AC, Article 17 forms its conclusion. The articles which follow are statements on questions which receive special treatment for practical reasons. Luther's *Confession* of 1528 also concludes with the last judgment.[1] Apart from the logic of closing any short summary of Christian teaching with the last judgment, its connection with the previous article should also be emphasized. The discussion on civil affairs is not seen in its proper perspective unless it is kept in mind that this world will pass away when Christ establishes his kingdom in glory. The AC adheres to the Apostles' Creed, but because of the Anabaptists, it was necessary to speak about the last things in more detail than the Apostles' Creed does. The article adds that the devil and the ungodly will suffer in eternity. This is not because of any particular interest in emphasizing the nature of the punishment. Luther's *Confession* states that the wicked together with the devil and his angels shall "ewiglich sterben" (perish eternally). The Schwabach Articles speak of Christ punishing the ungodly and condemning them eternally together with the devils. While the expressions may be different, their common bond is the belief of an eternal separation between the believers and the ungodly. This is the article's main point, which is further demonstrated by the condemnation of the Anabaptists, who had revived the ancient doctrine of apocatastasis. This doctrine, attributed especially to Origen, held that all things will be restored at the end of time, and that the devil himself

---

1. "Am letzten gleube ich die aufferstehen aller todten am Jüngsten tage / beyde der frumen und bösen / das ein iglicher daselbs empfahe an seinem liebe / wie ers verdienet hat / Und also die frumen ewiglich leben mit Christo / und die bösen ewiglich sterben mit dem teuffel und seinen engeln / Denn ichs nicht halte mit denen / so da leren / das die teuffel auch werden endlich zur seligkeit komen" (Finally I believe in the resurrection of all the dead at the Last Day, both the godly and the wicked, that each may receive his reward according to his merits. Thus the godly will live eternally with Christ and the wicked will perish eternally with the devil and his angels. I do not agree with those who teach that the devils also will finally be restored to salvation) (Clemen 3: 514, 38ff.; WA 26: 509; *LW* 37 [Philadelphia: Fortress, 1961], p. 372).

will be reconciled to God. In the first edition of the AC (*Na*), Origen's name was included.

In addition, the AC opposes those who believe that before the resurrection the righteous will rule on earth and suppress the ungodly. Here the AC attacks the idea of a "millennial reign." Shortly before the diet, proceedings had been taken against an Anabaptist who had entertained thoughts of a conquest of the Holy Land to establish an earthly, prophetic kingdom.[2] Even apart from such an occasion, however, the reformers are clearly opposed to the notion of establishing the kingdom of God on earth. Any such thing is prohibited by the doctrine of the two kingdoms. In addition, the actions of Thomas Müntzer had contributed greatly to the revulsion against this line of thought.

The Confutation naturally offers no objection to Article 17; and it receives no further commentary in the Apology, where Melanchthon simply repeats the content of the article. This lack of disagreement and an overview of the theological-historical context of the time of the Reformation are evidence that there was nothing serious at stake here. All that was necessary was to affirm the teaching of the church and to reject the contemporary deviations.

---

2. See W. A. Nagel, *Luthers Anteil an der Confessio Augustana,* Beiträge zur Förderung christlicher Theologie 34, 1 (1930), pp. 130f.

Article 18

• FREE WILL •

Text:

[On free will] our churches teach that man's will has some   1
liberty for the attainment of civil righteousness[1] and for the
choice of things subject to reason. However, it does not have   2
the power, without the Holy Spirit,[2] to attain the righteousness of God—that is, spiritual righteousness[3]—because natural man does not perceive the gifts of the Spirit of God (1
Cor. 2:14); but this righteousness is wrought in the heart   3
when the Holy Spirit is received through the Word. In Book   4
III of his *Hypognosticon* Augustine said these things in so
many words: "We concede that all men have a free will which
enables them to make judgments according to reason. However, this does not enable them, without God, to begin or

---

1. GT: "Äusserlich ehrbar zu leben" (to live an outwardly honorable life).
2. GT: "Ohn Gnad, Hilfe und Wirkung des heiligen Geists" (without the grace, help, and activity of the Holy Spirit).
3. GT: "Gott gefällig zu werden, Gott herzlich zu furchten oder zu glauben, oder die angeborene böse Lüste aus dem Herzen zu werfen" (making himself acceptable to God, of fearing God and believing in God with his whole heart, or of expelling inborn evil lusts from his heart).

(much less) to accomplish anything in those things which pertain to God, for it is only in acts of this life that they have freedom to choose good or evil. By 'good' I mean the acts 5 which spring from the good in nature, that is, to will to labor in the field, will to eat and drink, will to have a friend, will to clothe oneself, will to build a house, will to marry, will to keep cattle, will to learn various useful arts, or will to do whatever good pertains to this life. None of these exists without the 6 providence of God; indeed, it is from and through him that all these things come into being and are. On the other hand, 7 by 'evil' I mean such things as to will to worship an idol, will to commit murder," etc.

[Our churches condemn the Pelagians and others who 8 teach that without the Holy Spirit, by the power of nature alone, we are able to love God above all things, and can also keep the commandments of God insofar as the substance of the acts is concerned. Although nature is able in 9 some measure to perform the outward works (for it can keep the hands from theft and murder), yet it cannot produce the inward affections, such as fear of God, trust in God, patience, etc.][4]

In earthly matters, a person's will has **some liberty**. The expression is somewhat vague. Even when the subject is civil righteousness, caution is used. **Civil righteousness** implies obedience to the law and general decency (cf. the German text). Freedom of choice applies to things subject to *ratio* (**reason**), i.e., the things which pertain to civil life. It is a wholly different matter with the **righteousness of God,** however. Here the will can do nothing **without the Holy Spirit**. We are reminded again that righteousness before God is not an external righteousness, but a matter of the heart: **this righteousness is wrought in the heart** . . . . Seen against the background of Articles 4 and 5, this presents nothing new. The decisive question for the interpretation of the article is the understanding of the phrase **it does not have the**

---

4. The section in brackets was added in the first printed edition (*editio princeps*).

power, without the Holy Spirit. If it means merely that without the aid of the Holy Spirit a person cannot attain to a state of grace, the sentence expresses nothing which deviates from medieval tradition. Since it starts with the disjunction **however**, it must be possible to understand it as standing in opposition to the first sentence, which speaks of the province in which human beings possess a degree of freedom. Then, despite the cautious formulation, the meaning would be that before God a person has no freedom. The Pseudo-Augustinian citation (cf. *BK*, p. 73. note 2), which confines freedom completely to the "civil" arena seems to make the second option the preferable one.

Commentary

The question of the freedom of the will had been in the foreground from the very beginning of the Reformation. Luther's position remained adamant from the time of his *Lectures on Romans* (1515–1516) on. Already then he had totally denied the existence of *liberum arbitrium* (free will) in relation to God. He made this position clear in the disputation written at the same time, *De viribus et voluntate hominis sine gratia* (Of Men and Human Freedom Apart from Grace). Melanchthon had also vigorously defended the Lutheran position in the *Loci* of 1521. The reason a special article of the AC is devoted to the problem is due to the violent attack by their opponents, including Eck. Clearly, the primary concern of Article 18 is to maintain that the teaching of the reformers is not deterministic. This colors the article, both in form and in content. It contains two statements: (1) in earthly matters, a person possesses some freedom; (2) the righteousness of God is created by the Spirit who is received through the Word. In support of this, a Pseudo-Augustinian reference is cited as testimony to the article's agreement with church doctrine. Both statements regarding the will can be understood in harmony with Luther's teaching (cf. notes). Luther however, would never have begun with the freedom of the will in earthly matters, but with what was decisive, namely, that a person is able to do nothing in relation to God. As mentioned above, the words "not . . . without the Holy Spirit" could be construed to imply a cooperation between the person and grace, but it is at least possible to understand the article in harmony with Luther. The article's vague formulation must be accounted for by the church-political presuppositions of the AC.

The AC's caution is rewarded, for the Confutation approves the article without reservation. Thus, its authors claim, it befits Catholics to pursue the middle way, between the Pelagians and Manichaeans. It is an inhuman delusion to deny the freedom of the will in human beings, which each is able to experience himself. In closing, the Confutation cites a long series of Scripture passages which are supposedly supportive of this view, for example, "For you always have the poor with you, and whenever you *will* you can do good to them" (Mark 14:7). The example was chosen at random, but it is a typical one. In the Apology, Melanchthon is noticeably uneasy with this approval. He states that the various proofs which the opponents submit have little relevance to the issue. The language about a middle way does not please him either. Even though the principle of avoiding both Pelagianism and Manichaeism is certainly correct, he asks whether there is any difference between the Pelagians and his own opponents, since they both believe that human beings are able to love God, to do the good works which are required by the commandments, and to merit grace and justification with the help of reason without the Holy Spirit. Many absurdities follow from these Pelagian notions. Thus, Melanchthon adds, it is false to say that a person who does the works of the commandments apart from grace does not sin, for a bad tree cannot bear good fruit. There is no freedom in spiritual things, for the human heart cannot produce the works of the First Table without the Spirit. On the other hand, it is necessary pedagogically to speak of freedom regarding earthly matters. The teaching which Melanchthon is opposing here does not seem to correspond entirely to the teaching of the Confutation, however. To find the true object of his rebuttal, we must look at the school of Ockhamism.

In the theology of Gabriel Biel we encounter the concept of human free will which Melanchthon has in mind, and which Luther also polemicizes against. Biel maintains that, without grace, free will can do the good from a moral perspective, avoid mortal sin, and fulfill the divine commandments. Furthermore, one is able by one's own power to dispose oneself toward grace, since the intellect can acknowledge the good by itself, and the will can freely subscribe to it when it wills. One also is able to love God above all things without grace. It is conceded that many temptations threaten the will, so that one seldom is successful in doing all this by oneself. Even if one were to succeed, one is not thereby justified, for God demands that the fulfillment of the law must be by grace. It was especially this idea that enraged Luther, for thereby, he says, grace becomes nothing more than a new demand over and above the law: First is demanded the fulfillment of the law, and then that it occur by grace. Grace thereby is reduced to an additional demand.[5] In the first printed edition of the AC a condemnation of Pelagianism and "others" was added to Article 28 (the text in brackets). The teaching ascribed to these "others" corresponds exactly to Gabriel Biel's understanding and to the viewpoints Melanchthon charges the opponents with in the *Apology*.[6] There is certainly no doubt that Article 18 itself is directly opposed to the Ockhamistic doctrine of the will.

This judgment, however, affects only a part of the medieval tradition. In the theology of Thomas Aquinas, for example, there is no such great confidence in a person's own powers. He allows very little to be ascribed to the free will. Since the fall, according to Thomas, the will by itself is incapable of fulfilling God's commandments or turning itself to God unless God himself moves the will. Thomas, in other words, maintains that there is a free will, but it can accomplish nothing without God's help.[7] Now the question becomes whether such an understanding can be reconciled with the position of the reformers. It is important that this question be asked, because the answer will expose the true motifs of the reformers' teaching on the relationship between grace and free will. It is precisely the vague formulation of Article 18 which makes it necessary to go behind the text of the article in order to see the significance of this problem for reformation theology.

As far as Article 18 is concerned, the answer to the question depends on how the words *non . . . sine Spiritu Sancto* ("not . . . without the

---

5. See, e.g., *Disputatio contra scholasticam theologiam (Disputation against Scholastic Theology*, esp. theses 57–61; Clemen 5:324, 22ff.; *LW* 31 [Philadelphia: Fortress, 1957], p. 13). For Biel's ideas on the freedom of the will see *Collectorium super IV libros Sententiarum Lib. II*, dist. 23, 25, and 28.

6. See BK, p. 74, text-critical apparatus.

7. See *Summa Theologica* I, II, q. 109, esp. a. 2-4.

Holy Spirit") are interpreted. On the face of it, the article can be understood very nicely in harmony with Thomas. Melanchthon himself chose this route in later years. In the Augustana Variata the sentence in question was revised to read, "but spiritual righteousness is effected in us when we are helped by the Holy Spirit."[8] This statement can hardly be misunderstood. After 1535 Melanchthon maintained that the will cooperates in salvation. Three factors work together: the Word, the Holy Spirit, and the will.[9] Thus Melanchthon definitively parted company with Luther on this question.

It is indisputable that Luther's direct polemic on this question was initially directed against Ockhamism. Later, however, in his conflict with Erasmus, he faced an understanding which attributed a much more modest role to the will in one's relationship to God. As is known, this did not lead to any modification in Luther's position. It is useless to attempt to account for this by claiming that *The Bondage of the Will (De servo arbitrio)* occupies an exceptional position in Luther's authorship and therefore must be taken with a great deal of reservation. There is clear testimony that Luther fully acknowledged this work. It is difficult to unravel the lines of argument in the debate because various problems and ways of presenting them are intertwined. Especially perplexing is the fact that the problem of determinism/nondeterminism is often confused with the problem of grace and free will, as Melanchthon correctly points out in the Loci of 1559.[10] With respect to *The Bondage of the Will,* the fact is that Luther is faced with an understanding which is completely scholastic in origin. It has often been asked whether this did not result in fatal consequences for Luther by driving him to take extreme positions. This question cannot be addressed here. We must confine ourselves to the basic lines of thought.

The reason Erasmus opposes the idea of the bondage of the will is that he sees in it the abolition of human moral responsibility. An essential premise for him is that a person's relationship to God finds expression in the attempt to do God's will. Since the person is sinful, he or she is not capable of doing it by himself or herself, but this in no way alters the demand that a person must fulfill the law and exercise

---

8. Kolde: *Die augsburgische Konfession,* p. 179.
9. *Werke* 2/1, p. 243.
10. Ibid., p. 247.

righteousness by works. Thus the question becomes, how much does grace accomplish, and how much must a person do? Actually, the answer is mostly of academic interest. It is established that both God and the human being, grace and free will, contribute to salvation. How one is to distribute these roles more precisely is something that can be discussed, which Erasmus is eager to do. He is most comfortable with the understanding that relegates the will to a minimal place. The work is begun and completed by grace. The will is able only to give its consent to grace so that grace can complete the work which it has begun. Apart from grace, according to Erasmus, the will is capable of doing nothing. Grace is primary, the will is secondary.[11]

It seems, therefore, to be unfair to accuse Erasmus of being a Pelagian, or even of harboring views reminiscent of Gabriel Biel's, for example. Just the same, Luther attacks him with the greatest violence. For Luther the issue is not an interesting academic problem, but a matter of life and death. It is no exaggeration to say that in Erasmus's understanding he saw an insult to the gospel and to Christ. Clearly what is decisive for Luther is not *how much* one assigns to free will, but that one looks at salvation from this point of view at all. Erasmus is a long way from being a Gabriel Biel, but their way of presenting the problem is principally the same. From Luther's standpoint, therefore, which is a total rejection of precisely this way of presenting the problem, they are "birds of a feather."

Luther's attack is relevant solely to the question of what human beings are able to accomplish in relation to God. He maintains that it is self-evident that humans have some freedom with respect to earthly things. This, however, is useless in one's relationship to God, for it is simply impossible for a person to take a neutral position in the battle between God and Satan, even for one moment. In this battle a person is always engaged, always standing on one side or the other. Therefore the attempt to consider humans and their powers independently of this battle is a useless abstraction. Just as the person is subject either to God or to Satan, so also is the will. At the same time, it is important for Luther to maintain that this does not imply that a person acts under

---

11. Regarding Erasmus, see R. Bring, *Kristendoms Tolkningar* (Stockholm, 1950), pp. 170ff.

compulsion. Quite the contrary: the person chooses freely but without being able to alter the will. If Luther is to judge the teaching of Erasmus in the context of humanity's situation in the battle between God and Satan, he must deny that any such freedom exists. To allow this would require the assumption that there is such a thing as a "pure" will, a will which is not always "engaged," a will that does not by its very existence will something—and that, maintains Luther, is an impossibility. Without grace a person is in the power of sin, which means seeking self-advantage in everything, even in one's relationship to God. This self-centeredness means that a person is in Satan's power and does not wish anything else, because of ignorance of his or her true condition. Luther also rejects totally the idea that a person has any freedom in relation to God. Flesh and Spirit cannot be reconciled. Human beings are flesh through and through, in body and soul. It means nothing that the soul strives for what is noble and honorable, for this happens for the glory of humanity, not God. Consequently human beings do their worst when they do their best, for in doing these things they seek a glory which belongs to God alone. If thus even what is best in a person is flesh, then it follows that the human is altogether ungodly, for everything which is without God's Spirit is ungodly. In this context, therefore, it makes little difference whether one teaches that the free will is capable of doing everything or that it is only able to accomplish anything with the help of grace.

This does not mean that Luther actually disputes the existence of the type of striving in human beings which Erasmus speaks of. He simply appraises it completely differently. In the affirmation of a free will, Luther sees an attack on God, an attempt to arrogate a lordship to human beings which belongs to God. If such a phenomenon is to be found, says Luther, its mere existence is a testimony to the fact that humanity is in the power of Satan. Stated differently, what Erasmus calls "the free will" is precisely the person's attempt to make himself into God, that is, the strongest conceivable testimony that humanity is "curved in upon itself," in bondage to its own selfishness. The opposition between God and Satan, between grace and sin, is absolute. There is no spanning the chasm between them. The Confutation says that it is an inhuman delusion to deny human freedom. Luther's understanding can only be expressed by saying that it is an inhuman delusion to assert freedom, for thus one has written off humanity's only conceivable dignity, which consists in being totally dependent on the Creator.

Luther's doctrine of the bound will is not an extreme, idiosyncratic point of view, but simply another way of expressing the doctrine of justification by faith alone. For Luther the doctrine of the freedom of the will is an attempt to maintain the righteousness of the law. Thereby the gospel is abolished and Christ pushed aside. Therefore he enters the battle with all his might, for everything is at stake for him in this issue.

Returning to Article 18, we can see that, even if one understands the article as explained above, it is much more modest in its aim. Article 18 is intended first to prevent any deterministic misunderstanding, and second, to disassociate itself from the Ockhamistic doctrine of the will. Melanchthon undoubtedly wished to say nothing more in order to avoid creating any more discussion than absolutely necessary. This must be the reason why the article does not speak with the clarity on this subject which could have made it a direct continuation of Articles 4 and 5.

Article 19

• THE CAUSE OF SIN •

Text

[On the cause of sin] our churches teach that although God creates and preserves nature, the cause of sin is the will of the wicked, that is, of the devil and ungodly men. If not aided by God,[1] the will of the wicked turns away from God, as Christ says in John 8:44, "When the devil lies, he speaks according to his own nature."

The word **nature** here is a completely neutral expression, referring to the entire created world. Although God is the creator and therefore preserves nature, he nevertheless is not the cause of sin. It is solely the will of the wicked, **if not aided by God**. This expression is not completely clear. Does it mean that the will of the devil and the ungodly do not turn from God if God assists them? If so, it still seems that God, in one sense, does become responsible for sin. The article (naturally enough!) does not really answer the question it poses.

---

1. GT: "So Gott die Hand abgetan" (as soon as God withdraws his support).

Commentary

This article is tied to the previous one. Its purpose is to prevent any possibility of blaming the reformers for making God the cause of sin. Thus its primary purpose is negative. The AC does not seriously attempt to explain the origin of sin nor to go beyond what can be read in Scripture; Article 2 refers to the Fall. Here there is no attempt to elaborate further on original sin. The issue is rather sin as a continuous fact of life in the world. The statement "God creates and preserves nature" includes all human activity. As part of nature, all human activity depends upon the power of the divine Creator. Simply to include human activity within the compass of nature, however, is to say nothing as yet about the ethical or religious quality of such human activity, which is precisely the issue in the rejection of the notion that God is the cause of sin. In this context, the word *nature* is completely neutral; not in the sense that humanity as "nature" is able to stand outside the battle between good and evil for even an instant, but in the sense that "nature" is always qualified by "person," i.e., the human's disposition in the battle. It is possible to maintain that everything that happens in this world is dependent upon God's creative power, without making God the cause of sin, precisely because a human is more than "nature." That which qualifies the human being as person in the article is the term "the will." The will is the cause of sin. Of course, this offers no real explanation of evil whatsoever, but that is not its intention. It points out that the reformers' position on the sinful person's incapability of doing the good is not "Manichaeism." The evil will is not created by God.

The Confutation approves the article without reservation, and in the Apology Melanchthon is content to repeat the words of the article. In his recapitulation, however, he omits the phrase "if not aided by God." The phrase has also been dropped in the Augustana Variata. From the context it is not easy to determine more precisely what it means. The help which is spoken of could be a special divine assistance which prevents the will from turning to evil, i.e., a kind of actual grace. If this is its meaning, the phrase can be understood synergistically in the sense that the will is actually capable of doing the good with the help of God. Its omission in the Apology and in the Augustana Variata might indicate that Melanchthon had recognized the ambiguity. On the other hand, if its meaning is "apart from grace," it is self-evident from a Lutheran standpoint, in which case the phrase can be removed as superfluous. Clearly, the latter is most in harmony with Luther's understanding. He knows of no "grace" which is merely assistance to the human will and not justifying grace.

The background of this article is found in certain lines of thought set forth by Luther and Melanchthon, which had occasioned Eck to accuse them of making God the source of sin. He compiled some sentences from Melanchthon's *Annotations on the Letter to the Romans* in such a way that it appears as if Melanchthon maintains that God wills sin.[2] Eck could just as well have used *The Bondage of the Will* or the *Loci* of 1521 as the basis for his attack. Both speak of everything happening by necessity in a manner which at first glance appears to be a rigid determinism. If this were true, Eck's attack would, of course, be justified. The truth of the matter, however, is completely different. As mentioned in the discussion of Article 18, in *The Bondage of the Will* Luther occupies himself exclusively with the relationship between grace (understood as justifying grace) and human freedom. It is in this context that his thoughts on necessity must be understood. Behind everything that happens on earth is the creative power of God, which of necessity is in ceaseless activity. This is true, not only for the world of faith, but for the world of unbelief as well. Where unbelief exists, however, only evil acts can arise, and these evil acts happen by necessity, for since God is almighty, he cannot cease to work and drive humans to act, and since unbelief is evil, it can only do evil. From this it does not follow that the responsibility for evil can be attributed to God. Despite the fact that humans will always revert to sin, they do not act under compulsion. Humans do what is evil freely or willingly without being able to alter their wills. To say that everything happens by necessity does not mean, then, that God wills that humans must do evil, but that God cannot cease being almighty because humans are evil, and since humans are evil they can only do evil. The vicious circle is broken only when God gives the Spirit. Here we find ourselves at the limit of our comprehension: predestination. Into the source of God's will we have no right to inquire.

---

2. See *BK,* p. 75, note 1.

These thoughts can be reconciled very nicely with the position of Article 19. Apart from grace the human being is in the power of sin. The human being's will is never neutral but always wills *something*. Apart from grace it wills evil, and therefore what it does becomes sin. In other words, a person sins, not because God wills him or her to sin, but because the person is sinful. A final explanation of the origin of sin is not sought. Sin is spoken of as a fact. Because the human being is already sinful in basic disposition, sin is involved in everything he or she does. Thereby the article has rejected the notion that God should be the source of sin. That accomplishes the purpose of the article, and it seeks to do nothing further.

Article 20

• FAITH AND GOOD • WORKS

Text

Our teachers are falsely accused of forbidding good 1
works. Their publications on the Ten Commandments and 2
others of like import bear witness that they have taught to
good purpose about all stations and duties of life, indicating
what manners of life and what kinds of work are pleasing
to God in the several callings. Concerning such things 3
preachers used to teach little. Instead, they urged childish
and needless works, such as particular holy days, prescribed fasts, brotherhoods, pilgrimages, services in honor
of saints, rosaries, monasticism, and the like. Since our ad- 4
versaries have been admonished about these things, they
are now unlearning them and do not preach about such
unprofitable works as much as formerly. They are even be- 5
ginning to mention faith, about which there used to be marvelous silence. They teach that we are justified not by works 6
only, but conjoining faith with works they say that we are
justified by faith and works. This teaching is more tolerable 7
than the former one, and it can afford more consolation than
their old teaching.

Inasmuch, then, as the teaching about faith, which ought   8
to be the chief teaching in the church, has so long been
neglected (for everyone must grant that there has been profound silence concerning the righteousness of faith in sermons while only the teaching about works has been treated
in the church), our teachers have instructed our churches
concerning faith as follows:

We begin by teaching that our works cannot reconcile God   9
or merit forgiveness of sins and grace but that we obtain
forgiveness and grace only by faith when we believe that
we are received into favor for Christ's sake, who alone has
been ordained to be the mediator and propitiation through
whom the Father is reconciled. Consequently whoever trusts   10
that he merits grace by works despises the merit and grace
of Christ and seeks a way to God without Christ, by human
strength, although Christ has said of himself, "I am the way,
and the truth, and the life" (John 14:6).

This teaching concerning faith is everywhere treated in   11
Paul, as in Eph. 2:8, "For by grace you have been saved
through faith; and this is not because of works," etc.

Lest anyone should captiously object that we have in-   12
vented a new interpretation of Paul, this whole matter is
supported by testimonies of the Fathers. In many volumes   13
Augustine defends grace and the righteousness of faith
against the merits of works.[1] Ambrose teaches similarly in   14
De vocatione gentium [The Calling of the Gentiles] and elsewhere, for in his *De vocatione gentium* he says: "Redemption by the blood of Christ would become of little value and
the preeminence of human works would not be superseded
by the mercy of God if justification, which is accomplished
by grace, were due to antecedent merits, for then it would
be a reward for works rather than a free gift."[2]

Although this teaching is despised by inexperienced men,   15

---

1. GT cites Augustine's *De spiritu et litera (The Spirit and the Letter)* here.
2. GT does not have the citation from Pseudo-Ambrose.

God-fearing and anxious consciences find by experience that it offers the greatest consolation because the consciences of men cannot be pacified by any work but only by faith when they are sure that for Christ's sake they have a gracious God. It is as Paul teaches in Rom. 5:1, "Since 16 we are justified by faith, we have peace with God." This 17 whole teaching is to be referred to that conflict of the terrified conscience, nor can it be understood apart from that conflict. Accordingly inexperienced and profane men, who dream 18 that Christian righteousness is nothing else than civil or philosophical righteousness, have bad judgment concerning this teaching.[3]

Consciences used to be plagued by the doctrine of works 19 when consolation from the Gospel was not heard. Some 20 persons were by their consciences driven into the desert, into monasteries, in the hope that there they might merit grace by monastic life. Others invented works of another 21 kind to merit grace and make satisfaction for sins.[4] Hence 22 there was very great need to treat of and to restore this teaching concerning faith in Christ in order that anxious consciences should not be deprived of consolation but know that grace and forgiveness of sins are apprehended by faith in Christ.

Men are also admonished that here the term "faith" does 23 not signify merely knowledge of the history (such as is in the ungodly and the devil), but it signifies faith which believes not only the history but also the effect of the history, namely, this article of the forgiveness of sins—that is, that we have grace, righteousness, and forgiveness of sins through Christ.

Whoever knows that he has a Father reconciled to him 24 through Christ truly knows God, knows that God cares for

---

3. The last part of the section (following the Pauline citation) is lacking in GT.

4. GT inserts the following in the corresponding place: "Derselbigen viel haben erfahren dass man dadurch nicht ist zu Frieden kummen" (many of them discovered that they did not obtain peace by such means).

him, and calls upon God. He is not without God, as are the 25
heathen, for devils and ungodly men are not able to believe
this article of the forgiveness of sins; hence they hate God
as an enemy, do not call upon him, and expect no good
from him. Augustine, too, admonishes his readers in this 26
way concerning the word "faith" when he teaches that in
the Scriptures the word "faith" is to be understood not as
knowledge, such as is in the ungodly, but as confidence
which consoles and lifts up terrified hearts.[5]

Our teachers teach in addition that it is necessary to do 27
good works, not that we should trust to merit grace by them
but because it is the will of God.[6] It is only by faith that 28
forgiveness of sins and grace are apprehended, and be- 29
cause through faith the Holy Spirit is received, hearts are
so renewed and endowed with new affections as to be able
to bring forth good works. Ambrose says, "Faith is the moth- 30
er of the good will and the right deed."[7] For without the Holy 31
Spirit man's powers are full of ungodly affections and are
too weak to do works which are good in God's sight. Besides, 32
they are in the power of the devil, who impels men to various
sins, impious opinions, and manifest crimes. This we may 33
see in the philosophers, who, although they tried to live honest lives, were not able to do so but were defiled by many
manifest crimes. Such is the feebleness of man when he 34
governs himself by human strength alone without faith and
without the Holy Spirit.

Hence it may readily be seen that this teaching is not to 35
be charged with forbidding good works. On the contrary, it
should rather be commended for showing how we are enabled to do good works. For without faith human nature 36
cannot possibly do the works of the First or Second Commandments. Without faith it does not call upon God, expect 37

---

5. GT also refers to Heb. 11:1.
6. GT adds: "Und Gott zu Lob" (and to glorify God).
7. GT lacks the citation.

anything of God, or bear the cross,[8] but it seeks and trusts in man's help. Accordingly, when there is no faith and trust   38
in God, all manner of lusts and human devices rule in the heart. Wherefore Christ said, "Apart from me you can do   39
nothing" (John 15:5), and the church sings,   40

> Where Thou art not, man hath naught,
> Nothing good in deed or thought,
> Nothing free from taint of ill.

Since the commentary summarizes the article's contents, we may confine ourselves in the notes to a few comments on various details. Section 2: **manners of life** (*genera vitae*)—the various "estates," the relationships of each person to family, state, and church. The **duties** which are spoken of are those imposed by one's calling, one's official duties. In conjunction with the phrase **in the several callings**, these duties are clearly defined as those works performed in service to one's calling. Section 3 accuses the opponents of neglecting to speak of these duties. The implication is that not only is it incorrect to charge the Lutherans with forbidding works, but, in fact, they alone have restored works to their true place. Sections 15–18 refer to the experience of conscience: only the teaching of faith can bring comfort. This is not understood by those who imagine that Christian righteousness is identical with civil righteousness. In other words, if one sees only requirements for specific actions in the law's demand, i.e., outward integrity, one fails to understand the teaching about the righteousness of faith.

Sections 27–34 introduce a perspective on the relationship between faith and works of a different character from that of the rest of the article. For further elaboration on this, see the commentary. The article shows evidence of having been written later than the rest of the Confession, which explains its many repetitions of earlier themes.

---

8. GT adds: "Den Nächsten lieben, befohlene Ämter fleissig auszurichten, gehorsam zu sein, bose Lust zu meiden" (love one's neighbor, diligently engage in callings which are commanded, render obedience, avoid evil lusts).

Commentary

This article was also composed at a point in time when the AC was for the most part finished. Presumably, Melanchthon had considered it necessary to give this specific subject a more detailed treatment than the thesislike form in previous articles allowed, because the attacks had been especially strong here where the issue was the so-called practical life of the Christian.[9] Since the article is a further elaboration of the issue treated in Article 6, there is no reason to rehearse the Lutheran reformers' general position once more, which would simply be redundant. On the other hand, there are a number of details in this article which do deserve further comment.

The Confutation focuses its attack upon the understanding of the concept of merit. It protests that Christ's merit is not abolished by calling our works meritorious. This is so because our works are of no merit except by virtue of the merit of Christ's passion. Regarding the citation of John 14:6, "I am the way, the truth, and the life," in Article 20, the Confutation states that this is certainly true, but Christ has given an example for us to follow in the way of good works. In comparison to the rich exposition of Article 20, the answer must be said to lack substance. What is interesting is that the Christological basis of the concept of merit is emphasized so strongly. Much of Lutheran polemics, even Melanchthon's in the Apology, overlooks this starting point and unjustifiably identifies all talk of merit with Pelagianism. The antithesis of grace and merit, which is self-evident for us, is not applicable in Roman Catholic theology. Thomas Aquinas is a case in point.

It is a basic tenet for Thomas that faith is not a natural possibility for human beings. When a person comes to faith, it is due completely to grace. Nevertheless, faith is a meritorious act. Thus the concept of merit is introduced even into the concept of grace itself. The basis for this is that for Thomas it is self-evident that God cannot associate with human beings until they have been raised to a supernatural level. In the final analysis, the love of God can be directed only toward those who are worthy. Therefore a person must be able to demonstrate merit. However, since Thomas really does intend to affirm "grace alone,"

---

9. On the attacks, see also Eck's 404 Articles, which included a special section with the title, "Against Works," Articles 198-202; Gussman 1/1:96f.; ET, Reu 2:108.

he knows that it must be God alone who can make it possible for a person to merit salvation. That salvation must be merited is an unalterable fact for him, due to his understanding of God's righteousness as a *iustitia distributiva*, i.e., a righteousness which gives each what he deserves.[10] He defines meritorious works as follows: our acts are meritorious insofar as they spring from the free will moved by the grace of God. Faith is just such an act.[11] For the most part the reformers' polemic does not address a concept of merit such as the one presented here. This does not mean, however, that their position, viewed objectively, can be reconciled with the Thomistic one. Once again this contrast has its deepest roots in the reformers' Christology. For the human, the sole righteousness possible is the alien righteousness of Christ. Therefore, all merit, whether it be self-made merit or merit wrought with the help of grace, is excluded. In reality, as was demonstrated in connection with Article 4, justification is understood by the reformers as *total*—in a manner which is completely foreign to Catholic theology. The point is precisely that nothing can be added to it, and thus all talk about merit or anything similar is a sign that one does not trust in Christ alone and that demonstrates disregard for him. Works can add nothing to faith, even though they invariably follow from it.

In contrast to the understanding of works as meritorious, it was stated in Article 6 that they should be done because it is God's will. Here we learn a bit more about what is meant by works which are commanded by God. In §§1–3, works are given what the reformers deemed their rightful place, which is the calling. Having been justified by faith, the Christian is freed to serve God as coworker in creation, not with self-chosen inventions, but with those works which have been commanded. Melanchthon refers to various expositions of the Ten Commandments, of which Luther's should be noted. When Luther thought it necessary to speak of works, he generally referred to the Ten Commandments, precisely because they pointed to the neighbor.[12] In *The Freedom of a*

---

10. See A. Nygren, *Eros och Agape II* (1936), pp. 437ff. (ET, *Agape and Eros* [Philadelphia: Westminster, 1953], Part II, pp. 621ff.).

11. *Summa Theologica* II-II q. 2, a. 9, and q. 6.

12. First and foremost, *Von den guten Werken (Treatise on Good Works)*, 1520, and the Catechisms. Further references in *BK*, p. 75, note 2.

Christian, Luther speaks of being as a Christ to one's neighbor; i.e., in serving one's neighbor the Christian is not serving God, but, on the contrary, being united with God by faith, is participating in the work of God himself.[13] Luther actually likens this to the incarnation. Just as Christ became man, although as God he possessed all things, so faith becomes "incarnate" in love toward its neighbor, though it already has everything by having a gracious God.[14] The works of the Christian, therefore, are divine works, by virtue of faith, despite the sinfulness of the person. The works which are to be done are those works laid upon the person by his or her calling. For only in the calling, in relation to work and family, is a person positioned so that the focal point of ethics becomes the neighbor. Thereby, any attempt to distinguish between greater and lesser works is eliminated, since everything depends on whether it is done in faith. The true distinction between works occurs elsewhere, namely, in the distinction between works of faith and works of the law. Works of the law are all works by which persons in one way or another seek to justify themselves before God. Hence the rejection of "needless" works in Article 20 is primarily directed against works of satisfaction. The entire medieval ideal of piety and holiness is rejected here. This is expressed strongly in Article 27, "Monastic Vows," where, against the concept of the monastic life as a "state of perfection," it is asserted that Christian perfection is "honestly to fear God and at the same time to have great faith and to trust that for Christ's sake we have a gracious God; to ask of God, and assuredly to expect from him, help in all things which are to be borne in connection with our callings; meanwhile to be diligent in the performance of good works for others and to attend to our calling."[15] In other words, the issue is not "special" works, but in faith to know that God is present in all circumstances of daily life. It is a misunderstanding of the Lutheran ethic of vocation, however, merely to turn the medieval ideal of holiness on its head, so that one's calling occupies the place which works of satisfaction once held. This would mean that one's relationship to God

---

13. Clemen 2, pp. 24-27; WA 7: 35-38; LW 31 (Philadelphia: Fortress, 1957), pp. 364-367.

14. WA 40/1, 417, 15ff. and 427, 11ff. (*Lectures on Galatians*); LW 26 (St. Louis: Concordia, 1963), pp. 266f., 272f.

15. AC, 27 §49; *BC*, pp. 78-79.

would be mistakenly identified with one's relationship to one's neighbor. The idea of the calling means rather that the calling is the "place" where faith is to become incarnate, that is, where the neighbor is to be served. Precisely because works have nothing to do "in heaven," where faith alone rules, a person must not seek the greatest and best works, but must do the works at hand, which naturally commend themselves in the relationship between parents and children, lords and subjects, superiors and subordinates. It must be made clear, however, that these works are works of the Christian calling only because faith rests with God in heaven. "We conclude, therefore, that a Christian lives not in himself, but in Christ and his neighbor. Otherwise he is not a Christian. He lives in Christ through faith, in his neighbor through love. By faith he is caught up beyond himself into God. By love he descends beneath himself into his neighbor. Yet he always remains in God and his love, as Christ says in John 1[:51], 'Truly, truly, I say to you, you will see heaven opened and the angels of God ascending and descending upon the Son of man.' "[16]

In §§4–11, Melanchthon touches upon the opponents' doctrine of justification and repeats the Lutheran doctrine once again. It must be seen as an expression of his conciliatory tone that he declares it to be more tolerable when they speak of justification by faith *and* works than if they preach only works. This distinction is not very enlightening. It makes any sense only if it is understood in a purely pedagogical-psychological manner in the hope that there might be some for whom the true meaning of faith would emerge by the use of this formulation. The section on justification by faith contributes nothing new with respect to Article 4.

Following a few citations from the fathers (§§12–14) in support of the doctrine of justification, Article 20 proceeds to present the issue from a slightly different perspective. Sections 15–22 are an attempt to offer a sort of pragmatic "proof from conscience" for the doctrine of justification by faith. Only this can comfort the conscience. It is not possible to deal with all the problems which arise in this connection. It must be said, however, that here the spirit of Melanchthon emerges especially clearly. Luther could, of course, speak very earnestly about

---

16. *The Freedom of a Christian;* Clemen 2:27, 18ff.; *LW* 31:371.

the troubled conscience. The entire period of his life spent in the monastery was marked by this struggle. In his work as a physician of souls and as a preacher, he turns time and again to the question of the troubled person being comforted by faith in the forgiveness of sins. Luther never, however, makes this type of experience into a premise for, or even a part of, the *doctrine* of justification. It was his own personal experience that works brought no comfort to the conscience, but the decisive thing is that *truth* forbids either works or the law from having any place in the conscience. There is in this whole section a tendency to psychologize, which later became even stronger in Melanchthon's theology. One might express it in this manner: What for Luther was bitter personal experience and which for him formed the psychological background, became for Melanchthon the object of direct theological treatment in the doctrine of justification itself. This opens the door to the psychologizing of justification in Lutheran orthodoxy, characterized by the doctrine of the *ordo salutis* (order of salvation). As the dogmatic battles during the time after Luther's death would demonstrate, this resulted in a change of perspective which led away from Luther's understanding of the doctrine of justification. Interest became focused on "the person in the process of salvation," in which it became obvious that the perspective was egocentric—in contrast to Luther, for whom the true direction was always upwards toward God and outwards toward the neighbor.[17]

Sections 23–26 treat the concept of faith itself. The distinction employed here between believing "the history" and believing "the effect of the history," namely, the forgiveness of sins, has already been discussed under Article 4. As a further explanation of the concept of faith, however, Melanchthon introduces a reference from a Pseudo-Augustinian treatise on the concepts of *notitia* (knowledge) and *fiducia* (confidence or trust.)[18] In the context of Article 20 there is no doubt about their meaning. Here *notitia* stands for a sheer abstract idea, a concept of faith like the scholastic *fides informis*. In contrast, *fiducia* is supposed to designate faith, understood in Lutheran fashion.

---

17. For an outstanding account of this development, see Ragnar Bring, *Das Verhältnis von Glauben und Werken in der lutherischen Theologie* (Munich, 1955).

18. It is also possible that it stems from Augustine. See the reference in *BK*, p. 80, note 1.

The rest of the article is divided into two paragraphs. The first, §§27–34, emphasizes the necessity of faith with respect to good works, since it is the Holy Spirit, received by faith, who recreates the person and gives the person ethical powers. Primary emphasis is given to the contrast between the person who is renewed by the Spirit and the person who, in his folly, "governs himself by human strength alone." Thus far the paragraph expresses something central in the reformation understanding of "the new obedience." There is, however, one feature in the presentation which gives occasion for further reflection. The manner in which the obedience of faith as actual morality is set over against unbelief as immorality seems difficult to reconcile with Article 18, which states that the free will has a degree of power to exercise civil righteousness. In Article 20 the "philosophers" are denied the possibility of living "honest lives," since faith has been made the prerequisite for a moral life. This section is a moralistic reinterpretation of the Lutheran teaching on faith and good works. The psychologizing of the doctrine of justification, spoken of earlier, is plainly evident here. When good works are explained by the new "affections" which faith creates in the heart, then faith becomes the inner change which demands its outer continuation in the form of works. This moralistic understanding of works easily leads to the actual identification of the ethical with a "civil righteousness." This is a long way from Luther's distinction between works of faith and works of the law, which are indistinguishable from each other by any visible marks. From being "the good" in the good works, faith has become the cause of the "inherent" goodness of works, which represents a change of perspective.

The last paragraph, §§35–40, restates the understanding of good works in connection with faith as the fulfillment of the law. Apart from faith, one seeks only one's own advantage. Despite some cautionary remarks which need to be made on a few formulations, based on Luther's understanding and that of the rest of the AC, Article 20, on the whole, gives a clear presentation of justification, of faith, and of the source and nature of good works.

Article 21

• THE CULT OF SAINTS •

Text

[On the cult of saints] our churches teach that the re-   1
membrance of saints[1] may be commended to us so that we
imitate their faith and good works[2] according to our calling.
Thus the emperor[3] may follow the example of David in waging war to drive the Turk out of his country, for like David
the emperor is a king.[4] However, the Scriptures do not teach   2
us to pray to the saints or seek their help, for the only mediator, propitiation, highpriest, and intercessor whom the
Scriptures set before us is Christ.[5] He is to be prayed to,   3
and he has promised to hear our prayers. Such worship
Christ especially approves, namely, that in all afflictions

---

1. *Proponere* means especially "to set forth publicly."
2. GT: "Dass man der Heiligen gedenken soll, auf dass wir unsern Glauben stärken,
so wir sehen, wie ihnen Gnad widerfahren, auch wie ihnen durch Glauben geholfen
ist" (that saints should be kept in remembrance so that our faith may be strengthened
when we see what grace they received and how they were sustained by faith).
3. The GT adds: "seliglich und gottlich" (salutary and godly).
4. The GT adds: "(in kongiglichem Amt), welches Schutz und Schirm ihrer Un-
tertanen fordert" (of a royal office which demands the defense and protection of their
subjects).
5. The GT cites here 1 Tim. 2:5 and Rom. 8:34.

he be called upon. "If anyone sins, we have an advocate   4
with the Father," etc. (1 John 2:1).

This is about the sum of our teaching. As can be seen,   1
there is nothing here that departs from the Scriptures or the
catholic church or the church of Rome, insofar as the ancient
church is known to us from its writers. Since this is so, those
who insist that our teachers are to be regarded as heretics
judge too harshly. The whole dissension is concerned with   2
a certain few abuses which have crept into the churches
without proper authority. Even if there were some difference
in these, the bishops should have been so lenient as to bear
with us on account of the confession which we have now
drawn up, for even the canons are not so severe as to demand that rites should be the same everywhere, nor have
the rites of all the churches ever been the same. Among us   3
the ancient rites are for the most part diligently observed,   4
for it is false and malicious to charge that all ceremonies
and all old ordinances are abolished in our churches. But it
has been a common complaint that certain abuses were   5
connected with ordinary rites. Because these could not be
approved with a good conscience, they have to some extent
been corrected.[6]

The remembrance of saints may be commended to us: the saints
may be commended in the public worship service, especially in the
sermon. **May** (*potest*) indicates that this is not a matter of critical
importance. The German text is more explicit here. The purpose is
pedagogical. The saints serve as examples of faith and good works.
According to our calling: this phrase prevents the misunderstanding
that the saints are to be models of an imagined, otherworldly *status
perfectionis* (cf. Article 16). Rather, they are to be examples for en-
couragement in the works of one's calling. The citation of the emperor's
war against the Turk is pertinent, since it serves another purpose as
well, which is to attest to the confessors' loyalty to the emperor and

---

6. The conclusion of the GT is slightly more elaborate.

the fatherland. In this context one might also refer to Luther's writings concerning the Turks.

After this the article arrives at its decisive point. All invocation of and prayer to the saints are rejected as contrary to Scripture. Only Christ should be invoked. The expressions employed about Christ are obviously references to 1 Tim. 2:5 and Rom. 8:34, each of which is cited by the German text.

The conclusion of Part I of the Confession maintains first of all that nothing in the teaching of the confessors departs from the catholic church or the church of Rome **insofar as the ancient church is known to us from its writers**. *Scriptores* (**writers**) generally means the church fathers. H. Bornkamm interprets the phrase to mean "the ancient church up to early Scholasticism" (*BK,* p. 83, note 1). This is probably correct. On the basis of this conviction, the accusation of heresy is rejected. The whole question concerns **abuses** which have subsequently come about **without proper authority**, i.e., unwarranted either by Scripture or by the ancient church. It is confidently stated that the bishops ought to show leniency **on account of the confession**. The AC is supposed to have demonstrated clearly that the schism is groundless. The further modification, **which we have now drawn up**, is a useful reminder of the extent to which the AC is conditioned by the historical situation. On the question of diversity of rites, the following arguments are offered in favor of episcopal leniency: (1) Not even the canons demand complete uniformity. (2) History demonstrates that such uniformity has never existed. (3) The ancient rites are, for the most part, observed. (4) It is therefore false to charge that the Reformation leads to their complete abolishment. (5) The complaint about abuses had been common, and their removal had been necessary for reasons of conscience.

Commentary

The most remarkable aspect of this article is its placement. One might expect the question of the cult of saints to be first dealt with under the category of "abuses" in the second part of the AC. Nevertheless, the confessors considered the question together with the doctrinal articles. As the article demonstrates, the AC has a doctrine of the saints as well. They are to be remembered so they may serve as examples of faith and works for us. This imitation of the saints is understood completely in harmony with the view of life in the world set forth previously: "according to our calling." The AC has nothing else to say about how such "veneration" of the saints is to be done rightly. Invocation of the saints is rejected, on the basis of the fact that Scripture teaches us nothing about this but directs us to Christ alone. It is not surprising that the article is violently attacked in the Confutation. The article is utterly condemned as being in conflict with the universal church and the teaching of all the holy fathers. Next, a long series of scripture references follows, which supposedly testifies to the invocation of the saints, and princes and cities are called to see that their churches return to the teaching of the universal church.

In the Apology, Melanchthon derides the authors of the Confutation for their manner of using the Bible and also seeks to describe more precisely how the saints ought to be honored. In addition to imitating their faith and works, one must be particularly aware of how God's grace has proven to be strong in their weakness, which in turn strengthens our faith. This feature is set in opposition to the teaching that the merits of the saints are efficacious for our justification, which is an insult to Christ, our only mediator. Thus, the perspective from which the saints are viewed is completely transformed in conformity with the doctrine of justification. Imitation of the saints is no longer the way to perfection in the form of a higher life removed from earthly concerns, but a means to find one's rightful place in earthly existence, namely, within one's calling. The lives of the saints are no longer of benefit to us by virtue of their acquired merits, but as a testimony to God's mercy toward weak human beings. Thus contemplation of the saints becomes a proclamation of the gospel. In the Smalcald Articles, Luther states his position on this question. He rejects the invocation of saints as idolatry. It is, of course, possible that the saints in heaven pray for us, just as the angels and the saints on earth do, but it does not follow from this that we should pray to them. Once such idolatry has been removed, there are other ways in which you may appropriately honor them, but then they will soon be forgotten, for when they are no longer of benefit, no one will esteem and honor them out of love.[7] These

---

7. SA 2.3, "The Invocation of Saints" (*BK*, pp. 424f.; *BC*, p. 297).

words do not, however, express what Luther wished would happen. Perhaps the best example of his manner of treating such things is his exposition of Mary's song of praise, *The Magnificat,* of 1521. In his interpretation, the song of praise becomes a proclamation of the gospel, not of Mary. The basic viewpoint is established quickly. There are two kinds of people who cannot rightly sing the Magnificat, says Luther. The first are those who love God only when things go well for them, but who will not tolerate suffering or adversity. The second kind is even more dangerous. It is those who praise what they themselves have become by the goodness of God, so that they consider themselves better than other people. Mary is not like them. She does not seek her own ejoyment in the honor which God has permitted her to share, but keeps her spirit pure.[8] In this way the Magnificat becomes a proclamation of God's goodness toward poor and lowly mortals. It is God's grace toward Mary, who is unworthy, that we should praise. Mary does not desire that praise be directed to her, for thereby God's grace is diminished. If one would honor her, one should regard her low estate and marvel at God's exceedingly abundant grace toward her. Thereupon one should praise God, who acts this way toward poor and wretched human beings, and so learn to depend on God oneself, when one is despised and degraded. By elevating Mary into a sublime being, one destroys the comfort which Mary's words can bring.[9] Variations on this theme continue throughout the exposition. Thus it cannot be said that Luther has no place for the veneration of Mary and the saints, but rather that they are truly honored only when, in accordance with their example, one praises God for what God has done for them. In other words, the saints are to be venerated in such a way that their remembrance does not serve to elevate them, let alone invoke them, but rather to point to Christ, in whom alone they had their lives.[10]

Conclusion to Part I

Following the section on the cult of saints are some concluding remarks to the first part of the Confession. The thrust of these remarks

---

8. Clemen 2:143, 10ff.; WA 7:554f.; *LW* 21 (St. Louis: Concordia, 1956), pp. 307-308.

9. Clemen 2:156, 3ff.; WA 7:568f.; *LW* 21:323.

10. Cf. also Luther's *Sendbrief vom Dolmetschen und Anrufung der Heiligen,* 1530 (Clemen 4:190, 32ff.; WA 30/2: 643ff.).

corresponds completely to the Preface and the form of the articles. The confessors renounce all responsibility for the division in the church and lay it upon the bishops. When it is stated that the AC does not depart from the church of Rome, one must note the qualification, "insofar as the ancient church is known to us from its writers." The whole dissension is concerned with "certain few abuses." One must admit, perhaps, that the second part of the AC demonstrates that they are not so few after all! The reference to the fathers does not include Scholasticism. The historical perspective which is sustained throughout the AC may be stated thus: first and foremost a protest is being lodged against a series of recent abuses "which have crept into the churches without proper authority." Theologically, the confessors considered themselves in harmony with Holy Scripture and church tradition, but in conflict with the thought of the last three or four centuries. The AC, in other words, is presented as a defense of the church's faith against scholastic "modernism." Naturally, objections of one sort or another can be raised against this self-understanding when it is set forth in such a heavy-handed manner as it is here. On the other hand, it is clear that the concern of the Reformation is valid only if it occurs in the conviction that this is the church's concern, the same church which had now existed for 15 centuries. If the main concern of the Reformation were not the protest of the church, and thus also of the gospel, against the errors of the papacy and its abuses of power, then it would be nothing but an unfortunate mistake. The merits of this position will not be discussed here, but it must be noted that, no matter how many modifications are deemed necessary, the basic viewpoint of the AC is the only tenable one for any adherence to the reformers' confession. If one accepts these conditions, one must also draw the necessary consequences. The cause of the Reformation must not be allowed to be reduced to confessionalism.

Part II

ARTICLES IN WHICH AN ACCOUNT IS GIVEN OF THE ABUSES WHICH HAVE BEEN CORRECTED

• INTRODUCTION •

Text

Inasmuch as our churches dissent from the church cath-   1
olic in no article of faith but only omit some few abuses which
are new and have been adopted by the fault of the times
although contrary to the intent of the canons,[1] we pray that
Your Imperial Majesty will graciously hear both what has
been changed and what our reasons for such changes are
in order that the people may not be compelled to observe
these abuses against their conscience.

Your Imperial Majesty should not believe those who dis-   2
seminate astonishing slanders among the people in order
to inflame the hatred of men against us. By thus exciting the   3
minds of good men, they first gave occasion to this controversy, and now they are trying by the same method to increase the discord. Your Imperial Majesty will undoubtedly   4
discover that the forms of teaching and of ceremonies observed among us are not so intolerable as those ungodly
and malicious men represent. The truth cannot be gathered   5
from common rumors or the accusations of our enemies.
However, it can readily be judged that nothing contributes   6

---

1. GT: "(Missbräuche) welche zum Teil mit der Zeit selbs eingerissen, zum Teil mit Gewalt aufgericht" (some of the abuses having crept in over the years and others of them having been introduced with violence). The GT is shorter, omits mentioning the rumors and accusations, etc., and explains the necssary changes by stating that "Gottes Gebot" (God's command) requires them.

so much to the maintenance of dignity in public worship and
the cultivation of reverence and devotion among the people
as the proper observance of ceremonies in the churches.

   This section again takes up the theme of the conclusion of the first
part. The abuses are *novi* (**new**), i.e., unwarranted either by Scripture
or by the ancient church. Once again the confessors disclaim responsibility for the dissension, laying it at their opponents' feet.

Article 22

• BOTH KINDS •

Text

In the sacrament of the Lord's Supper both kinds are given   1
to laymen because this usage has the command of the Lord
in Matt. 26:27, "Drink of it, all of you." Christ has here man-   2
ifestly commanded with reference to the cup that all should
drink of it.

Lest anybody should captiously object that this refers only   3
to priests, Paul in 1 Cor. 11:20ff. cites an example from which
it appears that a whole congregation used both kinds. This   4
usage continued in the church for a long time. It is not known
when or by whom it was changed, although Cardinal Cu-
sanus mentions when the change was approved. Cyprian   5
in several places testifies that the blood was given to the
people. The same is testified by Jerome, who said, "The   6
priests administer the Eucharist and distribute the blood of
Christ to the people." In fact, Pope Gelasius commanded   7
that the sacrament should not be divided. It is only a custom   8
of quite recent times that holds otherwise. But it is evident   9
that a custom introduced contrary to the commands of God
is not to be approved, as the canons testify (Dist. 3, chap.

"Veritate" and the following chapters). This custom has been 10
adopted not only in defiance of the Scriptures but also in
contradiction to ancient canons and the example of the
church. Consequently, if any people preferred to use both 11
kinds in the sacrament, they should not have been compelled, with offense to their consciences, to do otherwise.
Because the division of the sacrament does not agree with 12
the institution of Christ, the processions which were hitherto
held are also omitted among us.

The German text contains no significant variants. Melanchthon
makes use of his knowledge of church history and canon law here.
Following the obvious references to **the command of the Lord** and
the situation in the congregation at Corinth, it is stated that distribution
under both kinds **continued in the church for a long time,** more
precisely, until the 13th century (see *BK,* p. 85, note 2). According
to Nicholas of Cusa, this "new form" goes back to the Fourth Lateran
Council, 1215 (see *BK,* p. 86, note 1). Distribution to the laity under
the form of bread only was first promulgated as church doctrine in
connection with the condemnation of John Hus at the Council of Constance (Session XIII: *Definitio de communione sub una specie,* Denzinger, 1198). Regarding Cyprian, see *BK,* p. 85, note 3. Hieronymus
(Jerome): "Sacerdotes quoque qui Eucharistiae serviunt et Sanguinem
Domini populis suis dividunt" (also priests who serve the Eucharist
distribute the blood of the Lord to the people; cited from Kolde, *Die
Augsburgische Konfession,* p. 59). **The canons** which are cited next
are from *Decretum Gratiani* (see *BK*). The final statement about the
discontinuance of **processions** (with the reserved host) was added after
the first edition (see *BK*).

The Confutation, of course, is completely unsympathetic. It attempts
to prove that communion *sub una specie* (under one form) had already
been in use during the time of the apostles! It could not be denied, of
course, that distribution *sub utraque* (under both) had existed, but,
referring to the Council of Constance, it is now maintained that it is
heresy to hold that the distribution of the cup to the laity is necessary.

Article 23

• THE MARRIAGE OF • PRIESTS

Text

    There has been common complaint concerning priests   1
who have not been continent. On this account Pope Pius is   2
reported to have said that there were some reasons why
priests were forbidden to marry but that there are now far
weightier reasons why this right should be restored. Platina
writes to this effect. Since priests among us desired to avoid   3
such open scandals, they took wives and taught that it was
lawful for them to contract matrimony. In the first place, this   4
was done because Paul says, "Because of the temptation
to immorality each man should have his own wife" (1 Cor.
7:2), and again, "It is better to marry than to be aflame with
passion" (1 Cor. 7:9). In the second place, Christ said, "Not   5
all men can receive this precept" (Matt. 19:11), by which he
declared that all men are not suited for celibacy because
God created man for procreation (Gen. 1:28). Moreover, it   6
is not in man's power to alter his creation without a singular
gift and work of God. Therefore those who are not suited   7
for celibacy ought to marry, for no law of man and no vow   8

can nullify a commandment of God and an institution of God. For these reasons our priests teach that it is lawful for them 9 to have wives.

It is also evident that in the ancient church priests were 10 married men. Paul said that a married man should be chosen 11 to be bishop (1 Tim. 3:2), and not until four hundred years 12 ago were priests in Germany compelled by force to live in celibacy. In fact, they offered such resistance that the arch-bishop of Mayence, when about to publish the Roman pon-tiff's edict on this matter, was almost killed by the enraged priests in an uprising. In such a harsh manner was the edict 13 carried out that not only were future marriages prohibited but existing marriages were also dissolved, although this was contrary to all laws, divine and human, and contrary even to the canons, both those made by the popes and those made by the most celebrated councils.

Inasmuch as the world is growing old and man's nature 14 is becoming weaker, it is also well to take precautions against the introduction into Germany of more vices.

Besides, God instituted marriage to be a remedy against 15 human infirmity. The canons themselves state that in later 16 times the old rigor should be relaxed now and then on ac-count of man's weakness, and it is devoutly to be desired that this be done in the case of sacerdotal marriage. And it 17 seems that the churches will soon be lacking in pastors if marriage continues to be forbidden.

Although the commandment of God is in force, although 18 the custom of the church is well known, and although impure celibacy causes many scandals, adulteries, and other crimes which deserve the punishments of just magistrates, yet it is a marvelous thing that nowhere is greater cruelty exercised than in opposition to the marriage of priests. God 19 has commanded that marriage be held in honor. The laws 20 of all well-ordered states, even among the heathen, have adorned marriage with the greatest praise. But now men, 21 and even priests, are cruelly put to death, contrary to the intent

of the canons, for no other cause than marriage. To prohibit 22
marriage is called a doctrine of demons by Paul in 1 Tim.
4:3. This can be readily understood now that the prohibition 23
of marriage is maintained by means of such penalties.

Just as no human law can nullify a command of God, so 24
no vow can do so. Accordingly Cyprian advised that women 25
who did not keep the chastity which they had promised
should marry. His words in the first book of his letters, Epistle
11, are these: "If they are unwilling or unable to persevere,
it is better for them to marry than to fall into the fire through
their lusts; at least they should give no offense to their broth-
ers and sisters."

The canons show some consideration toward those who 26
have made vows before attaining a proper age, and as a
rule vows used to be so made in former times.

The German text is somewhat more detailed in places, but regarding
basic content there is full correspondence.

The arguments which the article presents in favor of the marriage
of priests can actually be reduced to two. First, marriage is God's
ordinance, which humans have no right to alter. Second, experience
has shown how much suffering the demand of celibacy has caused.

Pope Pius: Pius II (Enea Silvio Piccolomini), see *BK*, p. 87, note
2. Following scriptural proofs and a general reference to God's ordering
of creation, historical arguments are presented. The episode involving
Siegfried of Mainz at the synods of Erfurt and Mainz in 1075, where
the demand of celibacy enjoined by Gregory VII was to be carried out,
is referred to also by Luther in *Exhortation to All Clergy Assembled
at Augsburg*, 1930 (*LW* 34 [Philadelphia: Fortress, 1960], p. 41, note
79; Clemen 4: 128; WA 30/2: 324). Apart from the peculiar reference
to the age of the world (§14), the rest of the article merely recapitulates
the arguments already advanced in different variations.

It is clear that the Confutation treats this matter with great intensity.
The demand of celibacy is justified initially by referring to tradition,
especially to the idea that sacerdotal service demands chastity. This
viewpoint has often been asserted, but it ought to be mentioned that

the Council of Trent does not expressly mention celibacy in the decree on ordination. On the other hand, the council denies that one who has renounced the vow of chastity can enter marriage on the grounds that he or she does not have the gift of chastity (Session XXIV, *Canones de sacramento ordinis,* canon 9, Denzinger, 1809; ET, Schroeder, p. 182). It is further asserted that it is *melius ac beatius* (better and more blessed) to remain celibate than to marry (ibid., Canon 10, Denzinger, 1810).

Article 24

• THE MASS •

Text

Our churches are falsely accused of abolishing the Mass.   1
Actually, the Mass is retained among us and is celebrated
with the greatest reverence. Almost all the customary cer-   2
emonies are also retained, except that German hymns are
interspersed here and there among the parts sung in Latin.
These are added for the instruction of the people, for cer-   3
emonies are needed especially in order that the unlearned
may be taught. Paul prescribed that in church a language   4
should be used which is understood by the people. The   5
people are accustomed to receive the sacrament together,
insofar as they are fit to do so. This likewise increases the   6
reverence and devotion of public worship, for none are admitted unless they are first heard and examined. The people   7
are also admonished concerning the value and use of the
sacrament and the great consolation it offers to anxious consciences, that they may learn to believe in God and ask for
and expect whatever is good from God. Such worship pleas-   8
es God, and such use of the sacrament nourishes devotion
to God. Accordingly it does not appear that the Mass is   9

observed with more devotion among our adversaries than among us.

However, it is evident that for a long time there has been 10 open and very grievous complaint by all good men that Masses were being shamefully profaned and applied to purposes of gain. It is also well known how widely this abuse 11 extends in all the churches, by what manner of men Masses are celebrated only for revenues or stipends, and how many celebrate Masses contrary to the canons. But Paul severely 12 threatened those who dealt unworthily with the Eucharist when he said, "Whoever eats the bread or drinks the cup of the Lord in an unworthy manner will be guilty of profaning the body and blood of the Lord." Accordingly when our 13 priests were admonished concerning this sin, private Masses were discontinued among us inasmuch as hardly any private Masses were held except for the sake of gain.

The bishops were not ignorant of these abuses. If they 14 had corrected them in time, there would now have been less dissension. By their own negligence they let many corrup- 15 tions creep into the church. Now when it is too late they are 16 beginning to complain about the troubles of the church, although the disturbance was brought about by nothing else than those abuses which had become so manifest that they could no longer be borne. Great dissensions have arisen 17 concerning the Mass, concerning the sacrament. Perhaps 18 the world is being punished for such long continued profanations of the Mass as have been tolerated in the church for many centuries by the very men who were able to correct them and were under obligation to do so. For in the Deca- 19 logue it is written, "The Lord will not hold him guiltless who takes his name in vain." Since the beginning of the world 20 nothing of divine institution seems ever to have been so abused for the sake of gain as the Mass.

To all this was added an opinion which infinitely increased 21 private Masses, namely, that Christ had by his passion made satisfaction for original sin and had instituted the Mass in

which an oblation should be made for daily sins, mortal and
venial. From this has come the common opinion that the 22
Mass is a work which by its performance takes away the
sins of the living and the dead. Thus was introduced a debate 23
on whether one Mass said for many people is worth as much
as special Masses said for individuals, and this produced
that infinite proliferation of Masses to which reference has
been made.

Concerning these opinions our teachers have warned that 24
they depart from the Holy Scriptures and diminish the glory
of Christ's passion, for the passion of Christ was an oblation 25
and satisfaction not only for original guilt but also for other
sins. So it is written in the Epistle to the Hebrews, "We have 26
been sanctified through the offering of the body of Jesus
Christ once for all," and again, "By a single offering he has 27
perfected for all time those who are sanctified."

The Scriptures also teach that we are justified before God 28
through faith in Christ. Now, if the Mass takes away the sins 29
of the living and the dead by a performance of the outward
act, justification comes from the work of the Mass and not
from faith. But the Scriptures do not allow this.

Christ commands us to do this in remembrance of him. 30
Therefore the Mass was instituted that faith on the part of
those who use the sacrament should remember what benefits are received through Christ and should cheer and comfort anxious consciences. For to remember Christ is to re- 31
member his benefits and realize that they are truly offered
to us; and it is not enough to remember the history, for the 32
Jews and the ungodly can also remember this. Conse- 33
quently the Mass is to be used to this end, that the sacrament
is administered to those who have need of consolation. So
Ambrose said, "Because I always sin, I ought always take
the medicine."

Inasmuch as the Mass is such a giving of the sacrament, 34
one common Mass is observed among us on every holy
day, and on other days, if any desire the sacrament, it is

also administered to those who ask for it. Nor is this custom 35
new in the church, for before the time of Gregory the ancients
do not mention private Masses but speak often of the common Mass. Chrysostom says that the priest stands daily at 36
the altar, inviting some to Communion and keeping others
away. And it appears from the ancient canons that some 37
one person or other celebrated Mass and the rest of the
presbyters and deacons received the body of the Lord from
him, for the words of the Nicene canon read, "In order, after 38
the presbyters, let the deacons receive Holy Communion
from the bishop or from a presbyter." Paul also commands 39
concerning Communion that one wait for another in order
that there may be a common participation.

Since, therefore, the Mass among us is supported by the 40
example of the church as seen from the Scriptures and the
Fathers, we are confident that it cannot be disapproved,
especially since the customary public ceremonies are for
the most part retained. Only the number of Masses is different, and on account of the great and manifest abuses it
would certainly be of advantage to reduce the number. In 41
former times, even in churches most frequented, Mass was
not held every day; as the Tripartite History testifies in Book
9, "Again, in Alexandria, the Scriptures are read and the
doctors expound them on Wednesday and Friday, and all
things are done except for the solemn remembrance of the
sacrifice."

Sections 4-9, 14-20, 24, 31-53 have been omitted in the German
text. In a few places the German text is more detailed without intro-
ducing anything essentially new.

For commentary on this article see R. Prenter, "Das Augsburgische
Bekenntnis und die römische Messopferlehre," *Kerygma und Dogma*
1 (1955): 42-58. The main ideas in Article 24 are rehearsed in the
chapter on Article 10, above. It is a great understatement to assert (§2)
that changes in the worship service are confined to occasional German
hymns. H. N. Clausen rightly notes that the attitude which is taken

toward the worship service in §3, that **ceremonies are needed especially in order that the unlearned may be taught**, tends to over-emphasize the intellectual (*Den Augsburske Confession*, p. 279). This corresponds well to Melanchthon's later concept of the congregation as a "coetus scholasticus" (assembly of learners). **For none are admitted unless**, etc. (§6): here the reference is to the previously mentioned ordinance of going to confession before communing. **Complaint by all good men** (§10): cf. *BK*, p. 92, note 2. Section §§10-13 in its entirety opposes private masses as "masses for profit." The section on bishops (§§14-20) serves to place responsibility for the abuses where it belongs.

It is not until §21 that the AC arrives at its main objection, which is that the Mass has been made into a sacrifice, thereby showing contempt for Christ. If the teaching about the sacrifice of the Mass and the sacraments' efficacy *ex opere operato* were true, then justification does not happen *ex fide* (by faith) but *ex opere missae* (by the work of the Mass; §29). Over against this it is maintained that the true character of the Mass is that of a remembrance of Christ (§§30–33). This does not mean that the Mass is nothing more than a memorial supper, for *historiam recordari* (to remember history) is not enough. The point is to remember Christ's benefits, i.e., to receive the forgiveness of sins by faith in Christ as the one who has made satisfaction once for all. Since this is the meaning of the Mass, it is (§34) always *communis missa* (the common Mass, Communion, as opposed to the private Mass). The number of Masses is determined by how often communion is desired. Section §§35–39 testifies to the truth of the phrase **Nor is this custom new in the church**. The conclusion (§§40–41) seeks once again to minimize the differences: **only the number of Masses is different**. In view of the preceding attack on the sacrifice of the Mass, this viewpoint can be maintained only with great difficulty.

Article 25

• CONFESSION •

Text

Confession has not been abolished in our churches, for 1
it is not customary to administer the body of Christ except
to those who have previously been examined and absolved.
The people are very diligently taught concerning faith in con- 2
nection with absolution, a matter about which there has been
profound silence before this time. Our people are taught to 3
esteem absolution highly because it is the voice of God and
is pronounced by God's command.[1] The power of keys is 4
praised, and people are reminded of the great consolation
it brings to terrified consciences, are told that God requires
faith to believe such absolution as God's own voice heard
from heaven, and are assured that such faith truly obtains
and receives the forgiveness of sins. In former times sat- 5
isfactions were immoderately extolled, but nothing was said
about faith. Accordingly no fault is to be found with our
churches on this point, for even our adversaries are forced 6
to concede to us that our teachers have shed light on the
doctrine of repentance and have treated it with great care.[2]

---

1. GT: "Dann es sei nicht des gegenwärtigen Menschen Stimme oder Wort, sondern Gottes Wort, der die Sunde vergiebt. Dann sie wird an Gottes Statt und aus Gottes Befehl gesprochen" (It is not the voice or word of the man who speaks it, but it is the Word of God, who forgives sin, for it is spoken in God's stead and by God's command).

2. GT: "Schicklicher dann zuvor in langer Zeit" (in a more fitting fashion than had been done for a long time).

Concerning confession they teach that an enumeration of sins is not necessary[3] and that consciences should not be burdened with a scrupulous enumeration of all sins because it is impossible to recount all of them. So the Psalm testifies, "Who can discern his errors?" Jeremiah also says, "The heart of man is corrupt and inscrutable." But if no sins were forgiven except those which are recounted, our consciences would never find peace,[4] for many sins can neither be perceived nor remembered.[5] The ancient writers also testify that such an enumeration is not necessary, for Chrysostom is quoted in the canons as saying, "I do not say that you should expose yourself in public or should accuse yourself before others, but I wish you to obey the prophet who says, 'Show your way to the Lord.' Therefore, confess your sins to God, the true judge, in your prayer. Tell him of your sins not with your tongue but with the memory of your conscience." The marginal note in *De poenitentia,* Dist. 5, 12 in the chapter "Consideret," admits that such confession is of human right.[6] Nevertheless, confession is retained among us on account of the great benefit of absolution and because it is otherwise useful to consciences.

    7

    8

    9

    10

    11

    12

    13

The article has been treated already in connection with Article 11. The Confutation objects to the introduction of the quotation of Chrysostom (§11) on the grounds that the issue addressed by it is public penance.

---

3. GT: "Dass man niemand dringen soll, die Sünde namhaft zu erzählen" (that no one should be compelled to recount sins in detail).

4. GT: "Wäre uns wenig geholfen" (we would be helped but little).

5. GT: "Die elend menschlich Natur steckt also tief in Sunden, dass die dieselben nicht alle sehen oder kennen kann" (Our wretched human nature is so deeply submerged in sins that it is unable to perceive or know them all).

6. GT: "Nicht durch die Schrift geboten, sondern durch die Kirchen eingesetzt" (is not commanded by the Scriptures, but was instituted by the church).

Article 26

• THE DISTINCTION OF •
FOODS

Text

It has been the common opinion not only of the people   1
but also of those who teach in the churches that distinctions
among foods and similar human traditions are works which
are profitable to merit grace and make satisfactions for sins.
That the world thought so is evident from the fact that new   2
ceremonies, new orders, new holy days, and new fasts were
daily instituted, and the learned men in the churches exacted
these works as a service necessary to merit grace and sorely
terrified the consciences of those who omitted any of them.
From this opinion concerning traditions much harm has re-   3
sulted in the church.

In the first place, it has obscured the doctrine concerning   4
grace and the righteousness of faith, which is the chief part
of the Gospel and ought above all else to be in the church,
and to be prominent in it, so that the merit of Christ may be
well known and that faith which believes that sins are for-

given for Christ's sake may be exalted far above
works and above all other acts of worship. Paul therefore
lays the greatest weight on this article and puts aside the   5
law and human traditions in order to show that the righteousness of a Christian is something other than works of
this sort; it is faith which believes that for Christ's sake we
are received into grace. This teaching of Paul has been   6
almost wholly smothered by traditions which have produced
the opinion that it is necessary to merit grace and righteousness by distinctions among foods and similar acts of worship. In treating of repentance no mention was made of faith;   7
only works of satisfaction were proposed, and the whole of
repentance was thought to consist of these.[1]

In the second place, these precepts obscured the com-   8
mands of God, for traditions were exalted far above the
commands of God. Christianity was thought to consist wholly
in the observance of certain holy days, rites, fasts, and vest-
ments. Such observances claimed for themselves the glam-   9
orous title of comprising the spiritual life and the perfect life.
Meanwhile the commands of God pertaining to callings were   10
without honor—for example, that a father should bring up
his children, that a mother should bear children, that a prince
should govern his country. These were regarded as secular
and imperfect works, far inferior to those glittering observances. This error greatly tormented the consciences of de-   11
vout people who grieved that they were bound to an imperfect kind of life—in marriage, in the magistracy, or in other
civil occupations—and admired the monks and others like
them, falsely imagining that the observances of such men
were more pleasing to God.

In the third place, traditions brought great dangers to con-   12
sciences, for it was impossible to keep all traditions, and yet
men judged these observances to be necessary acts of worship. Gerson writes that many fell into despair, and some   13

---

1. The GT omits the last sentence, on repentance.

even took their own lives, because they felt that they could not keep the traditions and, meanwhile, they had never heard the consolation of grace and of the righteousness of faith. We see that the summists and theologians gathered 14 the traditions together and sought mitigations[2] to relieve consciences; yet they did not altogether succeed in releasing them but rather entangled consciences even more.[3] Schools 15 and sermons were so preoccupied with gathering traditions that they have had no time to treat the Scriptures and seek for the more profitable teachings concerning faith, the cross, hope, the importance of civil affairs, and the consolation of sorely tried consciences. Hence Gerson and certain other 16 theologians greatly lamented that they were so hindered by these bickerings about traditions that they were unable to devote their attention to a better kind of teaching. Augustine 17 also forbids the burdening of consciences with such observances and prudently admonishes Januarius that he should know that they are to be as things indifferent, for these are his words.

Our teachers, therefore, must not be looked upon as hav- 18 ing taken up this matter rashly or out of hatred for the bishops, as some wrongly suspect. There was great need to 19 warn the churches of these errors which had arisen from misunderstanding of traditions. For the Gospel compels us 20 to insist in the church on the teaching concerning grace and the righteousness of faith, and this cannot be understood if men suppose that they merit grace by observances of their own choice.

Accordingly our teachers have taught that we cannot merit 21 grace or make satisfaction for sins by the observance of human traditions. Hence observances of this kind are not to be thought of as necessary acts of worship. Our teachers 22

---

2. Corresponding to *quaerere epiikias* (**sought mitigations**), GT reads "und Äquität gesucht" (also translated "sought mitigations" by Tappert [trans.]).

3. Lacking in GT.

add testimonies from the Scriptures. In Matt. 15:1-20 Christ defends the apostles for not observing the customary tradition, a tradition which was seen to be legalistic and to have a relationship with the purifications of the law,[4] and he says, "In vain do they worship me with the precepts of men." So he does not require an unprofitable act of worship.[5] Shortly afterward Christ says, "Not what goes into the mouth defiles a man." It is also written in Rom. 14:17, "The kingdom of God is not food and drink," and in Col. 2:16, "Let no one pass judgment on you in questions of food and drink or with regard to a festival or a sabbath." In Acts 15:10,11 Peter says, "Why do you make trial of God by putting a yoke upon the neck of the disciples which neither our fathers nor we have been able to bear? But we believe that we shall be saved through the grace of the Lord Jesus, just as they will." Here Peter forbids the burdening of consciences with numerous rites, whether of Moses or of others. And in 1 Tim. 4:1,3 Paul calls the prohibition of foods a doctrine of demons, for it is in conflict with the Gospel to institute or practice such works for the purpose of meriting grace through them or with the notion that Christian righteousness cannot exist without such acts of worship.

Here our adversaries charge that our teachers, like Jovinian, forbid discipline and mortification of the flesh. But something different may be perceived in the writings of our teachers, for they have always taught concerning the cross that Christians are obliged to suffer afflictions. To be harassed by various afflictions and to be crucified with Christ is true and real, rather than invented, mortification.

Besides, they teach that every Christian ought so to control and curb himself with bodily discipline, or bodily exercises and labors, that neither plenty nor idleness may tempt him to sin, but not in order to merit forgiveness of sins or

---

4. Lacking in GT.

5. GT: "So er nun dies ein vergeblichen Dienst nennt, muss er nicht notig sein" (Since he calls them vain service, they must not be necessary).

satisfaction for sins by means of such exercises. Such bodily 34
discipline ought to be encouraged at all times, and not merely on a few prescribed days. So Christ commands, "Take 35
heed to yourselves lest your hearts be weighed down with
dissipation," and again, "This kind of demon cannot be dri- 36
ven out by anything but fasting and prayer." Paul also said, 37
"I pommel my body and subdue it." By this he clearly shows 38
that he pommeled his body not to merit forgiveness of sins
by that discipline but to keep his body in subjection and fit
for spiritual things and for discharging his duty according to
his calling. Condemned therefore is not fasting in itself, but 39
traditions which with peril to conscience prescribe certain
days and certain foods as if works of this sort were necessary acts of worship.

Many traditions are nevertheless kept among us (such as 40
the order of lessons in the Mass, holy days, etc.) which are
profitable for maintaining good order in the church. At the 41
same time men are warned that such observances do not
justify before God[6] and that no sin is committed if they are
omitted without scandal. Such liberty in human rites was not 42
unknown to the Fathers, for Easter was kept in the East at 43
a time different from that in Rome, and when on account of
this difference the Romans accused the East of schism, they
were admonished by others that such customs need not be
alike everywhere. Irenaeus says, "Disagreement about fast- 44
ing does not destroy unity in faith," and Pope Gregory indicates in Dist. 12 that such diversity does not violate the
unity of the church. In the Tripartite History, Book 9, many 45
examples of dissimilar rites are gathered, and this statement
is made: "It was not the intention of the apostles to enact
binding laws with respect to holy days but to preach piety
toward God and good conversation among men."

---

6. GT adds here: "und lass man ohn Beschwerung des Gewissens halten soll" (and
that they are to be observed without burdening consciences).

The main points of this article were dealt with in the discussion of Article 15. Despite its length, the article contains nothing which in principle goes beyond the content of Article 15. The title is inadequate. The title in the Torgau Articles, "Of the Doctrines and Ordinances of Men," is much more to the point, as is the Apology's "Human Traditions in the Church." The rebuttal of the Confutation is weak. It attempts to justify its position by referring to the fact that all authority is from God, particularly the spiritual authority (!), which means that it must have the power to lay down laws.

Article 27

• MONASTIC VOWS •

Text

What is taught among us concerning monastic vows will   1
be better understood if it is recalled what the condition of
monasteries was and how many things were done in these
monasteries every day that were contrary to the canons. In   2
Augustine's time they were voluntary associations. Afterward, when discipline fell into decay, vows were added for
the purpose of restoring discipline, as in a carefully planned
prison. Many other observances were gradually added in   3
addition to vows. These fetters were laid on many, contrary   4
to the canons, before they had attained a lawful age. Many   5
entered this kind of life through ignorance, for although they
were not wanting in years, they were unable to judge their
own strength. Those who were thus ensnared were com-   6
pelled to remain, though some could have been freed by
appealing to the canons. This was the case in convents of   7
women more than in those of men, although more consideration should have been given to the weaker sex. Such   8
rigor displeased many good men before our time when they
saw that girls and boys were thrust into monasteries for their
maintenance and saw what unfortunately resulted from this

arrangement, what scandals were created, what snares were placed on consciences. They regretted that in such a   9
momentous matter the authority of the canons was utterly ignored and despised. To these evils was added the fact   10
that vows had such a reputation that it was clearly displeasing to those monks in former times who had a little more understanding.

They said that vows were equal to Baptism, and they   11
taught that they merited forgiveness of sins and justification before God by this kind of life. What is more, they added   12
that monastic life merited not only righteousness before God but even more, for it was an observance not only of the precepts but also of the counsels of the Gospel. Thus they   13
made men believe that the monastic profession was far better than Baptism, and that monastic life was more meritorious than the life of magistrates, pastors, and the like who, without man-made observances, serve their calling in accordance with God's commands. None of these things can   14
be denied, for they appear in their own books.

What happened after such people had entered monasteries? Formerly there had been schools of the Holy Scriptures and other branches of learning which were profitable to the church, and pastors and bishops were taken from them. Now everything is different, and it is needless to rehearse what is well known. Formerly people came together in monasteries to learn. Now they pretend that this kind of   16
life was instituted to merit grace and righteousness. In fact, they assert that it is a state of perfection, and they put it far above all other kinds of life instituted by God. We have re-   17
hearsed these things without odious exaggeration in order that our teaching on this topic may better be understood.

. In the first place, we teach concerning those who contract   18
matrimony that it is lawful for all who are not suited for celibacy to marry, for vows can not nullify the command and institution of God. This is the command of God, "Because   19
of fornication let every man have his own wife." Nor is it the   20

command only, but God's creation and institution also compel those to marry who are not excepted by a singular work of God. This is according to the text in Gen. 2:18, "It is not good that the man should be alone." Therefore those who obey this command and institution of God do not sin. 21

What objection can be raised to this? Exaggerate the obligation of a vow as much as one pleases, it cannot be brought about that a vow abrogates the command of God. 22
The canons state that every vow is subject to the right of a superior. How much less are those vows valid which are made contrary to God's commands! 23

If the obligation of vows could not be changed for any reason at all,[1] the Roman pontiffs would not have granted dispensations, for it is not lawful for a man to annul an obligation which is plainly derived from divine law. But the Roman pontiffs have prudently judged that leniency should be observed in connection with this obligation. Therefore, we read that they often granted dispensation from vows. Well known is the case of the king of Aragon, who was recalled from a monastery, and there is no want of examples in our time. 24 25 26

In the second place, why do our adversaries exaggerate the obligation or effect of a vow while they remain silent concerning the nature of a vow, which ought to be voluntary and chosen freely and deliberately? Yet it is not unknown to what an extent perpetual chastity lies in man's power. How few there are who have taken the vow spontaneously and deliberately! Before they are able to judge, boys and girls are persuaded, and sometimes even compelled, to take the vow. Accordingly it is not fair to argue so insistently about the obligation inasmuch as it is conceded by all that it is contrary to the nature of a vow to make a promise which is not spontaneous and deliberate. 27 28 29 30

Many canons annul vows made before the age of fifteen on the ground that before that age a person does not seem 31

---

1. Literally, "if there were no possible grounds for which they could be changed."

to have sufficient judgment to make a decision involving the rest of his life. Another canon, making a greater concession 32 to human weakness, adds a few years and forbids making a vow before the eighteenth year. Whether we follow one 33 canon or the other, most monastics have an excuse for leaving the monastery because a majority of them took vows before they reached such an age.

Finally, although the violation of vows might be rebuked, 34 yet it seems not to follow of necessity that the marriages of persons who violated them ought to be dissolved. For Au- 35 gustine denies that they should be dissolved in *Nuptiarum,* Question 27, Chapter I, and his authority is not inconsiderable, although others have subsequently differed from him.

Although it appears that God's command concerning mar- 36 riage frees many from their vows, our teachers offer still another reason to show that vows are void. Every service of God that is instituted and chosen by men to merit justification and grace without the command of God is wicked, for Christ says, "In vain do they worship me with the precepts of men." Paul also teaches everywhere that righteousness 37 is not to be sought for in observances and services devised by men but that it comes through faith to those who believe that they are received by God into favor for Christ's sake.

It is evident that the monks have taught that their invented 38 observances make satisfaction for sins and merit grace and justification. What is this but to detract from the glory of Christ and obscure and deny the righteousness of faith? It follows, 39 therefore, that the vows thus customarily taken were wicked services and on this account were void, for a wicked vow, 40 taken contrary to the commands of God, is invalid. As the canon says, no vow ought to bind men to iniquity.

Paul says, "You are severed from Christ, you who would 41 be justified by the law; you have fallen away from grace." Therefore those who would be justified by vows are severed 42 from Christ and fall away from grace, for those who ascribe 43 justification to their vows ascribe to their own works what properly belongs to the glory of Christ.

It cannot be denied that the monks taught that they were 44 justified and merited forgiveness of sins by their vows and observances. In fact, they invented greater absurdities when they claimed that they could transfer their works to others. If out of hatred anybody should be inclined to enlarge on 45 these claims, how many things could be collected of which even the monks are now ashamed! Besides all this, they 46 persuaded men that their invented observances were a state of Christian perfection. Is not this attributing justification to 47 works? It is no light offense in the church to recommend to 48 the people a certain service invented by men without the command of God and to teach that such service justifies men. For righteousness of faith, which ought especially to be taught in the church, is obscured when the eyes of men are blinded by these remarkable angelic observances[2] and this pretense of poverty, humility, and chastity.

Furthermore, the commands of God and true service of 49 God are obscured when men hear that only monks are in a state of perfection. For this is Christian perfection: honestly to fear God and at the same time to have great faith and to trust that for Christ's sake we have a gracious God; to ask of God, and assuredly to expect from him, help in all things which are to be borne in connection with our callings; meanwhile to be diligent in the performance of good works for others and to attend to our calling. True perfection and true 50 service of God consist of these things and not of celibacy, mendicancy, or humble attire. The people draw many per- 51 nicious conclusions from such false commendations of monastic life. They hear celibacy praised above measure, and 52 therefore they engage in their married life with a troubled conscience. They hear that only mendicants are perfect, and 53

---

2. *Illae mirificae religiones angelorum* (these remarkable angelic observances): The GT reads "Engelgeistlichkeit" (angelic spirituality).

therefore they have a troubled conscience when they keep their possessions or engage in business. They hear that it   54 is an evangelical counsel not to take revenge, and therefore some are not afraid to take vengeance in their private life since they are told that this is prohibited by a counsel and not by a precept. Others err still more, for they judge that   55 all magistracy and all civil offices are unworthy of Christians and in conflict with the evangelical counsel.

Cases can be read of men who, forsaking marriage and   56 the administration of the state, withdrew into a monastery. They called this "fleeing from the world" and "seeking a holy   57 kind of life." They did not perceive that God is to be served by observing the commands he has given and not by keeping the commands invented by men. A good and perfect   58 kind of life is one which has God's command in its favor. Concerning such things it was necessary to admonish men.   59

Before our times Gerson rebuked the error of the monks   60 concerning perfection and testified that it was a novelty in his day to say that monastic life is a state of perfection.

So there are many impious opinions which are associated   61 with vows: that they justify, that they constitute Christian perfection, that the monks observe both the counsels and the precepts, and that monks do works of supererogation. All these things, since they are false and useless, make vows   62 null and void.

The German text follows the Latin very closely. In the first edition, however, it was completely reworked (see *BK*, p. 119, note 3, in which the most important variants are given).

Beginning with a critique of the development of monasticism, especially of binding vows and the dedication of children to monastic life, the article continues with a general rejection. To speak of monastic life as a *status perfectiones* (**state of perfection**) leads both to works-righteousness and contempt for civil existence. Moreover, the distinction between God's commandments and evangelical counsels is rejected, together with works of supererogation. While in the other "abuse articles" all contain an evangelical teaching in place of what has been rejected, Article 27 concludes with a total rejection of monastic life. To the objection that only the abuses and a false understanding of monastic life should be rejected, one must ask what really is left once these are eliminated. The only possibility would be for a community to be created without binding vows, without "evangelical counsels," without references to "escaping from the world." Such a community, which could never even dream of being a state of perfection, or in any way being set over against life in the ordinary calling, however, can no longer reasonably be called a monastery (cloister). It must of course be noted that the article does not deny that celibacy can be God's will in special cases: *sine singulari Dei opera,* etc. (**a singular work of God**, §20).

The Confutation obviously cannot compromise here. Any criticism of monastic vows is ungodly.

Article 28

• ECCLESIASTICAL • POWER

Text

In former times there has been great controversy about   1
the power of bishops, and some have improperly confused
the power of the church with the power of the sword. From   2
this confusion great wars and tumults have resulted, while
the pontiffs, relying on the power of keys, not only have
instituted new forms of worship and burdened consciences
with reservation of cases and violent excommunications but
also have undertaken to transfer kingdoms of this world and
take away the imperial power. These wrongs have long since   3
been rebuked in the church by devout and learned men.
Accordingly our teachers have been compelled, for the sake   4
of instructing consciences, to show the difference between
the power of the church and the power of the sword, and
they have taught that on account of God's command both
are to be held in reverence and honor as the chief gifts of
God on earth.

Our teachers hold that according to the Gospel the power   5
of keys or the power of bishops is a power or command of
God to preach the Gospel, to remit and retain sins, and to

administer the sacraments. For Christ sent out the apostles   6
with this command. "As the Father has sent me, even so I
send you. Receive the Holy Spirit. If you forgive the sins of
any, they are forgiven; if you retain the sins of any, they are
retained." According to Mark 16:15 he also said, "Go and   7
preach the gospel to the whole creation."[1]

This power is exercised only by teaching or preaching the   8
Gospel and by administering the sacraments either to many
or to individuals, depending on one's calling. For it is not
bodily things that are thus given, but rather such eternal
things as eternal righteousness, the Holy Spirit, and eternal
life. These things cannot come about except through the   9
ministry of Word and sacraments, for Paul says, "The gospel
is the power of God for salvation to everyone who has faith,"
and Ps. 119:50 states, "Thy Word gives me life."[2] Inasmuch   10
as the power of the church bestows eternal things and is
exercised only through the ministry of the Word, it interferes
with civil government as little as the art of singing interferes
with civil government. For civil government is concerned with   11
other things than the Gospel. The state protects not souls
but bodies and goods from manifest harm, and constrains
men with the sword and physical penalties, while[3] the Gospel
protects souls from heresies, the devil, and eternal death.

Therefore, ecclesiastical and civil power are not to be con-   12
fused. The power of the church has its own commission to
preach the Gospel and administer the sacraments. Let it not   13
invade the other's function, nor transfer the kingdoms of the
world, nor abrogate the laws of civil rulers, nor abolish lawful
obedience, nor interfere with judgments concerning any civil
ordinances or contracts, nor prescribe to civil rulers laws
about the forms of government that should be established.
Christ says, "My kingdom is not of this world," and again, 14,15
"Who made me a judge or divider over you?" Paul also wrote   16

---

1. GT lacks Mark 16:15.
2. GT lacks Ps. 119:50.
3. GT lacks the words from here to the end of the paragraph.

in Phil. 3:20, "Our commonwealth is in heaven," and in 2   17
Cor. 10:4,5, "The weapons of our warfare are not worldly
but have divine power to destroy arguments," etc.

In this way our teachers distinguish the functions of the   18
two powers, and they command that both be held in honor
and acknowledged as gifts and blessings of God.

If bishops have any power of the sword, they have this   19
not as bishops under a commission of the Gospel, but by
human right granted by kings and emperors for the civil
administration of their lands. This however, is a function other than the ministry of the Gospel.

When one inquires about the jurisdiction of bishops, there-   20
fore, civil authority must be distinguished from ecclesiastical
jurisdiction. Hence according to the Gospel (or, as they say,   21
by divine right) no jurisdiction belongs to the bishops as
bishops (that is, to those to whom has been committed the
ministry of Word and sacraments) except to forgive sins, to
reject doctrine which is contrary to the Gospel, and to exclude from the fellowship of the church ungodly persons
whose wickedness is known, doing all this without human
power, simply by the Word. Churches are therefore bound   22
by divine law to be obedient to the bishops according to the
text, "He who hears you hears me."

However, when bishops teach or ordain anything contrary   23
to the Gospel, churches have a command of God that forbids
obedience: "Beware of false prophets" (Matt. 7:15), "If an   24
angel from heaven should preach any other Gospel, let him
be accursed" (Gal. 1:8), "We cannot do anything against   25
the truth, but only for the truth" (2 Cor. 13:8), and also, "Given   26
to me is the authority for building up and not for tearing
down." The canons require the same thing (II, question 7,   27
in chapters "Sacerdotes" and "Oves"). Augustine also says   28
in reply to the letters of Petilian that not even catholic bishops
are to be obeyed if they should happen to err or hold anything
contrary to the canonical Scriptures of God.

If they have any other power or jurisdiction to decide legal   29
cases (for example, pertaining to matrimony, tithes, etc.),

bishops have this by human right. When the bishops are negligent in the performance of their duties, princes are bound, even against their will, to administer justice to their subjects for the sake of maintaining public peace.

Besides, it is disputed whether bishops or pastors have 30 the right to introduce ceremonies in the church and make laws concerning foods, holy days, grades or orders of ministers, etc. Those who attribute this right to bishops cite as 31 evidence the passage, "I have yet many things to say to you, but you cannot bear them now. When the Spirit of truth comes, he will guide you into all the truth." They also cite 32 the example of the apostles who commanded men to abstain from blood and from what is strangled. Besides, they cite 33 the change from the Sabbath to the Lord's Day—contrary to the Decalogue, it appears. No case is made more of than this change of the Sabbath. Great, they say, is the power of the church, for it dispensed from one of the Ten Commandments!

Concerning this question our teachers assert, as has been 34 pointed out above, that bishops do not have power to institute anything contrary to the Gospel. The canons concede this throughout the whole of Dist. 9. Besides, it is against 35 Scripture to require the observance of traditions for the purpose of making satisfaction for sins or meriting justification, for the glory of Christ's merit is dishonored when we suppose 36 that we are justified by such observances. It is also evident 37 that as a result of this notion traditions have multiplied in the church almost beyond calculation, while the teaching concerning faith and the righteousness of faith has been suppressed, for from time to time more holy days were appointed, more fasts prescribed, and new ceremonies and new orders instituted because the authors of these things thought that they would merit grace by these works. So the peni- 38 tential canons formerly increased, and we can still see some traces of these in the satisfactions.

Again, the authors of traditions act contrary to the com- 39 mand of God when they attach sin to foods, days, and similar things and burden the church with the bondage of the law, as if in order to merit justification there had to be a service among Christians similar to the Levitical, and as if God had commissioned the apostles and bishops to institute it. For 40 thus some have written, and the pontiffs seem in some measure to have been misled by the example of the law of Moses. This is the origin of such burdens as this, that it is a 41 mortal sin to do manual work on holy days, even when it gives no offense to others, that certain foods defile the conscience, that fasting which is privative and not natural[4] is a work that appeases God, that it is a mortal sin to omit the canonical hours, that in a reserved case a sin cannot be forgiven except by the authority of the person who reserved the case, although the canons themselves speak only of reserving ecclesiastical penalties and not of reserving guilt.

Where did the bishops get the right to impose such tra- 42 ditions on the churches and thus ensnare consciences when Peter forbids putting a yoke on the disciples and Paul says that authority was given for building up and not for tearing down? Why do they multiply sin with such traditions?

Yet there are clear testimonies which prohibit the making 43 of traditions for the purpose of appeasing God or as if they were necessary for salvation. In Colossians 2 Paul says, 44 "Let no one pass judgment on you in questions of food and drink or with regard to a festival or a new moon or a sabbath." Again, "If with Christ you died to the elemental spirits of the 45 universe, why do you live as if you still belonged to the world? Why do you submit to regulations, 'Do not handle, Do not taste, Do not touch' (referring to things which all perish as they are used), according to human precepts and doctrines?

---

4. *Naturae* (**natural**) must be understood as an adjectival genitive. Thomas Aquinas (*Summa Theologica* II-II, q. 147, a. 1 ad 3) explains the term *ieiunium naturae* (fasting which is natural) as follows: "quo quis dicitur ieiunus antequam comedat" (according to which someone is said to be fasting prior to eating). An "actus virtutis" (act of virtue), on the other hand is "solum illud ieiunium quo quis, ex rationabili proposito, a cibis aliqualiter abstinet" (only that fast, according to which someone, because of a reasonable resolve, abstains from food to some extent) [trans. Justine Pierce]).

These have an appearance of wisdom." In Titus I Paul also says, "Not giving heed to Jewish myths or to commands of men who reject the truth." 46

In Matthew 15 Christ says concerning those who require traditions, "Let them alone; they are blind and leaders of the blind." He rebukes such services and says, "Every plant which my heavenly Father has not planted will be rooted up." 47 48

If bishops have the right to burden consciences with such traditions, why does Scripture so often prohibit the making of traditions? Why does it call them doctrines of demons? Was it in vain that the Holy Spirit warned against these? 49

Inasmuch as ordinances which have been instituted as necessary or instituted with the intention of meriting justification are in conflict with the Gospel, it follows that it is not lawful for bishops to institute such services or require them as necessary. It is necessary to preserve the doctrine of Christian liberty in the churches, namely, that bondage to the law is not necessary for justification, as it is written in the Epistle to the Galatians, "Do not submit again to a yoke of slavery." It is necessary to preserve the chief article of the Gospel, namely, that we obtain grace through faith in Christ and not through certain observances or acts of worship instituted by men. 50 51 52

What, then, are we to think about Sunday and about similar rites in our churches? To this our teachers reply that it is lawful for bishops or pastors to make regulations so that things in the church may be done in good order, but not that by means of these we make satisfaction for sins, nor that consciences are bound so as to regard these as necessary services. So Paul ordained that women should cover their heads in the assembly and that interpreters in the church should be heard one after another. 53 54

It is proper that the churches comply with such ordinances for the sake of love and tranquility and that they keep them, insofar as one does not offend another, so that everything in the churches may be done in order and without confusion. 55

However, consciences should not be burdened by sug- 56
gesting that they are necessary for salvation or by judging
that those who omit them without offense to others commit
a sin, any more than one would say that a woman sins by
going out in public with her head uncovered, provided no
offense is given.

Of the same sort is the observance of Sunday, Easter, 57
Pentecost, and similar festivals and rites. Those who hold 58
that the observance of the Lord's Day in place of the Sabbath
was instituted by the church's authority as a necessary thing
are mistaken. The Scriptures, not the church, abrogated the 59
Sabbath, for after the revelation of the Gospel all ceremonies
of the Mosaic law can be omitted. Nevertheless, because it 60
was necessary to appoint a certain day so that the people
may know when they ought to assemble, it appears that the
church designated the Lord's Day for this purpose, and it
seems that the church was the more pleased to do this for
the additional reason that men would have an example of
Christian liberty and would know that the keeping neither of
the Sabbath nor of any other day is necessary.

There are monstrous discussions concerning the mutation 61
of the law, concerning ceremonies of the new law, concerning the change of the Sabbath, all of which have arisen from
the false notion that there must be a service in the church
like the Levitical service and that Christ commissioned the
apostles and bishops to devise new ceremonies which would
be necessary for salvation. These errors crept into the 62
church when the righteousness of faith was not taught with
sufficient clarity. Some argue that the observance of the 63
Lord's Day is not *indeed* of divine obligation but is *as it were*
of divine obligation, and they prescribe the extent to which
one is allowed to work on holy days. What are discussions 64
of this kind but snares of conscience? Although they try to
mitigate the traditions, moderation can never be achieved
as long as the opinion remains that their observance is nec-
sary. And this opinion must remain where there is no un-

derstanding of the righteousness of faith and Christian liberty.

The apostles commanded that one should abstain from 65 blood, etc. Who observes this prohibition now? Those who do not observe it commit no sin, for the apostles did not wish to burden consciences with such bondage but forbade such eating for a time to avoid offense. In connection with the 66 decree one must consider what the perpetual aim of the Gospel is.

Scarcely any of the canons are observed according to the 67 letter, and many of them become obsolete from day to day even among those who favor traditions. It is not possible to 68 counsel consciences unless this mitigation is practiced, that one recognizes that canons are kept without holding them to be necessary and that no harm is done to consciences even if the usage of men changes in such matters.

The bishops might easily retain the lawful obedience of 69 men if they did not insist on the observance of traditions which cannot be kept with a good conscience. But now they 70 demand celibacy and will admit no one to the ministry unless he swears that he will not teach the pure doctrine of the Gospel. Our churches do not ask that the bishops restore 71 concord at the expense of their honor (which, however, good pastors ought to do), but ask only that they relax unjust 72 burdens which are new and were introduced contrary to the custom of the church catholic. Perhaps there were accept- 73 able reasons for these ordinances when they were introduced, but they are not adapted to later times. It is also 74 apparent that some were adopted out of misunderstanding. It would therefore befit the clemency of the bishops to mitigate these regulations now, for such change does not impair the unity of the church inasmuch as many human traditions have been changed with the passing of time, as the canons themselves show. However, if it is impossible to obtain a 75 relaxation of observances which cannot be kept without sin, we are bound to follow the apostolic injunction which commands us to obey God rather than men.

Peter forbids the bishops to be domineering and to coerce 76
the churches. It is not our intention that the bishops give up 77
their power to govern, but we ask for this one thing, that
they allow the Gospel to be taught purely and that they relax
some few observances which cannot be kept without sin. If 78
they do not do this, they must see to it how they will answer
for it before God that by their obstinacy they offer occasion
for schism.[5]

The basic content of the article is treated under Article 14. Limitations of space unfortunately prohibit further treatment of the many problems posed by the lengthy statement here. The notes given in *BK* provide the essential commentary. The article is, of course, completely unacceptable to the Confutation. Without going into details, it rejects the viewpoints set forth and maintains the essential aspects of medieval doctrine on the office of bishop.

A rejection of the papacy would also have belonged under Article 28. Given the tone of the AC, it is easy to understand why such a rejection is not found. It is clear, however, that by its teaching about the limits of episcopal authority the article implies a rejection. A pope who functions by the Word alone, who is obeyed for the sake of love, and who has no right to make laws for the church with divine authority is rather unthinkable. Only under these conditions, however, would he be acceptable from the AC's perspective. In this connection it should be noted that Melanchthon's *Treatise on the Power and Primacy of the Pope* should be considered as a supplement to the AC, rather than to Luther's Smalcald Articles (see *BK*, p. xxvi).

---

5. GT adds: "(Schisma), das sie doch billig sollen verhuten helfen" (Schism, which they should in truth help to prevent). Here, as in Article 27, the GT follows the Latin text very closely.

• CONCLUSION[1] •

Text

We have now reviewed the chief articles that are regarded   1
as controversial. Although more abuses could be mentioned,
to avoid undue length we have discussed only the principal
ones.[2] There have been grave complaints about indul-   2
gences, pilgrimages, and misuse of excommunication. Parishes have been troubled in many ways by indulgence sell-
ers. There have been endless quarrels between parish
ministers and monks about parochial rights, confessions,
burials, and countless other things. We have passed over   3
matters of this sort so that the chief points at issue, being
briefly set forth, may more readily be understood.

Nothing has here been said or related for the purpose of   4
injuring anybody. Only those things have been recounted   5
which it seemed necessary to say in order that it may be
understood that nothing has been received among us, in
doctrine or in ceremonies, that is contrary to Scripture or to
the church catholic. For it is manifest that we have guarded
diligently[3] against the introduction into our churches of any
new and ungodly doctrines.

---

1. There is no heading in *BK*. Here the heading is the one used in the earlier
reproductions of the AC for the sake of form.

2. GT adds: "daraus die anderen leichtlich zu ermessen" (the others can readily be
weighed in light of these).

3. GT: "Mit allem Fleiss, mit Gottes Hilf (ohne Ruhm zu reden)" ([to speak without
boasting] that we have diligently and with God's help).

Conclusion

In keeping with the edict of Your Imperial Majesty, we have desired to present the above articles in order that our confession may be exhibited in them and that a summary of the doctrine taught among us may be discerned. If anything is found to be lacking in this confession, we are ready, God willing, to present ampler information according to the Scriptures.

6

7

Your Imperial Majesty's faithful subjects:

JOHN, duke of Saxony, elector
GEORGE, margrave of Brandenburg
ERNEST, with his own hand
PHILIP, landgrave of Hesse, subscribes
JOHN FREDERICK, duke of Saxony
FRANCIS, duke of Lüneburg
WOLFGANG, prince of Anhalt
Senate and magistrate of Nuremberg
Senate of Reullingen

• SELECTED •
BIBLIOGRAPHY

Sources

Bornkamm, Heinrich, editor. *Die Bekenntnisschriften der Evangelisch-lutherischen Kirche,* 3rd edition. Göttingen, 1956. Included are the Schwabach, Marburg, and "Torgau" Articles, as well as the plan for the preface and the manuscript *Na.*

Denzinger, H. J. C., and Schönmetzer, A., editors. *Enchiridion Symbolorum: Definitionum et Declarationum de Rebus Fidei et Morum.* 36 edition. Barcinone: Herder, 1976.

Gussmann, Wilhelm, editor. *Quellen und Forschungen zur Geschichte des Augsburgischen Bekenntnisses.* Volume 1:1-2, Leipzig/Berlin, 1911; volume 2, Kassel, 1930.

Immenkötter, Herbert, editor. *Confutatio der Confessio Augustana.* Corpus Catholicorum. Münster, 1979.

Jacobs, Henry Eyster, translator. "Reckoning of the Faith of Ulrich Zwingli" (translation of *Fidei Ratio).* In Jacobs, *The Book of Concord.* Philadelphia: The United Lutheran Publication House, 1911.

Luther's works:

    Clemen, Otto, editor. *Luthers Werke in Auswahl.* 8 volumes. Bonn, 1912–1933; Berlin, 1955–1956.

    D. Martin Luthers Werke: Kritische Gesamtausgabe (Weimar edition). Weimar: 1883—.

    Luther's Works. American Edition. 55 volumes. Philadelphia: Fortress, and St. Louis: Concordia, 1955–1986.

Melanchthons Werke in Auswahl. Edited by R. Stupperich. Gütersloh, 1951—.

Schroeder, H. J. *Canons and Decrees of the Council of Trent: Original Text with English Translations.* St. Louis/London: B. Herder, 1955.

Reu, Johann Michael. *The Augsburg Confession: A Collection of Sources with an Historical Introduction.* Chicago: Wartburg, 1930.

Tappert, Theodore, translator and editor. *The Book of Concord.* Philadelphia: Fortress, 1959.

Literature

Burgess, Joseph A., editor. *The Role of the Augsburg Confession: Catholic and Lutheran Views.* Philadelphia: Fortress, 1980.

Ebeling, Gerhard. *Der Lauf des Evangeliums und der Lauf der Welt. Die Confessio Augustana einst und jetzt, in: Lutherstudien III,* pp. 339–65. Tübingen, 1985.

Forde, Gerhard O. *Justification by Faith: A Matter of Death and Life.* Philadelphia: Fortress, 1982.

Forell, George W., and McCue, James F., editors. *Confessing One Faith.* Minneapolis: Augsburg, 1982.

Gritsch, Eric, W., and Jenson, Robert W. *Lutheranism: The Theological Movement and Its Confessional Writings.* Philadelphia: Fortress, 1976.

Hoffmann, Fritz and Kuhn, Ulrich, editors. *Die Confessio Augustana im ökumenischen Gespräch.* Berlin, 1980.

Iserloh, Erwin, editor. *Confessio Augustana und Confutatio. Der Augsburger Reichstag 1530 und die Einheit der Kirche.* Münster, 1980.

Lohse, Bernhard and Pesch, Otto Hermann, editors. *Das "Augsburger Bekenntnis" von 1530. Damals und Heute.* Mainz, 1980.

Maurer, Wilhelm. *Historical Commentary on the Augsburg Confession.* Translated by H. George Anderson. Philadelphia: Fortress, 1987.

Meyer, Harding, editor. *Augsburgisches Bekenntnis im ökumenischen Kontext.* Stuttgart–Berlin, 1980.

Meyer, Harding and Schütte, Heinz, editors. *Confessio Augustana. Bekenntnis des eines Glaubens. Gemeinsame Untersuchung lutherischer und katholischer Theologen.* Paderborn and Frankfurt, 1980.

Mildenberger, Friedrich, *Theology of the Lutheran Confessions.* Translated by Erwin L. Luecker. Philadelphia: Fortress, 1983.

Nagel, William. *Luthers Anteil an der Confessio Augustans.* Gütersloh: Bertelsmann, 1930.

Plitt, Gustav. *Einleitung in die Augustana.* 2 volumes. Erlangen: A. Deichert, 1867-1868.

Schlink, Edmund. *Theology of the Lutheran Confessions.* Translated by Paul F. Koehneke and Herbert J. A. Bouman. Philadelphia: Fortress, 1961.

Seeberg, R. *Lehrbuch der Dogmengeschichte.* Erlangen and Leipzig: A. Deichert, 1895-1898.

Thieme, K. *Die Augsburgische Konfession und Luthers Katechismen.* Giessen: A. Töpelmann, 1930.

• INDEX OF SUBJECTS •

Anabaptists, 69, 94, 103, 110, 168
Augustana variata, 20, 117f., 191
Baptism, 44, 46, 103f., 136, 144
Church, 54f., 89ff., 99ff., 153
—unity of, 24f., 89, 91f., 95f., 153
Eucharist. *See* Lord's Supper.
Faith, 60-64, 82-87, 91-92, 104, 111, 117, 119, 139, 149, 195, 202, 229; *see also* Word of God, and Faith
—*fides caritate formata,* 71, 85
—*fides historica,* 60, 86
Grace, 61, 71, 86, 108, 110, 126, 147f., 150, 185, 192, 199
—*dispositio ad gratiam,* 65, 137, 143, 147, 149, 185
—*gratia praeveniens,* 63
Incarnation, 34, 51, 73, 76, 94, 122, 147, 200f.
Justification, 45-68, 81-89, 105, 110, 140, 189
—according to Thomas, 199f.
—according to Trent, 63f.
—imputed, 59-63
—in medieval theology, 45f.
Law, 66, 161, 165, 185
—law and gospel, 66, 141
Lateran Council, 114, 127-128, 131, 133, 216
Lord's Supper, 88-126, 215-216
—opus operatum, 76, 106, 119, 124, 147, 149f., 223-224

—sacrifice of the Mass, 52, 79, 119, 124
Merit, doctrine of, 63, 64, 199
Nature, human
—natural power, 44, 54
—nature and person, 191
—*status naturae,* 46, 59-60
Nature of Christ
—essence and work, 57
—nature and person, 54f.
Office, churchly, 69-80, 98, 101, 151-158, 241f.
—of clergy, 78, 132f., 153
—of spiritual and secular, 166-177
Ordination, *character indelebilis,* 79, 101, 155
Ockhamism, 62, 137f., 184
Person
—of God, 32, 35
—of Christ, 53
Predestination, 74, 77, 192
Redemption, 37, 52, 59, 87
Repentance, 105f., 109, 128, 163, 227
Sacraments, 69-80, 99, 107, 128
Sacrifice of the Mass. *See* Lord's Supper.
Sin, 40-49, 132f., 173, 187f.
Spirit, 39, 51-53, 70-71, 83, 94, 181f., 188
Trent, Council of, 20, 47, 52, 64, 83, 125, 131-132, 143, 150, 219f.
Trinity, 31-39

Will, 64f., 85, 181f., 191
Word of God, 60f., 71-72, 101, 105f.,
  126, 129, 132, 152, 208f.
  —of consecration, 71, 75f., 107f.
  —and faith, 60, 74, 98, 108, 117, 119-
  123, 147

—and sacraments, 149f.
—service of, 78f., 97
—and Spirit, 71-72, 123
Works
  —of faith, 82, 162, 173, 194-204
  —of the law, 66, 108, 201

• INDEX OF NAMES •
(SELECTED)

Augustine, 41, 45, 181, 195, 230, 234,
  237, 243
Biel, Gabriel, 184 185
Bucer, Martin, 35, 62, 73
Carlstad, 72, 121f., 130, 165, 168
Denck, Hans, 38f., 142
Eck, Johann, 16, 34, 105, 117, 153, 168,
  192, 199

Erasmus, 186
Müntzer, Thomas, 168, 180
Ockham, 43; see also Ockhamism
Thomas Aquinas, 42, 84f., 185, 199, 245
Zwingli, Huldrich, 15, 47, 54, 74, 76,
  79f., 111, 115, 121, 146

DATE DUE		
AUG 1 4 1998		
MAR 2 4		
MAY 3 0 2009		